The Slums
of Aspen

NATION OF NEWCOMERS
Immigrant History as American History

General Editors: Matthew Jacobson and Werner Sollors

LISA SUN-HEE PARK AND
DAVID NAGUIB PELLOW

The Slums of Aspen

Immigrants vs.
the Environment in
America's Eden

NEW YORK UNIVERSITY PRESS
New York and London

NEW YORK UNIVERSITY PRESS
New York and London
www.nyupress.org

First published in paperback in 2013

References to Internet websites (URLs) were accurate at the time of writing. Neither the author nor New York University Press is responsible for URLs that may have expired or changed since the manuscript was prepared.

Library of Congress Cataloging-in-Publication Data
The slums of Aspen : Immigrants vs. the Environment in America's Eden /
Lisa Sun-Hee Park and David Naguib Pellow.
p. cm. — (Nation of newcomers: immigrant history as American history)
Includes bibliographical references and index.
ISBN 978-1-4798-3476-1 (paper : alk. paper)
ISBN 978–0–8147–6803–7 (cloth : alk. paper) — ISBN 978–0–8147–6804–4
(ebk.) — ISBN 978–0–8147–6865–5 (ebk.)
1. Aspen (Colo.)—Emigration and immigration—Government policy.
2. Emigration and immigration—Environmental aspects.
3. Environmental policy—Colorado—Aspen. 4. Environmentalism—
Political aspects—Colorado—Aspen. 5. Aspen (Colo.)—Race relations.
6. Immigrants—Colorado—Aspen—Social conditions.
I. Park, Lisa Sun-Hee. II. Pellow, David N., 1969–
JV6930.A76S58   2011
305.9'069120978843—dc23   2011017988

New York University Press books are printed on acid-free paper, and their binding materials are chosen for strength and durability. We strive to use environmentally responsible suppliers and materials to the greatest extent possible in publishing our books.

Manufactured in the United States of America

10 9 8 7 6 5 4 3 2 1

CONTENTS

ACKNOWLEDGMENTS

First and foremost, we would like to thank the immigrant residents of the Roaring Fork Valley who participated in this project by sharing their time and wisdom with us. We also greatly appreciate the thoughtful contributions of the many people and organizations in the Roaring Fork Valley who helped make this book possible. They include the Aspen Historical Society, Catholic Charities in Glenwood Springs, Scott Chaplin and the staff of the Stepstone Center, Peter Jessup, Alice Hubbard Laird, Mike McGarry, Marie Munday, Terry Paulson, Luis Polar, George Stranahan, and Felicia Trevor.

At the University of Colorado–Boulder, where we began this project, we thank our friends and colleagues in the departments of Ethnic Studies, Women's Studies, and Sociology. We were also fortunate to work with a wonderful group of student researchers: Sonya Maria Johnson, Alex Urquhart, and Traci Brynne Voyles. We would like to extend a special note of gratitude to Traci and Alex for their invaluable research assistance and enthusiasm for this project. At the University of California–San Diego, Ethnic Studies Department, we continued this project with the student research assistance of Gloria Angelina Castillo, Miya Saika Chen, Monica Cornejo, Mohan Kanungo, Juliana (Jewels) Smith, and Angelic Willis. We completed the book at the University of Minnesota, Department of Sociology, thanks to the time and other key resources we were generously provided there.

Along the way, there were a number of scholars and archivists who provided key support, including Cawo Abdi, Julian Agyeman, Ron Aminzade, Richard Delgado, Kenneth Gould, Teresa Gowan, Michiko Hase, David Hays, Lynn Hudson, Patricia Limerick, Alanna Aiko Moore, Jennifer Pierce, Jane Rhodes, Malcolm Rohrbough, Allan Schnaiberg, Rachel Schurman, Rachel Silvey, Duane Smith, Stephen Snyder, Jean Stefancic, Leanne Walther, and Linda White.

Finally, we are grateful for the enthusiastic support of Eric Zinner, editor in chief, NYU Press, and Ciara McLaughlin, assistant editor. Our book benefited tremendously from David Lobenstine's careful editing, and we are honored to be a part of Matthew Frye Jacobson and Werner Sollors's book series.

ABBREVIATIONS

Alternatives for Community and Environment (ACE)
merican Indian Movement (AIM)
American Smelting and Refining Company (later renamed ASARCO)
Asistencia Para Latinos (Assistance for Latinos/APL)
Aspen Valley Community Foundation (AVCF)
Bureau of Land Management (BLM)
Californians for Population Stabilization (CAPS)
Carbondale Council on Arts and Humanities (CCAH)
Colorado Alliance for Immigration Reform (CAIR)
Committee on Women, Population and the Environment (CWPE)
Conservation International (CI)
Criminal Alien Program (CAP)
Earth Liberation Front (ELF)
Federation for American Immigration Reform (FAIR)
Immigration and Customs Enforcement (ICE)
Immigration and Nationalization Service (INS)
International Monetary Fund (IMF)
Locally Unwanted Land Uses (LULU)
National Asian Pacific American Legal Consortium (NAPALC)
North American Free Trade Agreement (NAFTA)
Political Ecology Group (PEG)
Roaring Fork Area Adult Literacy Program (RFAALP)
Roaring Fork Legal Services (RFLS)
Sierrans for U.S. Population Stabilization (SUSPS)
Southern Poverty Law Center (SPLC)
Zero Population Growth (ZPG)

Introduction

Environmental Privilege
in the Rocky Mountains

On December 13, 1999, the City Council of Aspen, Colorado—one of the country's most exclusive recreational sites for some of the world's wealthiest people—unanimously passed a resolution petitioning the U.S. Congress and the president to restrict the number of immigrants entering the United States. The language of the resolution suggests that this goal could be achieved by enforcing laws regulating undocumented immigration and reducing authorized immigration to 175,000 persons per year, down from the current annual level of between 700,000 and one million.[1] One of their primary reasons for encouraging tougher immigration laws was the purported negative impact of immigrants on the nation's ecosystems.

Concerns about immigration's environmental impacts generally include such broad issues as urban/suburban sprawl, the loss of urban green space, and overdevelopment of wilderness and agricultural lands. In Aspen, more specific complaints include everything from car exhaust pollution associated with older model vehicles many immigrants drive (since workers drive anywhere from thirty to one hundred miles to labor in Aspen's tourist industry), littering in mountain caves where some homeless immigrant workers sleep since affordable housing is nonexistent (the average sale price of a single family home in Aspen in 2000 was $3.8 million[2]), to having too many babies (i.e., overpopulation), which some fear will contaminate the pristine culture that accompanies the stunning ecology of the Rocky Mountains. With an unemployment rate of 1.5 percent (in

2000), Aspen experienced severe labor shortages, and Latinos and other immigrants filled the many low-paying, seasonal jobs within the service industry. And, while there are a wide number of nationalities represented in the immigrant service economy of the Roaring Fork Valley, we focus on Latinos who comprise the majority of immigrants in the area.

The narratives that define immigration (particularly from Latin America) as a leading ecological threat also expose a profound irony: the everyday reality of this playground for the rich depends enormously upon low-wage immigrant labor. The luxury goods and services that distinguish Aspen, that make it a "world-class" resort town, are possible in large part because of the workers from all over the world who clean the goods and deliver the services and care for the people who buy them. In some respects, this is a bizarre story of a town that prides itself on being environmentally conscious, whose city council can approve the construction of yet another 10,000-square-foot vacation home with a heated outdoor driveway, and simultaneously decry as an eyesore the "ugly" trailer homes where low-income immigrants live. In other respects, this is a familiar story of America's continuing clash between people of different races and classes, who rely on each other and yet cannot figure out how to live with each other. In still other respects, this is a story of the future, about the increasingly brutal inequality that will only become more pronounced as we negotiate the fast-paced global economy and its flows of money, ideas, and people.[3]

From 2000 to 2004, we traveled up and down Aspen's social pecking order. We conducted extensive archival and interview-based research to understand how people experience these contentious social issues. Our goal was to better understand the growing economic and racial inequalities from new vantage points, specifically from the perspective of environmentalists and immigrants. Our mission is to shed new light on these controversies, and to raise what we hope will be innovative, constructive questions that point to productive solutions.

Scholars and activists have, for four decades, presented evidence that people of color, as well as poor, working class, and indigenous communities face greater threats from pollution and industrial hazards than other groups. Environmental threats include municipal and hazardous waste incinerators, garbage dumps, coal-fired power plants, polluting manufacturing facilities, toxic schools, occupationally hazardous workplaces, substandard housing, uneven impacts of climate change, and the absence of healthy food sources. Marginalized communities tend to confront a disproportionate volume of these threats, what researchers and advocates have labeled *environmental injustice* and *environmental racism*.[4] These communities are also more likely to be impacted by extractive industrial operations such as mining, large dams, and timber harvesting, as well as "natural" disasters like flooding, earthquakes, and hurricanes.[5] We observe these patterns at the local, regional, national, and global scale, and the damage to public health, cultures, economies, and ecosystems from such activities is well documented.[6] For example, immigrants and people of color in California's Silicon Valley live in communities with disproportionately high concentrations of toxic superfund sites and water contamination, and work in jobs that expose them to disproportionately high volumes of hazardous chemicals.[7] In Chicago, African Americans and Latinos live in neighborhoods with disproportionately high numbers of garbage dumps and other environmental hazards,[8] and we see this pattern holding true for Asian Americans, Native Americans, and working-class whites nationally.[9] The field of environmental justice studies has emerged as a means to consider the historical and contemporary drivers of environmental inequalities, its many manifestations, and as a vehicle to address this problem through research, action, and policy. Environmental justice studies span the fields of history, sociology, anthropology, law, communication, economics, literature, ethnic studies, public health, architecture, medicine, and many others. Activists and policymakers have also produced a great deal of research on environmental justice issues and have drawn on the work of scholars to pass laws and introduce state and corporate policies, which would confront some of the most glaring aspects of environmental injustice in the United States and globally.

Scholars have also demonstrated how communities have responded to such ecological violence creatively through protest, art, science, and sustainable development projects. Such work underscores how environmental injustices shape the politics of race, class, indigeneity, citizenship, gender, sexuality, and culture.[10] While these studies reveal the hardships and suffering associated with environmental inequality and environmental racism, fewer studies consider the flipside, or source, of that reality: *environmental privilege*. Over the last several years we have been developing this concept, inspired by the work of scholars like William Freudenburg, Kenneth Gould,

George Lipsitz, and Laura Pulido.[11] We argue that environmental privilege re-sults from the exercise of economic, political, and cultural power that some groups enjoy, which enables them exclusive access to coveted environmen-tal amenities such as forests, parks, mountains, rivers, coastal property, open lands, and elite neighborhoods. Environmental privilege is embodied in the fact that some groups can access spaces and resources, which are protected from the kinds of ecological harm that other groups are forced to contend with everyday. These advantages include organic and pesticide-free foods, neighborhoods with healthier air quality, and energy and other products siphoned from the living environments of other peoples. In our study, we show how environmental privileges accrue to the few while environmental burdens confront the many, including lack of access to clean air, land, water, and open spaces.

If environmental racism and injustice are abundant and we can readily observe them around the world, then surely the same can be said for envi-ronmental privilege. We cannot have one without the other; they are two sides of the same coin. The authors of the groundbreaking United Nations Millennium Ecosystem Assessment articulate the relationship between environmental injustice and environmental privilege quite powerfully:

> In numerous cases, it is the poor who suffer from the loss of environ-mental services due to the pressure exerted on natural systems for the benefit of other communities, often in other parts of the world. . . .The impact of climate change will be felt above all in the poorest parts of the world—for example, as it exacerbates drought and reduces agricul-tural production of the driest regions—while greenhouse gas emissions essentially come from rich populations.[12]

Where there is pesticide poisoning of agricultural workers and eco-systems as a result of multinational chemical companies producing and forcing these toxins onto laborers and global South communities (via aid packages from international financial institutions), somewhere those who profit from these actions may be living and working in pesticide-free spaces, eating organic foods (the term "global South" is a mainly a social—rather than strictly geographic—designation meant to encom-pass politically and economically vulnerable communities). While some people are forced to live next door to a paint factory, a landfill, or an incinerator and breathe air that contributes to asthma and various respiratory diseases, others have the luxury of spending time in second homes in secluded semirural environs and can marvel at the fresh air they take in during a morning walk. Deforestation in the Amazon and Indonesia produces wood and paper products for people in far away places who live in far more comfortable surroundings, while the indigenous peoples whose land produces such goods confront genocide. Environmental privilege not only feeds off of environmental injustice, it *is* environmental injustice. The French journalist Hervé Kempf puts it this way: "We must . . . understand that the ecological crisis and the social crisis are two faces of the same disaster. And this disaster is implemented by a system of power that has no other objective than to maintain the privileges of the ruling classes."[13]

Environmental privilege exists whenever environmental injustice occurs. In Minnesota, residents receive much of their heating and cooling from the Xcel Energy Corporation and Manitoba Hydro, both of which supply that energy from hydroelectric dams built on the lands of the Métis and Cree First Nations in Canada. As their hunting grounds and sources of fishing were disrupted in the wake of dam construction and flooding, these indigenous communities have faced economic, social, psychological, cultural, and ecological devastation. Dawn Mikkelsen's film *Green Green Water* explores this story in depth and urges Minnesota residents who enjoy the benefits of hydro-powered electricity to reflect upon the price that Canadian indigenous nations pay for their southern neighbors' creature comforts. Environmental privileges like this are difficult to witness, but they are rarely questioned because of the social distance between those who receive them and those who suffer the consequences. In fact, few Minnesotans have any idea where their energy comes from.

The international trade in hazardous waste reveals environmental privilege and racism on a global scale. As the volume of industrial chemical pollutants expanded during the post–World War II economic boom in the global North, environmental movements in Europe and the United States pushed for greater regulation of these materials through legislative mechanisms like the Clean Air and Clean Water Act, and the founding of the U.S. Environmental Protection Agency. In response, rather than fundamentally changing the way they functioned, many transnational firms instead shifted their dirtiest operations and most hazardous products to lands and markets in the global South. Other firms simply began dumping their chemical wastes in these communities. For example, as activists and industries in the United States and Europe came to realize how intensely toxic electronic wastes like old computers are, these parts have been shipped overseas to Ghana, Nigeria, India, Pakistan, China, Brazil, and the Philippines, where they are used for manufacturing new products under highly hazardous conditions, or just dumped: meadows, farmland, market places, neighborhoods, and bodies of water in these nations are now filled with the polluting carcasses of electronic garbage from rich communities, presenting significant threats to public health and ecosystems. Many observers have called this practice "toxic colonialism" or global environmental racism. While we agree with this characterization, it only focuses on one end of the process. The problem began in the global North, where the flipside of environmental racism—environmental privilege—drives this practice from within some of the wealthiest and most elite communities on earth.

Environmental privilege is readily observable in many contexts nationally and globally. Therefore, what we witnessed in Aspen is not unique to that particular city. The discourse, cultural politics, and policymaking in Aspen and the surrounding Roaring Fork Valley are familiar to those that can be found in various historical moments and across geographic spaces.

While racially and economically marginalized people living in poor rural towns, inner cities, inner ring suburbs, and on reservations do battle with polluting industries and intransigent governments, those living in wealthy enclaves enjoy relatively cleaner air, land, and water—and as important, often believe they have *earned the right* to these privileges. Aspen, Colorado, and many other places in the United States are classic examples of environmental privilege and deserve closer consideration as sites for understanding the roots of environmental justice struggles. The case of Aspen illustrates the importance of understanding poverty and environmental inequality by getting out of the ghetto and into places where racial and economic privilege are enjoyed. That certain communities face greater environmental harm is indeed a social problem, but the accompanying social problem is that others benefit from this harm through environmental privilege. We must examine the other side of environmental degradation and understand the communities that have come to expect a pristine world (and the army of workers who make such a world possible), in order to expose the source and persistence of environmental injustice.

Aspen and the Roaring Fork Valley is just one of the planet's many sites built as a refuge from undesirable people and as a place where nature can be manipulated for the convenience and enjoyment of a handful of elites. Aspen is environmental privilege at work.[14]

Saving the Environment, Aspen Style

Terry Paulson, an Aspen City Council member and also a longtime immigration critic and self-avowed environmentalist, hailed the 1999 resolution as an important milestone for Aspen. He received support and guidance from nationally prominent nativist organizations, which seek to control immigration in various ways, using public protest and legislation. These organizations include the Carrying Capacity Network and the Center for Immigration Studies, whose staff reportedly told Paulson "other communities haven't had the courage to do so. . . . Because many current immigrants are members of minority groups in the U.S., attempts to limit immigration may be seen as racist."[15] Paulson wasted no time in calling for an expansion of the resolution beyond the city of Aspen. He announced his intention to launch a statewide campaign to "promote overpopulation awareness" and declared, "If we address population and do something about it, everything else will fall in line."[16]

Aspen, located in Pitkin County, Colorado, successfully persuaded the county to follow the city's lead, and in March 2000, the county commissioners voiced unanimous approval for a "population stabilization" resolution. The commissioners were largely inspired by a presentation Mr. Paulson gave, in which he screened *Immigration by the Numbers*, a film produced by the influential nativist organization NumbersUSA.[17] The Aspen City Council document "A resolution of the city of Aspen, Colorado, supporting population stabilization in the United States" cleverly combines classic nativist language around immigration with ideas that most politically progressive persons could embrace. The resolution includes the following statements regarding environmental and labor conditions in the United States:

> The population of the U.S. is six percent of the world's population, consuming up to 25 percent of the world's natural resources.

[The U.S. government should begin] requiring equitable wages and benefits for workers and community environmental protections to be part of all free trade agreements.

[T]he people of the United States and the City of Aspen, Colorado envision a country with . . . material and energy efficiency, a sustainable future, a healthy environment, clean air and water, ample open space, wilderness, abundant wildlife and social and civic cohesion in which the dignity of human life is enhanced and protected.

The council wanted Aspen to be a "city beautiful," a beacon of sustainability and social responsibility, where the activities of the U.S. government and corporations would have positive impacts both locally and globally. But how do we get there? This is where nativism enters the picture:

Population growth generated by mass immigration to the United States causes increasing pressures on our environment and forces local governments and communities to spend taxpayers' dollars for additional schools, health care facilities, water disposal plants, transportation systems, fire protection, water supplies, power generation plants and many other social and environmental costs.

Following this logic, immigration becomes the major cause of our ecological crises. The resolution goes on to state: "The ability of the United States to support a population within its carrying capacity is now strained because of population growth."[18]

At the end of the resolution the city council called on the federal government to "immediately stabilize the population of the United States . . . by mandated enforcement of our immigration laws against illegal immigration, thereby promoting the future well being of all the citizens of this Nation and the City of Aspen."[19] The cultural and racial overtones are clear, as the resolution references Europe as the model for sustainability. Specifically, the text states that the United States has "the highest population growth rate of the developed countries of the world. Most European countries are at zero or negative population growth."[20] Interestingly, many European nations and Japan now consider their low birthrates a social problem given the diminishing domestic labor pool and subsequent increased dependence on immigrants. Terry Paulson sponsored the resolution with the following opening statement:

Fellow Council Members. This resolution we will be considering for adoption tonight could be the most important consideration we will ever make as representatives of our constituents and their children. In October, I attended and participated in a conference at the Aspen Institute, called The Myth of Sustainable Growth. At that conference, I had the privilege of hearing a remarkable talk, "Population, Immigration and Global Ethics," by Jonette Christian, from Mainers for Immigration Reform. Jonette is a family therapist by profession, giving her a very special perspective on this matter before us. Here is some of what she said: "We have agitated, confused and deluded ourselves with the illusion that we are being overwhelmed by many, many problems—when in fact we have primarily only one. But it is the one that terrifies us the most, and we handle that terror by chattering endlessly about everything else. Denying . . . [ignoring] and minimizing population growth in the 1990s is a *hate crime against future generations*, and it must end." Please, join me . . . by passing this resolution as written, and thereby insuring a sustainable future for America and her children.[21]

Similar initiatives have been proposed in numerous states and cities across the West and Southwest. There are a number of common threads that are evident in these campaigns. First, the primacy of native-born or white children is invoked as part of a larger moral imperative, and population or immigration control is portrayed as a difficult but necessary mission to be carried out by a few brave souls. Second, immigrants are cast as the main source of our social and ecological ills, and doing nothing to stem the tide of immigration is characterized as a " hate crime" against future generations of Americans—again, the implication is that "Americans" comprise those identified as native-born and white. In this way, discriminatory anti-immigrant actions are not just recast as a patriotic duty; white Americans who oppose these measures are portrayed as perpetrating violence against their own race.

What is interesting here is that these are privileged communities claiming victim status. A Roaring Fork Valley area progressive activist and educator told us: "Environmental racism is when people of color are dumped on. But here, especially in Aspen, we have rich white folks who are saying *we're* getting dumped on! So it's like the idea has been totally turned around and upside down." In other words, Aspenites are essentially crying "reverse environmental racism" because they view immigrants not only as a cause of environmental harm, but as a kind of social contamination, a form of pollution harming whites.[22]

Shortly thereafter, the city of Aspen experienced a momentary embarrassment when it was reported that its resolution was featured on the website of the American Patrol—a nativist organization whose founder, Glenn Spencer, is a nationally known ultraconservative activist who lobbied vigorously for the passage of California's Proposition 187 (denying public benefits to undocumented immigrants) and who wrote an infamous letter to the *Los Angeles Times* in 1996 stating that "Chicanos and Mexicanos lie as a means of survival."[23] The American Patrol website also contained a radio production titled "The Mexican Conquest of California," claiming a conspiracy between Mexican Americans and the Mexican government to retake the U.S. Southwest and rename it "Aztlán."[24] In response to this and other reports of concern about the resolution, the Aspen City Council took great pains to stress that the initiative "was not racially motivated."[25]

Four months later, the Pitkin County commissioners passed a nearly identical resolution. However, a number of additional statements stand out and reveal the tensions and affinities between nativism on one hand, and cynical notions of ecological sustainability and social responsibility on the other. The county resolution contained the following statements: "Immigration is the leading cause of population growth in the Unites States. Population is the leading cause of environmental degradation."[26] Thus, by implication, immigration must be the primary driver of ecological degradation. The resolution continues with the declaration that "Legal and illegal immigration combined is too high for assimilation."[27] This claim is followed by population statistics that paint a picture of an Anglo society overwhelmed by brown people from south of the border. The clear implication is a cultural fear that the Southwestern United States could be the target of a *reconquista* or a reconquering by Mexico. The resolution continues:

> The Board of County Commissioners recognizes the value of diversity and the contributions of immigrants since the arrival of the first settlers many centuries ago. We also recognize and deplore the exploitation of immigrants through violations of the Fair Labor Standards Act, such as minimum wage and overtime. We specifically reject the notion that

immigrants (legal and not) are disproportionately criminal or bad people. Nonetheless, we believe immigration, both legal and illegal, should
be restrained. The United States has a responsibility to promote family
planning opportunities worldwide, to require our trade partners to treat
their laborers humanely . . . to respect our shared environment . . . [and]
provide financial support of programs designed to assist Third World
nations with family planning utilizing all methods of education and con-
traceptives available. . . . Pitkin County accepts its responsibility to work
to improve working and living conditions, both locally and throughout
the world, through appropriate regulations that support multi-cultural
education programs, that conserve natural resources worldwide, that
move toward greater energy efficiency in production and use of goods
and services, and that exhibit social responsibility.[28]

Beneath Pitkin County's rhetoric lies a disturbing view of "social responsibility." The family-planning claims in particular are troubling considering
the history of such efforts by U.S. government agencies and their links to
sterilization campaigns among women of color in the United States and
the global South.[29] But we believe that along with the rest of the text—and
like the Aspen resolution—it underscores the long-standing link between
nativism and environmentalism in the United States and elsewhere.

As Aspen councilmember Tom McCabe cautioned, "The planet's a finite
resource. . . . We can't indefinitely welcome people and expect to maintain
our quality of life."[30] And that is precisely the point: Aspenites and others
in privileged places across the United States want to protect their "quality
of life," which includes resources and wealth derived from the ecosystems
that only they have access to and from the hard work of others. This is
what makes environmental privilege work: the disconnection between the
way of life in a place like Aspen, and the social and environmental relationships that make that lifestyle possible. It is no wonder that the U.S.
environmental movement finds itself in a state of crisis, with many residents holding such organizations beneath contempt for elitist politics and
righteous views of a world that they refuse to share with others.[31]

While we do not doubt that humans, including immigrants, contribute
to strains on ecosystems, we find the intense focus on immigrants mis-
placed. This focus instead functions to benefit other actors and institutions who likely contribute a great deal more to environmental harm. We

should remember that European immigrants and internal European American migrants—along with the U.S. military, the federal government, and many extractive industries—produced inordinate damage to the American West long before contemporary battles began over preserving this fabled landscape. The story of the California Gold Rush and the later gold and silver rushes in the Rocky Mountains offer ample evidence.[32] Urban theorist Mike Davis considers much of the intermountain West a "national sacrifice zone" as a result of U.S. military activities that have taken place in the region over the years; many scholars and scientists have ignored or underestimated this position. Uncovering this reality and challenging dominant images of the region, Davis considers the impacts of "militarism, urbanization, the Interstate highway, epidemic vandalism, mass tourism, and the extractive industries' boom-and-bust cycles."[33]

Making Sense of Aspen

What is the meaning of this conflict in Aspen, Pitkin County, and the surrounding towns of Colorado's Roaring Fork Valley, and why does it matter? We see the turmoil in the Roaring Fork Valley as part of the larger, and less recognized, problem at the intersection of immigration and environmental politics in the United States. We like to think that our environmental movement is as pristine and unblemished as Mother Earth. But the reality is far closer to the state of our planet today: sullied by our ignorance, corrupted by our ideologies, threatened by our own self-interests. Environmental and nativist movements share a great deal of common ground, far more than most progressives and liberals would like to believe.

Examples abound of the links between efforts to "save" the earth and efforts to control certain groups of people. The more we look, the more we see that both of these practices intersect with discomforting frequency. Environmental and nativist movements in the United States have been historically racist, classist, and patriarchal, and these efforts have been rooted in biological, natural, and social scientific ideas of how the world should be. Consider that the creation of many of this country's national parks was made possible through the explicit removal or containment of Native American tribes.[34] The feminist scholar Betsy Hartmann calls this

"coercive conservation," the violent expulsion of local people from what become wilderness preserves. The environmental group Conservation International (CI) is notorious for supporting such practices. Hartmann reports
that CI works with the World Wildlife Fund and USAID (both groups are
infamous for their focus on population control in the global South) and
the Mexican government in Chiapas to remove people—often Zapatista
communities of indigenous peoples—from "illegal" settlements to restore
parts of the Lacandon Forest. This policy, paired with the Mexican government's alleged forced sterilization of many women in the region, reinforces
the simplistic contention of the region's CI director, that deforestation is
the direct result of population growth: "It's obvious that the main problem
is overpopulation."[35]

Thus, environmentalists and nativists have historically shared a preoc-
cupation not only with population control but also with erecting and reinforcing borders to support conservation efforts. These preoccupations are
some of the many reasons why mainstream environmentalism remains a
largely culturally exclusive cause. The mainstream environmental movement has been incapable of building a mass following in this nation precisely because it refuses to embrace a broader agenda of social justice. In
fact, the movement has more often supported policies that benefit and reflect the desires of privileged groups. The unfortunate ideological fixation
on population control—one of the core aims of nativism—has crippled the
environmental cause in this nation.

Drawing on the work of scholars studying immigration and race in the
United States, we view nativism as part of a system of discourses and actions that seek to promote the interests of native-born peoples in opposition to other populations on the grounds of their foreignness.[36] "Foreignness" need not be strictly defined as non-native born, since people of color
born in the United States have been defined throughout our history as
foreign in cultural terms.[37] And while some forms of nativism may not be
overtly racist, the justification for inclusion or exclusion of certain groups
almost always comes down to race. Indeed, race cannot be separated from
nativism because the meaning of legal and full social citizenship (i.e., belonging) in the United States has always been racialized.[38]

Extending this concept to the realm of environmental politics, we
use the term "nativist environmentalism," which we define as a political
movement that seeks racial exclusivity in places deemed to have special

ecological and racial or cultural significance. Nativist environmentalism is a form of racism rooted in a sense of entitlement to places imbued with particular socio-ecological importance. In other words, while traditional nativists defend "their" nation's borders because they believe they are the truly rightful inhabitants, nativist environmentalists do the same when it concerns the confluence of environmental and cultural entitlements. It is environmentalism with a racial or cultural inflection, and nativism with an ecological inflection. Nativist environmentalism is the ideological force at the nexus of the nativist and environmental movements, a politics that threatens to damage both our social fabric and our planet.

Nativist environmentalism is a phenomenon that supports not only racial exclusion but also environmental privilege—the notion that one group should have near-exclusive enjoyment of precious ecological resources such as open space, national parks, ocean—and lakefront real estate, clean air, clean land, and clean water.[39] Environmental privilege is a key ecological dimension of social inequality that has gone largely unnoticed by social scientists, as we have almost entirely focused on the problem of disadvantage in studies of environmental inequality and environmental racism. Communities of color and working-class communities are more likely than others to suffer from an overburden of industrial pollution from factories, landfills, chemical plants, and the like, and are more likely to bear the brunt of ecosystem resource extraction activities and the impact of "natural" disasters. But if we are to fully understand inequality, then we must examine both disadvantage and advantage, misery and luxury, and poverty and wealth. Within our current economic system, environmental privilege cannot exist without environmental injustice.

Nativist environmentalism and environmental privilege are further linked and reinforced by a common view of environmental politics and social change we call "the Aspen Logic." The Aspen Logic is a worldview that people across the mainstream political spectrum embrace, but one that is particularly prominent in liberal and Democratic political circles. The idea is that environmentalism and capitalism are entirely compatible and not in fundamental opposition. In fact, within the Aspen Logic, true capitalism is the kind of economic system that pays closer attention to nature's limits and needs while never sacrificing profits. By extension, the only path to ecological sustainability is by embracing a kinder, greener capitalism. The Aspen Logic suggests that we can achieve ecological goals without confronting the brutality and violence that capitalism necessarily imposes on people and ecosystems. We can attain sustainability without challenging racism, class hierarchies, patriarchy, and nativism. The Aspen Logic is the defining philosophy of the mainstream environmental movement and, we believe, a primary reason why so few real advances toward improving the health of our planet have been made.

The Aspen Logic is hard at work in the en vogue fixation with the so-called green economy. The fundamental problem with an idea like green capitalism is that it presumes that capitalism is, at root, a just system that only needs regulation and reform. We reject this premise for what should be obvious reasons: because capitalism is a hierarchical, violent system of production, consumption, commerce, and governance that inherently views people and ecosystems as variables to be manipulated for the benefit of a minority. The same can be said of many socialist nations whose leaders have committed the same folly. Therefore green capitalism does not result in a transformed society marked by ecological sustainability and social justice because (1) it is not possible and (2) because that is not the goal. The goal of green capitalism is to maintain the current social order and perhaps appease and co-opt some of its liberal critics. Many progressive and liberal individuals would probably recoil at the idea of green racism. But that is exactly what nativist environmentalism is: a political ideology that seeks to subvert ecosystems to the needs of certain people while punishing others. Capitalism, whether green or mean, is no different. Environmental privilege can be challenged only when larger systems of power are undone.

We speak of nativist environmentalism to make clear that we are not referring to all environmentalists—just those who (implicitly or explicitly) support nativist ideas. There *are* environmental groups whose members reject nativism, racism, environmental privilege, and the Aspen Logic. Unfortunately, they do not have the ear of the media, Congress, the White House, and other policymakers.

As we grapple with how to sustain both our planet and its many peoples, the story of Aspen becomes a disturbing window into what is happening every day all over our country. We believe that the planet's health can be improved only if we also take care of the people who live on it. In the sections below, we highlight four essential themes that underscore the importance of this conflict in the Roaring Fork Valley: (1) the paradox of immigrant labor markets in a global economy; (2) national immigration politics in the United States; (3) the racist and nativist roots of U.S. environmentalism; and (4) the interlinked practices of inclusion and exclusion in environmental politics.

The Paradox of Immigrant Labor in a Global Economy

There is an important paradox that underlies the presence of immigrants in the United States: the simultaneous economic dependence upon and social contempt for low-income immigrant labor.[40] Social contempt frequently reinforces the invisibility of immigrant labor—the informal, "off the books," and hidden nature of much of the work newcomers do in this country. Recent events in Aspen signal that this region is an important case study for illuminating the complexities of policies regarding immigrant labor, environmental protection, and poverty in our increasingly global society. Many low-income immigrant workers experience a double-edged sword: they enter the United States as a result of growing transnational markets, but at the same time they face anti-immigrant legislation that punishes their arrival and existence. The significant rise in the Latino population has fueled a nationwide political backlash against Latino immigrants and bilingual education.

As we spent time in Aspen, we found that many people use the environment as a way to promote a particular romantic image of the Roaring Fork Valley as a pristine, post-industrial refuge. Such romance, however, is built on the backs of "unskilled" immigrants. There is nothing romantic about a Mexican dishwasher or landscaper who makes just enough money to scrape by, or the trailer park in a flood zone on the outskirts of town where many of these workers live. These conditions are both essential and invisible to the production of Aspen. Immigrant labor makes Aspen, according to its wealthy residents, "heaven on earth," but keeping immigrants in the back room, as it were, away from the public eye allows elites a chance to enjoy the natural surroundings without the distraction of undesirable social elements.

Local policies, such as population-stabilization resolutions, are reflections of the paradox of immigrant labor and its uncomfortable reminders of invidious social inequalities. These actions by local governments are important signposts of things to come and are worthy of serious public and scholarly consideration. Research on the future of immigrant labor requires that we examine the "new Latino immigration," which includes understudied destinations such as the Rocky Mountain West.[41] As many scholars and business leaders have noted, continued economic globalization (primarily the liberalization of barriers to trade and finance) fuels both the demand for cheap immigrant labor and maintains the pool of willing migrant workers.[42] Following this trend, Aspen has experienced a growing number of immigrant workers. Our years of data gathering illustrated how the growing presence of low-income Latino immigrant workers challenged core social meanings that have constructed the image of Aspen as a pristine place of refuge away from the polluted, unsavory central cities. This image is essential to the continued economic prosperity of Aspen's tourist industry. In response to the ideological disturbance created by the presence of poor ethnic migrants, various stakeholders in the region constructed a range of policies to address "the problem" and to reassert the importance of maintaining Aspen's social, cultural, and ecological image. And, as business and government officials in tourist destinations know all too well, image is everything.

Increasing global capital expansion has had an accompanying effect of growing class inequalities, resulting in the contraction of the middle class in Aspen and the surrounding area. The exorbitant cost of living, accompanied by a depression of wages, has driven the native-born middle – and working-class populations out of the area. In this respect, this exclusive mountain resort is indicative of a growing number of towns and cities that find themselves increasingly dependent upon two economic extremes: a tourism-based economy of the wealthy, and those who serve them, many of whom are immigrants. The inequalities are stark and ever present. The visual images that gloss Aspen magazine covers feature stretch Range Rover limousines, black-tie fund-raisers, world-class ski slopes, and film celebrities who live part of the year in multimillion dollar, single-family homes. At the same time, Aspen is also a place where foreign-born workers drive thirty to one hundred miles round-trip daily to work in low-status jobs for low wages with few benefits. Many of these workers live in deplorable housing conditions, including cars, campers, and even caves. Our research focuses on Aspen and Colorado's Roaring Fork Valley as an entree to a larger discussion of the place and persistence of the immigrant working poor in the global economy.

National Immigration Politics in the United States

Nativism in the United States has a long history. Benjamin Franklin was well known for his anxieties about German immigrants coming to Pennsylvania in the 1750s. He once wrote, "Unless the stream of their importation could be turned they will soon so outnumber us that all the advantages we have will not be able to preserve our language, and even our government will become precarious."[43] John Jay—one of the authors of the Federalist Papers and later a Supreme Court Justice—suggested in New York's Constitution that the state erect "a wall of brass around the country for the exclusion of Catholics."[44] Under the 1798 Alien Act, President John Adams was given the power to deport anyone he considered "dangerous" to national security. The list of anti-immigrant policies in the United States from its origins to the present is too lengthy to consider here, but it makes one thing clear: as much as this country may be a "nation of immigrants," it has also always been a nation of nativists.[45]

Nativism grew intensely in the 1990s due to a combination of factors. The nation experienced a growing sense of economic insecurity, an increasing rift between the rich and the poor, and an increase in immigration. Census predictions for the year 2000 and beyond continued to stress that whites would become the minority in several states (which did happen), feeding a growing anxiety among many European Americans. Moreover, economic globalization, free trade agreements, and the intensified privatization of public resources contributed to economic insecurity, declines in real wages, a continued disempowerment of the labor movement and unions, a major rise in the temporary employment sector, and significant cutbacks in the social safety net including welfare and health care funding.[46] Taken together, these dynamics fueled nativist movements and sentiment in the contemporary era.

Some of the principal fears among the U.S. citizenry include the idea that immigrants are "taking jobs" away from native-born persons; that immigrants place a strain on public services (such as welfare or general assistance); and that immigrants threaten the cultural fabric of the nation by introducing new languages, religions, and new racial/ethnic political power blocs. The associated anti-immigrant backlash has been virulent, punctuated at the policy level by the passage of California's Proposition

INTRODUCTION   19

187, Arizona's Senate Bill 1070 (giving local law enforcement the authority to profile Latinos for possible deportation), a series of "anti-solicitation" ordinances targeting immigrant day laborers in cities around the nation, the Immigration Act of 1996 ("Illegal Immigration Reform and Immigrant Responsibility Act"), the Welfare Reform of 1996 ("Personal Responsibility and Work Opportunity Reconciliation Act"), the Antiterrorism and Effective Death Penalty Act of 1996, and the proliferation of "English only" legislation (or proposals) in several states around the nation.[47] On a broader public or popular cultural level, we observe the continued rise and dominance of nativist rhetoric in newspaper reporting and editorials, on conservative AM talk radio shows, in popular music, videos, and movies.[48] On the street and the Internet we see a rise in hate crimes and interpersonal violence directed at immigrant populations and those perceived to be foreign born. The border vigilante group, the Minuteman Project, has grown considerably in the wake of the anti-immigrant hysteria of recent years, and many hate groups including the Ku Klux Klan credit the immigration debate with their recent revival in membership.[49] These groups have focused more and more on the "threat'" of immigration from Mexico in particular—with rhetoric of the coming *reconquista* of the American Southwest. Such traditional nativist fears have only been compounded and intensified by the fallout associated with the al-Qaeda attacks of September 11, 2001 and the ensuing "War on Terror."[50]

Moreover, during the 1990s, there was a marked rise in hate crimes against other groups. According to the National Asian Pacific American Legal Consortium (NAPALC) there was a 13 percent increase in reported anti-Asian incidents between 1998 and 1999 alone. That consortium found that South Asians were the most targeted among Asian Americans and that vandalism was the most common form of anti-Asian discrimination. This trend has continued. There was a huge spike in anti-Asian hate crimes and violence in 2001, following the attacks of September 11, 2001, with South Asians—particularly Indians and Pakistanis—receiving a disproportionate level of abuse, including Sikh men who wear turbans and long beards, two of the symbols that have come to be associated with terrorism in the media, despite the fact that Sikhs are not Muslims. That year there were 507 bias-motivated hate crimes against Asian Pacific Americans, with threats, vandalism, arson, rape, and assaults with baseball bats, metal poles, and guns.[51] These patterns occur not only in U.S. cities and in immigrant-owned stores and small businesses but at universities and colleges as well. For example, in the 1990s, anti-Asian vandalism at California's Stanford University included such threats as "rape all oriental bitches," "kill all gooks," and "I'm a real white American."[52] In February 2008, the day before the National Day of Remembrance of the internment of thousands of Japanese Americans during World War II, a student newspaper at the University of Colorado–Boulder published a column stating "If it's war the Asians want . . . It's war they'll get." The column advocated forcing Asian Americans to perform demeaning acts and suggested that they should be "hogtied."[53] The column was published on the eve of the university's Diversity Summit. Such violence, both verbal and physical, marks certain spaces as legitimate only for certain groups.

The recent upsurge of anti-immigrant sentiment is, in fact, nothing new at all. Such popular anger against newcomers has been a continuous hallmark of U.S. history, in which ordinary citizens, labor unions, politicians, journalists, academics, the courts, and environmentalists have all vigorously participated.[54] Immigrants are blamed for producing strains on the carrying capacity of local, regional, national, and global ecosytems.[55] Politicians, talk show hosts, foundations, best-selling authors, and even environmentalists have made this claim, which is interesting: much of the evidence reveals that many immigrant communities are actually exposed to pollution (created by others) at higher rates than their privileged citizen counterparts. In our haste to blame immigrants for environmental decline, we should not forget that immigrants often pay the price of modern "progress" in the form of environmental racism, via pesticides exposure and residential proximity to locally unwanted land uses (LULUs) such as power plants.[56] Latinos also experience higher risks of exposure to lead-paint poisoning and asthma in New York, a lack of access to parks and public transportation, and significant threats to land ownership in the American Southwest as a result of federal energy policies.[57] In Aspen, with regard to the issue of ecological footprints, the extravagance of the wealthy, white, part-time residents in that city is part of its lore and lure; immigrants are only there to support the leisure economy.

The contentious debate regarding immigrants and the environment continues. From the intensity of the discourse, it appears that this issue elicits some core anxieties among native-born Americans.

Racist and Nativist Roots of U.S. Environmentalism

Proponents of immigration control policies often define their actions as courageous because they make these decisions despite the historically racist implications of population control. The Aspen councilman Terry Paulson stated, "This is one of those touchy subjects that no one wants to talk about."[58] The former Colorado governor Richard Lamm—a part-time Aspen resident and supporter of the resolution—addressed the issue of cultural sensitivity and immigration policy by saying, "It's not a question of compassion. It's a question of what kind of country do we want to leave our children."[59] Using a similar argument to stress the urgency of immigration control, Paulson described the "denial" of population growth's negative impacts as a "hate crime" against future generations. In effect, an argument of reverse discrimination is made on behalf of native-born, white children. This priority of preserving an intergenerational legacy is a vital tool for diffusing the specter of race and racism, one that shadows population control arguments. In this way, environmental politics plays a central role as ecological preservation is cast as an imperative for the survival of the next generation of white Americans. The questions of preservation for whom and for what purpose are critical in the nativist agenda, but are always reduced to the simple "citizen/white versus immigrant/other" framework. Environmentalism, then, allows nativists to remove race from the conversation and provide a safer, more comfortable grounding for the white majority calling for drastic limits on immigration.

Thus, environmentalism plays a crucial role as a solution, particularly because it can obscure the growing racialization of poverty in the idyllic, staunchly Democratic-voting, resort town of Aspen. Environmentalism, as a palatable rationale for anti-immigrant policies, brings together the strangest of bedfellows—the compassionate liberal activist with the rational social conservative. As a social movement, environmentalism brings with it a checkered past, due largely to its links with nativist movements. The alleged negative environmental impact of immigration is a charge levied by many nativist organizations, a dimension of America's recurring anti-immigrant backlash with deep historical roots.[60]

The innocent claim that environmentalists in the Roaring Fork Valley only want to "preserve our way of life" is belied by the fact that such a lifestyle requires the domination of the environment and of certain groups of people (e.g., people of color, immigrants, and workers who make such privileges possible for the wealthy and mostly white elite). It also underscores an enduring belief that there are essential differences between people of varying ethnic, racial, and national backgrounds. Recall the language from the Pitkin County resolution on population stabilization, which stated "Legal and illegal immigration combined is too high for assimilation."

A number of scholars have described this kind of language as a core part of the "new racism," one that no longer relies on outdated and abhorrent biological notions of superior versus inferior peoples. Instead, the new racism is based on the idea that there are insurmountable and incompatible *cultural* distinctions between peoples.[61] As the sociologist Howard Winant notes, "the reinterpretation of racialized differences as matters of culture and nationality, rather than as fundamental human attributes somehow linked to phenotype, turns out to justify exclusionary politics and policy far better than traditional white supremacist arguments can do."[62] The new racism is a critical component of the "post-racial" (or "colorblind") approach to race that has been sweeping the nation for some time—since civil rights legislation formally outlawed public acts of racism.[63] Post-racial perspectives on racial inequality deny the *existence* of race and therefore are inherently blind to racism. People and institutions approaching race in this way can, at the same time, employ the new racism to argue that certain groups are unassimilable based on other characteristics (language, religion, nationality, etc.).[64]

While we agree with scholars writing about the new racism that many biological notions of racial difference have given way to other frameworks, our focus on the immigration-environment nexus reveals that such ideas are unfortunately not entirely outdated. In the case of the Roaring Fork Valley and the general immigration-environment debate, we observe both cultural and biological arguments at work: nativist environmentalists claim that nations must obey the *laws of nature* in order to achieve (and not threaten) the "natural" biological balance of population and environment. This is what terms like "carrying capacity" and "population-environment balance" mean. These are cultural ideas masked as scientific facts and are therefore not open to debate in the minds of advocates. It is crucial to understand how the environment fits into and influences racial and immigration conflicts today because biology still plays a significant role.[65]

Inclusion, Exclusion, and Environmental Politics

The geographer David Sibley bluntly writes that Western society is based on exclusion.[66] But the flipside of exclusion is inclusion, so every act that repels others sends a message of belonging to those who are "like us." Even so, it is more than just about the persecution of one community so that another community gains power. It is more insidious and disturbing than that. In 1984 President Ronald Reagan launched a media campaign titled "It's Morning Again in America," which offered rosy images and remembrances of 1950s suburban, white neighborhoods basking in peace and harmony (all this at a time of serious political and racial discord).[67] This kind of imagery has clear parallels to the nativist environmentalist vision of the future and is indeed about exclusion of some groups while building walls and boundaries to include a select few. Inclusion of this kind is also about building community, about creating strong, meaningful ties and social networks among elites so that they can enjoy their lives and find comfort in this world. Unfortunately, that inclusion appears to be dependent upon exclusion and domination of others. Sibley writes that "The human landscape can be read as a landscape of exclusion. . . . Because power is expressed in the monopolization of space and the relegation of weaker groups in society to less desirable environments."[68] He suggests that we take a closer look at the "curious practices" of the "majority . . . who consider themselves to be normal or mainstream" in order to uncover "the oddness of the ordinary."[69] Similarly, the historian Patricia Limerick contends, in thinking about U.S. history, "it has become essential to follow the policy of cautious street crossers: Remember to look both ways."[70]

Sibley catalogues ways in which whiteness has been equated with purity and hygiene in the colonial world, and how dark skin and people racialized as the "other" were equated with filth, dirt, uncleanliness, and therefore placed outside of civilized society (e.g., Roma, African Americans, Irish, Aborigines, and Jews as rats, and others associated with pigs, cockroaches, trash, and sewers). This ideology extends itself to perhaps the greatest challenge for the environmental movement in the United States: the underlying cultural, racial, and economic elitism of environmentalism that often consciously and blatantly associates clean environments with whiter and wealthier people.

The classical sociologist Thorstein Veblen characterized society's elites as people who relegate lower-status groups to menial labor, even though such jobs are the foundation of a society. The higher-status people often engage in what Veblen famously termed "conspicuous consumption"—a wasteful use of resources and money to maintain a visible standard of social prestige.[71] It is regrettable and dangerous that nativist environmentalists in the Roaring Fork Valley and elsewhere refuse to target the role that elite conspicuous consumption plays in ecological degradation.

Another aspect of conspicuous elite behavior and its effects on inequality concerns U.S. foreign policy. Scott Chaplin, a Roaring Fork Valley social justice activist, wrote a guest editorial in a local newspaper echoing the thoughts of many progressives and immigrant-rights advocates. Specifically, he made an association between U.S. foreign and economic policy and the rise of immigration:

> Most immigrants coming to the United States . . . come here due to the lack of economic opportunity in their countries. . . . Unfortunately the lack of economic opportunity in many "developing" countries has been caused in no small part by U.S. foreign policy, which for too long has created a sad legacy of oppression and poverty in the world by placing corporate interests ahead of democracy and human rights concerns. . . . What do we as citizens of the United States owe the people of these countries for overthrowing or undermining their democracies? What do we owe them for supporting their wealthy elite at the expense of the economic opportunity that could have been available to the majority of their citizens? . . . Can we really take a high moral stand and say to those who want to immigrate here, "Yes, we may have destroyed your democracies and created economic hardship for you, but we need to protect our environment, so you can not come here."[72]

Scholars and journalists have produced books, studies, and reports that support Chaplin's contention that, generally speaking, U.S. policy in Latin America since the late nineteenth century has frequently involved a series of anti-democratic practices aimed at geopolitical and economic dominance that instill terror among publics and unparalleled political destabilization.[73] For example, in many Latin American nations, U.S.–supported state violence laid the groundwork for free-market economic reforms in the 1980s and 1990s, which mandated lower tariff barriers, cut social services, privatized public utilities, increased unemployment, and widened the gap between the rich and the poor. These reforms were demanded by the International Monetary Fund (IMF) to not only facilitate the payment of large foreign debts incurred during the dictatorships but also to make it easier for transnational corporations to penetrate domestic markets and exploit the land and labor of ordinary Latin Americans. Undocumented immigration to the United States is just one of the consequences.

Environmental Privilege and the Resort

The resort vacation spot and second-home getaway has an appeal that few people with the means to access such places can resist. This is nothing new. In a pioneering study of histories of environmental justice struggles in the United States, Dorceta Taylor locates what we would call environmental privilege in this country, dating back to the its earliest days. For example, Taylor describes how, since the seventeenth century, wealthy elites of New York and New England responded to the environmental turmoil of the cities by privatizing or acquiring green space, building large country estates clustered among other rich residents in exclusive enclaves on the edge of urban areas, and excluding undesirables (Jews and people of color) from these spaces and social networks.[74] One of the many places those elites established was the "summer colony," known as the Hamptons. In *The End of the Hamptons*, Corey Dolgon explores the dynamics of environmental privilege through the lens of conquest and resistance that characterizes class struggles on Long Island's East End. Dolgon makes a compelling point regarding the significance of that exclusive resort community. He argues, "studying Long Island's East End is important precisely because the area exhibits social forces and cultural experiences similar to those that exist elsewhere in the region, in the nation, and in the world."[75] He states that while the pressing issues found on Long Island are common, such high-profile locations as the Hamptons provide an "animated" site to bring together a complex narrative of power, property, and place. We would argue that Aspen is another key "animated" site for exploring these issues as they relate to race, immigration, citizenship, and the

environment. The stories of the Hamptons and Aspen are important because we see that environmental privilege is quite common, and that it is
always contested at some level.

The AOL Travel website recently announced its "Top Ten American Resort Towns and Weekend Getaways." The Hamptons made the top of the
list, followed by Aspen at number two. The entry on the Hamptons states,
"The old-money mansions and picturesque villages share acreage with
farms, vineyards and forests" and refers to our town of choice in Colorado
with the following declaration: "ultimate luxury in Aspen is not the exception, it's the rule." The rest of the list includes Palm Springs (California),
Jackson (Wyoming), Key West (Florida), Cherry Hills Village (Colorado),
Hilton Head Island (South Carolina), Newport Beach (California), Lake
Geneva (Wisconsin), and Sandpoint (Idaho). Featured attractions invari-
ably involve hiking, beaches, horseback riding, spas, ski lodges, boating, ca-
noeing, "world-class golf," galleries, boutiques, "fine restaurants," "upscale
activities," "an absence of retail businesses . . . underscoring the echelon
of your surroundings," "austere beauty," and "breathtaking scenery."[76] We
could add Martha's Vineyard, Vail, Pebble Beach, Miami Beach, and many
other towns to this list. We see Aspen mirrored everyday at numerous
other centers of environmental privilege around the nation.

Using Aspen as a strategic site, our goal is to contribute to a larger discussion of the sociological links among immigrant labor, the environment,
and race and class inequalities within the global economy. The increasingly globalized reach of market economies contributes to the continuing presence of working poor, immigrant communities across the United
States and many other global North communities.

While one of our primary emphases is the politics of immigration—not
immigrants themselves—throughout this book we consider the immigrant
worker's experience of living the existence of someone whose labor is embraced while his or her social existence is often cursed. In the course of our
research, we found ourselves in a fortunate position in which immigrant
workers—some of whom were in quite vulnerable situations—trusted us
with their personal stories of immigration, work and labor, and raising
families. They gave us candid reflections on how they survive, whom they
work for, and the nature of local politics. We were able to gain their trust
because of our relationships with well-respected community leaders from
social service, religious, media, and advocacy organizations. While most

Latino immigrants in the Roaring Fork Valley come from Mexico, many others also traveled from Central and South America. Most of them work long hours in hotels, for landscaping services, in food service institutions, or in construction. It was clear in our interviews that depending on one's social position and immigration status, Aspen is an entirely different place for different people. It was evident that one's privilege and position within the very distinct racial and class hierarchy dramatically affects one's sense of geography. As one interviewee replied in response to our question as to whether he finds time to enjoy the famous Rocky Mountains that surround the valley: "Mountains? What mountains?"

1

The Logic of Aspen

While our geographic focus extends throughout Colorado's Roaring Fork Valley, all valley roads ultimately lead to Aspen. There is the physical road, Highway 82, which is the main path to Aspen, connecting that city with Snowmass, Woody Creek, and the "down valley" communities of Basalt, Carbondale, Glenwood Springs, Rifle, and Parachute. There is also the so-called road of influence, politics, opportunity, and money that leads to Aspen, the Pitkin County seat where affluence and glitter outweigh anything you can find down valley. Aspen, it seems, offers something for everyone: work for immigrants, inspiration and funding for environmentalists and intellectuals, and a playground for the rich. And so it is there we begin our story.

Aspen sits high in the Rocky Mountains and is a mecca for skiers, hikers, nature enthusiasts, environmentalists, classical music lovers, and economic, political, and cultural elites from around the world. Jane Fonda, Arnold Schwarzenegger, Don Henley, Don Johnson, Barbie Benton, Melanie Griffith, Kevin Costner, John Kerry, Ross Perot, and Jesse Jackson are known to vacation, exercise, own homes, or raise money in Aspen.[1] Aspen's sister cities are Chamonix, France; Davos, Switzerland; and Garmisch-Partenkirchen, Germany.[2] The average price of a home here was around $4 million in 2007,[3] and locals attend free seminars at the Aspen Institute on "how to pay no estate tax to the IRS."[4]

Aspen's year-round residential population is just under 6,000, but in July and August the number of people in town can reach nearly 30,000, when the various summer festivals are held. While skiing may be what Aspen is most famous for, the summer season rivals the popularity of its winter activities.

The town of Aspen from above. Photo by L. S. Park

Student musicians playing in downtown Aspen. Photo by L. S. Park

The Aspen/Snowmass *Food and Wine Classic* is a major extravaganza spon-sored every year by *Food and Wine* magazine (Snowmass is the closest town north of Aspen). The event promotes intensive consumption and opulent lifestyles. But for years the main summer attraction has been the Aspen Music Festival. This gathering features numerous musicians playing in or-chestras, quartets, and other combinations, and allows tourists and locals a chance to enjoy classical music in a relaxed, bucolic atmosphere.

People travel from around the world to attend this event and the festival's organizers create slick brochures and websites to market it. The 2002 publicity captured many of the issues we highlight in this book. The theme for that year was "Voices of Expatriates":

> For centuries artists have left their native countries to seek creative homes—places that nurtured them and, more importantly, their work. The stories are many: Composers as varied as Joseph Haydn, Ludwig van Beethoven, Gustav Mahler, Serge Rachmaninoff, Bela Bartok, Arnold Schoenberg, and Igor Stravinsky all worked far from their homelands. . . . This summer, the Festival goes on its own journey of discovery to explore the sometimes aching, sometimes exultant voices of these expatriate artists. . . . This summer . . . journey to a place where music surrounds you. Discover a deeper understanding of an art form you love. Experience the soul of the music expressed in all its bare beauty. Return home changed, quietly but profoundly. Come be refreshed, come be connected, come be changed. In Aspen, classical music pours out like sunshine. It lives and breathes *like the nature that surrounds it—filling the mountain air* with the sounds of five full orchestras, countless chamber combinations, 1,000 musicians, and up to eight performances a day, all in one quiet little mountain town. *This organic combination of music and nature stems from the Festival's belief that it is the unhurried beauty of nature* that allows for the creative growth of musicians—and ultimately then of music itself. Artists from all over the world come to Aspen to take a break from their everyday lives and rejuvenate, collaborate, experiment and experience the joy of really connecting with music again.[5]

Aspen is a place where expatriate musicians are welcomed. And Aspen is a place where people from around the world are beckoned for relaxation, rejuvenation, and the enjoyment of nature's beauty. That is, unless you happen to be an immigrant laborer whose very purpose is to make possible and facilitate that rendezvous with Mother Earth for the rest of Aspen's visitors.

On any given day one can walk the streets of Aspen and see purebred dogs adorned with bejeweled collars drinking water from bowls provided by cafés, and people inside such establishments casually drinking coffee and juice. The Anglo workers are in front and Latinos are back in the

kitchen. People fresh from their plastic surgeon's offices stroll the prom-
enades wearing clothes from high-end boutiques, while a snow-capped
mountain towers in the background. This is a great getaway, if you can
afford it.

In May 2009 we walked, drove, and biked through Aspen's neighborhoods and marveled at the size of the homes there, including new homes
under construction, which appeared to be oblivious to the recent devasta-
tions in the housing market and our nationwide and global recession. As
always, there were numerous Latino men doing landscaping and remodel-
ing work in the community. We observed Latinas walking from house to
house, as they finished one domestic service job and moved to the next.
On the grounds of the Aspen Institute and the Aspen Meadows, the same
pattern prevailed: Latino men landscaping, Latinas cleaned the guest
rooms. Both Latino men and women worked in the dining service operations at the institute's restaurant.

As we strolled through downtown Aspen, we saw tourists and residents
mingling, shopping, and eating. On Hyman Avenue, people streamed in
and out of the Wheeler Opera House, which sits opposite a row of upscale
restaurants. On Mill Street, just a block from the historic Hotel Jerome, a
blonde woman in casual clothes jumped into the drivers' seat of a pickup
truck with a sign on the door that read "Nordic Gardens Landscape Services." Two Latino men climbed into the back, apparently heading out to a
job with their boss.

Across from the Pitkin County Library we saw the county sheriff's office on the corner of Main Street and Galena, flanked by Aspen law enforcement's vehicles of choice: Toyota Highlander hybrid fuel SUVs. Situated between the sheriff's offices and the library, there is an open area and
brick walkway for tourists to take in the mountain views, high above the
Roaring Fork River. The middle of this spot is punctuated by a public art
piece "El Conquistador," a shiny, silver-colored, metal sculpture of a conquistador on horseback, a celebration of the Spanish conquest of the New
World.

Shoppers have their choice of various upscale businesses like Dior, Bulgari, Louis Vuitton, Gucci, and Prada, as well as a host of furriers, jewelers,
art galleries, and sports shops selling gear for whitewater rafting, skiing,
and snowboarding. Roots, the Canadian clothing line with a prominent
shop along Galena Street, is clearly for the young and hip demographic.

A display sign outside the door features a photograph of a fashion model in a verdant background with the caption "It's sexy being green." On the same block, we see three Latino men fixing the roof and gutter on top of an espresso and wine bar as white patrons relax below them with laptops and lattés. We take it all in while sitting on a public bench made from recycled materials.

A headline—"Aspen is a Fashion Show"—in the *Aspen Times* newspaper one winter day summed up much of what that city means to a lot of people.[6] In another publication, the author Hal Clifford writes:

> In the pantheon of North American ski resorts, Aspen reigns near the pinnacle. It offers four ski areas, unparalleled dining and nightlife, year-round performing arts and what the hoity-toity like to call "world-class shopping." For some, shopping is Aspen . . . Bulgari, Ralph Lauren, Chanel, Christian Dior, Fendi[7]

George Stranahan, an Aspen-area philanthropist and progressive social activist, described his adopted hometown this way:

> It's a cute town, a fabulous area for fishing, climbing . . . pure physical attraction. . . . It's pretty good if that's what you like. Aspen is a façade like Disneyworld. It's solid, but it is a façade. . . . It's not a reality, it's an entertainment industry.[8]

One evening we spoke with a bartender at a favorite watering hole in downtown Aspen. Nearing closing time on a slow night, she relayed some of her more memorable moments as a seasonal worker.[9] She told us stories about teenagers and preteens from wealthy families coming into the bar running up tabs of several hundred dollars, carrying $4,000 Prada purses, and bragging about how they paid for these accessories with their own personal Platinum Visa cards. According to the bartender, the employees at the bar are basically told "don't even check their IDs, it's fine."[10] She recalled an episode when there was a party on the second floor of the bar. A "Fortune 500 guy" was hosting the event, at which the guests ran up a bill of over $10,000 on alcohol. When she gave him the bill, he gave her a credit card. She asked him for his ID and he reportedly "had a fit" and said, "Do you have any idea who I am? I could buy this bar, this whole building right now, if I wanted to!" She remarked to us, "The wealthy people in Aspen are so wealthy that they look down on the movie stars. The wealthy people here often ask if the Hollywood stars want *their* autographs! Goldie Hawn, Barbie Benton, and others have wealth that is trivial compared to some of these folks."

A newspaper advertisement from Coates, Reid, and Waldron realtors who sell luxury estates in the area featured a $1 million *discount* on a home with an original price tag of $10,990,000. A red slash runs through the price, followed by the new much lower price of $9,990,000: "Located in the prestigious and gated Starwood Subdivision, this 8 bedroom/8 bath estate boasts almost 13,000 square feet of luxury living space, dramatic views of all four ski areas, indoor swimming pool and outdoor tennis court."[11] Another home, selling for $7.5 million boasts "over 39 private acres" of land in a "small, private, and prestigious subdivision just minutes from Snowmass Village and downtown Aspen."[12] The emphasis on privacy, exclusive access to mountain vistas, and open space are reflections of environmental privilege.

The following comes from an advertisement for yet another private facility in Aspen called the Maroon Creek Club:

> There are Privileges. And then there are Privileges. There is a lot of talk about private club membership. We don't believe that sharing a condominium and being one of more than 200 other visitors with the same "privileges" is all that private and exclusive. So if you're looking for privacy, exclusivity and membership privileges, you owe it to yourself to check out Maroon Creek Club's New Lodging Program. With two new ways to call Aspen home. . . . Ahhh, the real privileges of membership in Aspen's most exclusive private golf and tennis club: 32 winter memberships from $140,000, 16 Gold memberships from $475,000. You owe it to yourself to arrange a private tour.[13]

Privilege is apparently a highly competitive, multilayered sport. For most people, a private, exclusive club in Aspen is simply redundant.

Another advertisement printed in many of the area's publications is for Aspen Aviation, Inc., a private "on-demand" air charter company. The text reads: "Imagine flying on your schedule, in your own private aircraft, with no airline hassles, and no lost luggage. Experience our outstanding service, with our Aspen-based aircraft and crews, at rates more affordable than you may imagine."[14] And if you cannot afford a private jet, then there are plenty of other airlines that can get you to Aspen. *SkyWest Magazine*—SkyWest airlines' official in-flight publication—featured an article on Aspen that offers an alluring vision for anyone needing a getaway to enjoy the beauty of the Colorado Rockies. The article calls Aspen "Mother Nature's playground":

> Here the outdoor life is the life. . . . Of course, not everything about Aspen is so active. It's also possible to spend leisurely hours at a pampering spa, run your toes through the grass in one of many downtown pocket parks, listen to impromptu concerts on downtown street corners or watch children revel in the dancing waters of the Hyman Avenue fountain. . . . Aspen on a shoestring: Whether you're craving wide-open adventure or community culture, some of the best things about Aspen are free. Hike through the Maroon Bells–Snowmass Wilderness, fly-fish the Roaring Fork River, or stroll downtown for window-shopping and people-watching. Other complimentary benefits to Aspen life include wine and cheese receptions at the Aspen Art Museum, lawn seating for Aspen Music Festival concerts, Thursday night concerts on Fanny Hill in Snowmass and guided nature walks atop Aspen Mountain.[15]

The display of wealth and conspicuous consumption in Aspen is legendary.

In 2004, the Aspen Valley Hospital announced that it would begin offering discounts on cosmetic surgery procedures in order to drum up business.[16] Dr. Dennis Cirillo has a cosmetic surgery practice on Main Street in Aspen, specializing in "facelifts, eye work and breast enhancements." According to Cirillo, facelifts are the most common procedures requested. He noted that many of his clients have second homes in Aspen or visit regularly for recreation and rejuvenation. His office routinely provides patients with tickets to the ballet, theater, or symphony to make the recovery process more enjoyable. Many of his patients come to him so that they can relax, get a facelift, see a show, and return home looking "refreshed."[17] And, of course, skiing is part of everyday life during the winter season. As one Aspenite told us "I have skis here sitting in my office, it's very culturally acceptable to run out over your lunch hour and take a couple of runs."[18]

Even the homes in the trailer parks sell for $300,000 and up, and professionals like doctors, architects, and lawyers are among the residents there.[19] A critical Aspenite tells us, "It's the Twilight Zone up here when you start looking at real estate. It's just incomprehensible. There's no way that a person who is reliant on the income from a job could ever purchase here."[20] One Aspen City Council member told us, "Unfortunately . . . it *is* a resort community. And it is not unlike a community like Beverly Hills . . . or even Manhattan, where people who work there can't afford to live there."[21] A writer put it this way: "Aspen may be the only ski town that has become a verb. To Aspenize, in the eyes of those who live elsewhere, is to destroy a nice little ski town with conspicuous wealth, development, and self-indulgence."[22]

The philanthropist George Stranahan responded to our question "Is there affordable housing in this town?" with "Hell, no. No. You can't be a line cook at maybe twelve dollars an hour and find a renters program. It's not going to work very well."[23]

Despite the fact that 95 percent of the city's population is white, and despite the eagerness of Terry Paulson and others to restrict Aspen's population, you don't have to be white to live in Aspen, or to own a second, third, or fourth home there.[24] Enough wealth and fame can buy you access, as proved by David Robinson, a former San Antonio Spurs star. Robinson, who is African American and wealthy, has a second home in Aspen. Consider the case of Saudi Prince Bandar, who obtained permission from the city council to build a 56,000-square-foot home he calls Hala (which he says is the Arabic word for "welcome"). Bandar gave donations of $820,000 to various charities in Aspen just before his proposal came before the council. In some people's view, this was nothing less than a bribe. But Dick Butera, a realtor, developer, and co-owner of Aspen's landmark Hotel Jerome, declared that Bandar's "palace" (as some called the house) would have a positive economic ripple effect, which would trickle down to the common person, including children (in the form of school taxes) and construction workers (jobs from building the house) and via the funding boost to local charities.[25] The resulting structure is larger than the White House, with fifteen bedrooms, sixteen bathrooms, a private barbershop and beauty salon, and enough space to host a party for 450 revelers and a staff of twelve servants.[26]

Like many of Aspen's wealthiest denizens, this is just one of multiple homes Bandar owns around the world, which means he is rarely in town. The ecological footprint involved in building and maintaining such a structure for someone who rarely visits Aspen might give one pause, considering that the same city council that allowed a special exception for Hala condemned working-class immigrants as the real ecological threat. When, in 2007, Bandar decided to sell the house for $135 million—the most expensive single-family residential property on the market in the United States that year—the message was clear: "non-billionaires need not apply."[27] This means that even Aspen's traditional Hollywood-star set is increasingly finding it difficult to purchase or maintain a residence in the area.

Many other Aspen area elites have equally extravagant approaches to home, hearth, and the ecosystem. Most elite jet-setters with homes in the area spend little time there, but often want their multimillion-dollar domiciles ready for them whenever they arrive. One Snowmass property manager told a journalist that his job was to look after vacation homes while their absentee owners were out of town. Most of the properties he managed were empty forty-five weeks of the year, "[y]et they had to stay heated so the pipes wouldn't freeze and their swimming pools, as a rule, were heated continuously—not drained—so they'd be ready for use when the owners arrived."[28] Gerhard Andlinger is an Aspen resident. He is also a multimillionaire financier who violated land-use codes when—in the process of constructing his home—he "dug and hauled away an entire hillside" and "built a trench through habitat without the necessary permits." He thought this was perfectly reasonable for what he calls his "cabin"— a 7,500-square-foot luxury home that sits on a 157-acre lot. The county objected when he moved more than 10,000 cubic yards of dirt, which he termed an "agricultural improvement" that would allow him to more easily "keep an eye on his horses."[29] Yet the city and county still hold firm in their view that population control is the real key to ecological sustainability.

To the average Aspenite, though, excesses like Andlinger's seem ordinary. One local mother we spoke to described her child's future school in town:

> They're in the process of building a $41 million high school . . . and I'm pretty confident that the schools are going to be probably better. For a couple of reasons. One is, they have a lot of money . . . every kid in the new high school will be furnished with a brand new laptop computer. . . .

The city is also building a $3 million . . . ice rink facility . . . that was donated by a group of wealthy individuals here [and it will be] right in front of the high school . . . it will be a community center that will have an Olympic-sized hockey rink and pool and so on.[30]

At the same time, Aspen's reputation for environmentalism and new-age spirituality is highly regarded.[31] As the director of the Aspen Valley Community Foundation told us, "We have a ton of environmental nonprofits in this small area."[32] With a penchant for Eastern philosophies (and their Westernized derivatives), this area is a veritable theme park for people seeking spiritual rejuvenation through outdoor activities and access to motivational speakers, gurus, and spa treatments. In 2004, Snowmass hosted the Snowmass Wellness Experience. They welcomed a visit from the yoga guru Bikram Choudhury and the best-selling author and "spiritual savant" Deepak Chopra, which allowed locals to revel in the "mind-body-spirit connection for which the 'Aspen Idea' is so justifiably famous."[33] The session also featured speakers on Feng Shui and Ayurvedic healing.

Running through so much of the story that Aspen tells eagerly about itself is the Aspen Logic. The marriage of capital growth and environmentalism has been a hallmark of this area for years, far ahead of current initiatives by large corporations such as Walmart. Auden Schendler, director of environmental affairs at the Aspen Skiing Company—known to Aspenites as "SkiCo"—is a staunch believer and practitioner of the Aspen Logic. He boasts, "We don't just have one green building; we have a green development policy and many green buildings. We don't just buy renewable energy; we're currently exploring a new goal of 25 percent renewable power, and now we're making clean power on the hill with our hydroelectric station on Snowmass."[34] And SkiCo has the awards to prove it.[35] Consistent with the feel-good spirit of the Aspen Logic, Aspen's airport and post office are both outfitted with solar panels.

The Aspen Logic is a match made in heaven for "green consumers" who wish to maintain their high-status lifestyle while supporting environmental causes. *Aspen Magazine* published a story about locals who have been bitten by the scooter bug:

But how green our town is extends beyond organic produce to the trend of environmentally friendly scooters. . . . Not only are they the most stylish

way to get around in the summer, they also make parking in our con-
gested downtown considerably easier. In the summertime, Aspen proves
that Rome isn't the only place where scooters rule. "My Italjet gets a kabil-
lion miles to the gallon. I never fill it up," says Maria DeGraeve, manager of
the Aspen Bulgari store and avid scooter rider. "And it's a lot more ecologically friendly than my SUV." Valerie Alexander, who works for Bluegreen,
says riding the vintage Vespa takes her to another place. "I feel like I
should be in Europe, heading to lunch with the girls, scarf blowing in the
wind, and a baguette in my backpack—except I'm in Aspen."[36]

The references to Rome and Europe are consistent with a long and conscious history of constructing U.S. ski towns as faux-Bavarian or Alpine
villages of the Rockies. The father of modern Aspen, Walter Paepcke, lov-
ingly referred to the town as an American Salzburg. After World War II,
ski resort promoters deliberately marketed these developments as European ski resorts within the American West, thus securing environmental
privileges by making invisible those people of color who worked or lived
in these places.[37] It is also interesting that Ms. DeGraeve is self-congratulatory about her scooter usage, yet unconcerned that she still owns and
drives an SUV. The article continues:

> Part-time Aspenite Celeste Fenichel chose her scooter's color to match
> her turquoise jewelry. She spends most of the year in London—where
> she drives luxury SUVs—with her husband and two sons. But while
> Fenichel is in Aspen during the summer, she can often be seen riding
> her Vespa to her tennis matches at the Maroon Creek Club.[38]

The breeziness of the article's prose is endemic to the plethora of promotional journalism written about Aspen. This story, like so many others, rev-
els in a self-congratulatory air that is as bright and shiny as Aspen's own
crisp mountain air. The message is clear: in Aspen, you can have it all. You
can take pride in riding a scooter but still drive an SUV. Environmental responsibility and conspicuous consumption are entirely compatible.

The unexamined environmental privilege is what makes Aspen so at-
tractive to its elite residents. A casual sampling of Aspen area bumper
stickers (generally on old Volvos as well as SUVs and other second or third
cars) revealed a range of political themes:

"If you're NOT an environmentalist you're totally insane."

"Be Green: Help the Earth Live."

"NATIVE" [with the Colorado Rocky Mountains as the background].[39]

"No Vacancy" [with the Colorado Rocky Mountains as the background].

"What schools need is moment of science" [as opposed to the Religious
    Right's "moment of *silence*"]

"Replenish the Earth: Prevent Excess Births."

The owners of each of these bumper-stickered vehicles likely view themselves as politically progressive. Each sticker embraces a message that is
antiwar or peace loving, in favor of smart growth, slow growth, no growth,
and ecological sustainability. Yet they also seek to maintain environmental
privileges by excluding others from these places and reflect an unexamined refusal to sacrifice political power or material wealth.

Regarding Aspen's claim to ecological purity, George Stranahan is more
critical. He stated, "there's a little gray haze over Aspen in the summer. We
are one pollutin' son of a bitch. Everybody who comes up here, everyone
gets a rental car. I guess the [ecological] impact is the tourism."[40] Recent
reports of the environmental toll on land and waterways associated with
mountain climbing, hiking, snowmaking, fishing, backpacking, snowmobil-
ing, snowshoeing, skiing, and other off-road recreational activities in Colorado's mountains would certainly support Stranahan's contention.[41] Even
"nature loving" activities have negative environmental impacts.

Stranahan was also clear as to the state of class inequality in town:

> The economic diversity in Aspen is . . . there's no poverty in Aspen. The
> rest of the world is looking at this huge divide between 5 percent of the
> people who have 90 percent of the money and 95 percent of the people
> who have nothing. When in Aspen, you're not going to see the people at
> the bottom. So we don't have an economic diversity, we're a very strati-
> fied class structure.[42]

Regarding Aspen's racial demography (or lack thereof), city council member Tony Hershey had this to say:

> Aspen is a very wealthy community, frankly it's a very white commu-
> nity, just because David Robinson from the [San Antonio] Spurs had a

house here doesn't make us integrated, you know. It's frankly, unusual to see a black person. There was a comedian that I went to see the other night, and he's staying at the St. Regis [Hotel]. And he said "I was in the hotel room when the maid came in, and she was white, and I went like 'Who are you?,' and she's like 'Who are *you*?!'" Joking because, there's no black people here. . . . We had a crime wave two summers ago. . . . And it turns out there were two young high school Aspen kids. And these were serious crimes, armed robbery of a supermarket and stuff, and immediately it was like "Oh those Mexicans were involved." And it was sort of a wake-up call for some people because, hey, they weren't Mexicans, they were Aspen . . . white kids. But, it was an unfortunate thing, there's been some crime and some people point their finger at the poor people.[43]

Aspen is a mountain town where many people live a larger-than-life existence, where liberals and progressives flock to enjoy themselves and express their love of nature and New-Age fads, and where the ugliness of capitalism and racism is expressed and exposed from time to time.

Living Down Valley

The separation of Aspen and "down valley" towns is both real and an artifact. It is real in that Aspen is the pinnacle of wealth and glitter in the Roaring Fork Valley. It is an artifact because the valley is, to a degree, a single community that represents great social diversity. As one resident told us, "The valley is a very, very small community and, in some respects, is one community although it is comprised of a series of small towns starting at the upper valley in Aspen and then you move down."[44]

The Roaring Fork Valley, situated in western Colorado, is bisected by an eighty-mile corridor defined by the Roaring Fork River and its tributaries, including the Crystal and Frying Pan Rivers. The valley is surrounded by mountains on all sides, in particular the Elk Mountains, Aspen Mountain and the Maroon Bells, which are southwest of Aspen, and Mount Sopris, which stands on the northwest edge of the region. Aspen sits at the highest point in the valley, at approximately 8,000 feet above sea level. The city literally looks out over the valley. As you leave Aspen on Highway 82, you head northwest—down valley. You first hit Snowmass, Woody Creek, Basalt, Carbondale, Glenwood Springs, and then Rifle and Parachute going west on Highway 70. This stretch along the Roaring Fork River has developed around mining and tourism since the 1880s. The names of many towns reflect Colorado's role as a major mining hotspot and a key site in the violent exploitation and settlement of the American West. Some towns and communities are named after minerals (Basalt, Marble, Leadville, Carbondale, Gypsum, Silt, Redstone) or weapons (Gunbarrel and Rifle).

As you leave Aspen's cultivated downtown heading north on Highway 82, you come to Snowmass, where life looks essentially the same as Aspen but with a few less designer shops. The town of Woody Creek is nearby and easy to miss since it is unincorporated and quite small. The town has a legendary bar—the Woody Creek Tavern. Woody Creek is famous for its superstar residents like Don Henley, Don Johnson, the late Hunter S. Thompson, and more recently, Nancy Pelosi. Farther down 82 you hit Basalt, a town of less than 3,000 residents, a high cost of living, and a great location for trout fishing and mountain biking. This is also the town that passed a pro-immigration resolution in response to Aspen's nativist resolution. In February 2001 the Basalt city council's resolution acknowledged the positive contributions of immigrants; promoted equal rights for all workers (both documented and undocumented); sought amnesty for people in the country without papers; and called for the federal immigration process to be streamlined so that immigrants might move along the path to legal citizenship more easily. Jon Fox-Rubin, a Basalt City Council member, related:

> To me it just really scapegoats immigrants when we white people driving around in our sport utility vehicles consuming the American lifestyle are phenomenally out of proportion with the Latinos that are living in our community. . . many of them are commuting on the bus or carpooling in relatively large numbers and living very efficiently. The single issue thinking behind the Aspen resolution was "my environment, my local backyard environment is worth more than the global environment." So that was the impetus for our resolution.[45]

Down the road from Basalt, you come to Carbondale, perhaps the most relaxed town in the valley. There are 5,000 residents and a sizable immigrant and Latino population, great Mexican restaurants, a number of mobile home communities, and a large public park that the locals often use. Carbondale has become a bedroom community for many workers who spend their days in Aspen, and the average incomes are much less than those found farther up the valley. In the Bonanza trailer park, the average monthly salary of its mostly Latino immigrant residents was $2,000, which is a poverty wage in the Roaring Fork Valley. Just under half of the Bonanza residents earned less than $1,300 each month.

This town celebrates its growing artist community and has inspiring vistas with Mount Sopris towering above, just to the south—the area's most imposing natural landmark. In many ways, much of Carbondale sees itself as the ecologically conscious town that Aspen wants to be. It is a place where restaurants serve dandelions with fresh-from-the-farm entrees, where few streetlights are allowed so as to reduce "light pollution" at night, and where low-flow toilets are the order of the day. The Stepstone Center for Social Justice director and Carbondale councilmember Scott Chaplin laughs as he describes the environmental perspective that is emblematic of his town:

> In that sense, our town is a little bit ahead of Aspen in some ways, in that we haven't sprayed pesticides in our parks for about eight years now. There's a strong environmental ethic in this town. We're talking about getting solar powered hot water in the swimming pool. We've made the dandelion the town flower because if you have dandelions, it's a good sign that you're not using chemicals. . . . I think there's more of a feeling here in Carbondale that this is a community for people *and* the environment, and in Aspen it's more like they don't care so much about people, they just want the environment![46]

The town of Carbondale is an important site in the immigration and environment debate. In many ways, it is where much of the opposition to Aspen's nativist environmentalism has emerged. The Stepstone Center for Social Justice, Mountain Folks for Global Justice, and other pro-immigrant, environmental justice, and social justice groups are based there. Carbondale has a "crunchy granola" reputation that is more down to earth than Aspen. For example, while the Aspen Institute invites world dignitaries to discuss philosophy, the arts, and the benefits of economic globalization, Carbondale prefers hosting its annual Mountain Fair, which looks like a countercultural gathering from another era. As one local activist told us, "Carbondale is a bunch of old hippies. And has a pretty fierce western independence kind of thing like 'what do you mean I can't smoke pot in the park?'"[47]

Local organizers also regularly bring in speakers like the progressive author and activist Jim Hightower, who was cheered on by Carbondale's strong, left-leaning community as he characterized president George W. Bush's administration as a group of "kleptocrats" who were responsible for "stealing our democracy."[48] On a Monday evening when we were visiting Carbondale, a group of activists marched down Main street with a twelve-foot figure of George W. Bush with faux flames rising out of the back of his pant legs, while people chanted "liar, liar, pants on fire." This was part of a national campaign dreamed up by Ben Cohen, co-founder of the Ben & Jerry's ice cream corporation, as a tactic for raising public awareness of the "credibility gap" associated with the Bush regime's foreign policy decisions. The protest went well and received local support, but it also resulted in a police citation for having the wrong kind of lights on the trailer carrying the Bush figure.[49]

Continuing down the valley, Glenwood Springs is the next stop. Glenwood sits at the confluence of the Colorado and the Roaring Fork rivers and is most famous for its hot springs and caverns. Tourists, athletes, and the infirm have enjoyed the hot springs for more than a century. This city of 9,000 people is a major destination for mountain bikers, anglers, and water sports enthusiasts. If you approach Glenwood from Interstate 70, you can see tourists white-water rafting and kayaking on the Colorado River. The smell of sulfur fills the air and is a bit jarring, but you quickly get used to it once you feel the warmth of the hot springs. Glenwood is also the home of the Colorado Mountain College, which serves many Latino and immigrant youth. In addition, Glenwood where *La Unión*, a progressive, monthly, bilingual newspaper is based. Luis Polar said he gave the paper that name because "I want this paper to reflect unity. Unity among cultures, unity among races, and unity among people."[50] Glenwood Springs has a strong and progressive social-services sector that works with immigrants and their families to find employment and to offer childcare and other needs. The connection to nature is no less serious here than anywhere else in the valley. For example, a hunter from Glenwood Springs was recently sentenced to 120 days in jail and a $27,500 fine after he illegally shot and killed a bighorn ram.[51]

Continuing west on Highway 70, you drive past Rifle (population 10,000) and reach the end of the Roaring Fork Valley in Parachute, Colorado (population 1,000). Both towns have Latino populations of about 20 percent; median and family incomes are fairly low in these communities, which are struggling to maintain a tax base. Since the mid-1990s, the town of Rifle has grown into a bedroom community where many immigrants from Mexico, Honduras, and other Latin American nations live when they are not working in Aspen, sixty miles up valley. Rifle was also the site of a violent anti-Latino migrant killing spree in 2001 (which we discuss later in this chapter).

The mobile home parks in the valley are often tucked away beyond or under a grove of trees, a way of making sure the working-class and immigrant populations living there are not too noticeable to the tourists or the local elites. In one park we saw in Glenwood Springs, the homes are lined up in two rows along a dirt road and are barely visible from highway 82. The homes are neatly kept, but there is not a lot of activity in the neighborhood because the residents are rarely home since they are at work all day. Looking out over Glenwood Springs from the campus of Colorado Mountain College—which sits atop a small mountain—you are struck by how well the mobile home communities and their immigrant residents are hidden from view.

In 2006 Tom Brokaw, the NBC correspondent, did a series of stories on immigration in the twenty-first century. One of his stops was the Roaring Fork Valley. Brokaw spoke with a construction-company owner who hired undocumented immigrant workers at $12–14 per hour. That's not a bad wage, except for the high cost of living in the valley and that many of these workers must send money back home to family in Latin America.[52] Many workers and employers we spoke with agreed that $14 per hour was the high end of the wage spectrum.

While it is impossible to know how many undocumented persons are in the region, there are estimates available. Michael Comfort, the deputy district director for the Immigration and Nationalization Service (INS) in the late 1990s, estimated that between 35,000 and 45,000 undocumented persons live in Colorado.[53] The Pew Research Center estimates the undocumented immigrant population of Colorado to be 4.5 percent of the state's workforce, but the number in the Roaring Fork Valley is likely much higher.[54] Garfield County contains many of the Roaring Fork's down-valley towns like Carbondale, Glenwood Springs, Rifle, and Parachute. The

Roaring Fork Valley mobile home park. Photo by L. S. Park

Latino population of the county is 17 percent of the county's 55,000 residents. The government estimates that there are 6,700 undocumented persons in the county, or 8.2 percent.[55] With Latinos making up nearly one-fifth of the county's population, and undocumented persons constituting half of that number, immigrants are an important part of the region's culture and economy. Aspen sheriff deputy Marie Munday underscored this point when she estimated that there are 20,000 Latinos (documented and undocumented) in the entire Roaring Fork Valley, which includes Garfield, Pitkin, and Summit counties.[56]

Jessica Dove, a local Anglo woman who works as an educational advocate for immigrant communities, described the ethnic and racial terrain of the valley:

If you'd like a general picture of the immigrant community, I can tell you that they come from all over. The vast majority is Mexican, of course, but there are also Salvadorans—they tend to be documented because there was an amnesty program a while ago. We also have a number of Argentines and Peruvians as well, both of which are very used to mountain living, having done so in their home countries. They come here to work during the ski season, and I suspect most find other work during the off-season. We also have a number of folks coming from Uruguay and Paraguay. The Ski Company has a real racket—they've been able to recruit folks from Argentina to be ski lift operators and ski instructors for as low as $8/hour. These are jobs that used to pay much more in the past. There is a small Asian community that works mostly in restaurants. Many of them are working toward legal status in the United States. . . . There are not very many African Americans . . . and in terms of Anglos, they are often second-homeowners and have personal staffs at their homes—nannies, cooks, gardeners, and cleaners, etc. These Anglos actually contribute a great deal to the local employment just by employing large staffs of immigrants to do their personal services. There is also a working business-class in the area as well, which is mostly white and not necessarily wealthy.[57]

Much of the present-day immigrant and second-generation Latino population in the Roaring Fork Valley traces its roots to the 1980s when businesses recruited temporary workers from south of the border to come north for employment in the booming tourist sector. Instead of returning after a few years, many of these migrants remained, brought their families (or created families here), found friends, and created a community.[58]

Up-Valley and Down-Valley Politics

Since down-valley communities are more affordable than Aspen, this is where most of the immigrant population lives. And, as is the case in many other parts of the country, the environmental privileges of the wealthy exist alongside greater environmental risks affecting the poor and people of color. Jon Fox-Rubin explains the situation in Basalt:

Most of the affordable housing that we have is in the form of mobile homes, and they are in a floodplain. One of the key issues that we have is helping move those households out of the floodplain and into other affordable housing. And that price that they have there is very hard to beat. We're looking at moving people out of harm's way without moving them downstream or out of the community. A lot of them are working-class people that go to Aspen everyday . . . in a variety of service-related jobs. . . . A large fraction of the people are Latinos. We probably have about a hundred mobile homes. And then the low-end area is probably the most precarious . . . because that's the north end of the flood plain.

The precarious nature of immigrant housing is indicative of their uncertain existence in the community. Their segregated, subpar living conditions fix the Latino immigrant community on the lowest rung of the social hierarchy. In addition, local zoning laws, even in politically progressive towns like Basalt, function as constant reminders lest they forget. Fox-Rubin observed:

We have regulations on how many unrelated people can live in a household. I think that it's going to be an uphill battle because there's a lot of education required. There aren't any Latinos on our town council. There's a lot of implicit—I guess you would call it—institutionalized racism issues that white communities have. We don't realize that our policies are essentially unfair and have a racist component. (Interviewer: And you would say that that's prominent in Basalt politics?) Yes.[59]

From Hurricane Katrina in the Gulf Coast region to communities affected by hydroelectric power on nearly every continent to Roma settlements outside Central and Eastern European cities, marginal populations frequently face the environmental injustice of living in floodplains or in areas at risk of flooding from waterways and dams. This is a result of political and economic inequalities.[60]

Down-valley communities are an integral part of Aspen's existence, providing immigrant labor, white-collar workers, housing, and new opportunities for growth and investment. Down valley activist and council member Scott Chaplin states, "There's always been this Up Valley/Down Valley tension. They're providing more of the funding for the bus system, so they think they're doing us a favor. But we're housing most of their workers, so we think we're doing them a favor."[61] Affordable housing is nonexistent in Aspen, whereas other Roaring Fork communities are trying to implement housing programs for working people out of sheer necessity. The industries employing immigrants throughout the valley are largely in the service sector—hotels, restaurants, and grocery stores—and landscaping and construction. While the wages in Aspen are relatively high, even for low-end service work, they do not adequately compensate a worker for the high cost of living there. Alice Hubbard Laird—a city council member in Carbondale and a well-respected environmental advocate in the valley— stated that the Aspen "billionaires are pushing the millionaires out!"[62]

The various down valley communities are all grappling with their very different roles concerning a number of pressing and interrelated issues: housing, employment, and immigration. But the mainstay of public concern and conversation in the valley is growth and its impact on the environment and quality of life. And, of course, growth is inseparable from the politics of immigration, housing, and employment. From Aspen to Parachute, whether it is embraced or repelled, growth is the thing. The owner of an inn in Glenwood Springs told us:

> It's like everyone has a connection to the construction industry here in this town. My husband is in the industry, so that colors my perceptions of growth. My parents live in Glenwood Springs and my sister does too. My kid goes to school in Carbondale . . . and everyone has either a job in education, medical services, or construction here. There has been an ongoing proposal for a golf course over the hill here, and initially all the nearby residents were protesting it, but since we are in construction we understand why people want to build, so we're of two minds on that.[63]

As much as Aspenites complain about overcrowded trails, ski slopes, and roads, the rest of the valley is facing growing pains and pleasures as well. The towns of Basalt and Carbondale are sites of rising local concerns and hopes over massive growth.[64] This growth is not necessarily driven by international migration, but rather by commercial and residential development intended to serve affluent *internal* native-born migrants from other parts of the valley, state, and nation.[65] And much of the development in Carbondale and Basalt is funded and controlled by Aspen-based businesses. One recently completed project is the River Valley Ranch, a golf-and-residential development in which the Aspen Skiing Company is a major investor. Another Aspen-based developer, Mark Kwiecienski, is building Ten Peaks Meadows, a residential development that "targets the upper-end niche in the down-valley market." Sirous Saghtoleslami is yet another Aspen developer who is building Fox Run Meadows, "a project that includes 17 two-acre, single-family-home lots, seven lots of between 10 and 14 acres, and seven caretaker units."[66]

The environmental ethic and growth imperative are often at odds down valley, but some creative efforts are underway in places like Basalt. As Jon Fox-Rubin told us:

> [W]e have a pretty unique setup here. We're bordered by some Division of Wildlife lands, some Forest Service land, some BLM (Bureau of Land Management) land, and several ranches. We have made some progress . . . on acquiring some key open-space parcels that are migration corridors for big game. . . . We have one very large ranch that was developed into a golf course, which is kind of a leading-edge environmental golf course. It has one of the lowest pesticide uses in the country, things called phyto-islands, which are diverse islands of native species that synergistically exist. So on one hand it's an environmental success, and on the other hand it took out a tract of land that was open space that was deer habitat and, in the summer, hay and cattle ranches . . . the ranchers that owned that, they made a little bit of money but the developers made a heck of a lot of money.[67]

It appears that this project achieved the multiple goals of environmental conservation, expansion of golfing greens, and profit-making for developers. It is also likely that the project would have gone forward only if developers themselves had approved it.

In the face of increasing concerns around growth, immigration, and environmental sustainability, the Roaring Fork Valley becomes an ever-more complex community—a patchwork of cultures linked by a common economy and a stunning ecology—in which its residents' day-to-day lives could not be more different.

Immigrant Life and Politics

Aspen's evolution as the ultimate elite retreat was possible only as a result of its parallel narrative: the evolution of an undesirable but essential workforce. The Latino immigrants who make tourism possible are the latest generation of laborers working in the relentless machinery of extractive industry. And today, in Colorado's Roaring Fork Valley just as in the rest of America, these immigrants are embroiled in a love-hate relationship with the U.S. citizenry. Earlier we mentioned the double bind in which many immigrants find themselves, as providers of labor that is both sought after and despised, welcomed by much of the business community but condemned by nativists who see their influence as alien, suspect, and socially impure.

During the 1990s, most of the Mexican workers in the Roaring Fork Valley came from the northern state of Chihuahua, south of El Paso. In the early 2000s, many newcomers traveled from the southern coastal states of Guerrero, Nayarit, and Michoacan (to say nothing of those folks from Guatemala, Honduras, El Salvador, and other points farther south). These hometown differences matter greatly among many Mexicans, but for most U.S. residents they're all "just Mexicans."[68]

The numerous hurdles faced by migrants frame much of their lives. From our perspective in the United States, we often lose sight of the difficulties in their home countries that make the daunting and dangerous trip north seem necessary. But that decision is only the beginning. One means of understanding some of the enormous obstacles and hardships some immigrants face is to consider Mike Davis and Alessandra Moctezuma's concept of multiple borders.[69] In writing on the tensions between Mexican immigrants and nativist whites in Southern California, Davis and Moctezuma describe the "first border" as the official national boundary between the United States and Mexico.[70] The "second border" is often a moving target, including those dragnets and detention centers that the Border Patrol and the Immigration and Customs Enforcement (ICE, formerly the INS) set up at various checkpoints in the interior of the United States.[71] This "second border" consists of those activities carried out by law enforcement agencies that track, detain, and deport immigrants within the States.

As if crossing the first border were not dangerous enough,[72] along the second border ICE performs regular sweeps through communities, patrols the Interstate highway system, and conducts raids on businesses and homes throughout the interior. Profiling and stopping vans with immigrants traveling into the United States have become routine for ICE authorities. In May 2000, forty-seven undocumented persons were apprehended from three vans, which were traveling on Interstate 70 in Colorado near the Roaring Fork Valley.[73] Local officials like Garfield County sheriff Tom Dalessandri stated, "This is an example of why we need INS agents in our area and why we need a facility placed here."[74] As we'll see, the ensuing controversy over locating an INS/ICE facility in the valley was explosive and reflected the intensity on all sides of the immigration debate in the area.

The detention and deportation stories of immigrants are numerous, and they epitomize the terrible bind in which many of today's newcomers find themselves. A Mexican woman living in a down-valley town reported that law enforcement officials stopped her for not wearing a seatbelt while driving. She was immediately detained and deported by immigration officials, who left her on a bridge between El Paso, Texas, and Ciudad Juarez, Mexico. As a result, her three young children were forced to remain in the United States and live with a relative who had a record of domestic abuse.[75] Rico Torres, a community advocate working for Catholic Charities (a social service organization in the Roaring Fork Valley) noted that he has spoken with about thirty clients who related stories about themselves or loved ones being deported for minor crimes. In January 2000, twenty-one undocumented persons were apprehended in a single traffic stop in the Valley.[76] These actions produce major strains within communities and families that are already living from paycheck to paycheck.

Drug smuggling has, for years, been the primary rationale for border militarization and immigrant surveillance, and plays an important role in justifying the continued expansion of the size and power of the federal ICE agency. Virginia Kice, an ICE spokesperson, indicated that ICE's main focus is on "trying to disrupt the criminal smuggling networks and lead investigations."[77] According to Kice, Colorado is an important site of illicit smuggling of migrant workers:

> We found that Colorado is a huge over-ground smuggling state for undocumented persons (particularly along the I-70 corridor), and this led to the development of our Quick Response approach. What this means

is we have an information system so that if a local sheriff suspects that someone is illegal, they can call it in to a Clearinghouse Law Enforcement Center in Vermont that we have and get all the information they need immediately—we'll tell them if the person has a record of immigration law violations. It's connected to all officers around the country. This is a "force multiplier," a new technology. Human smuggling is a big focus . . . the volume is huge and the profits are huge as well. There has been a tenfold increase in the price of smuggling across the border in the last decade. This is a multibillion dollar industry.[78]

The connection to national security and the threat of attacks on civilians is also always present in these conversations. Kice cautioned us, "No matter what your politics are, one thing is true: the people who come here illegally, who sneak across the border, we don't know who they are, so this is why we need Homeland Security." The assumption is that anyone and everyone crossing the U.S. border could be a security risk. There is also an assumption that those who reside in the United States with citizenship are "known" and without risk. The repeated use of language such as "sneaking," "illegal," and "smuggling," is common among those working to foster a perceived association between immigration and crime.[79]

We should note that ICE detention centers have become one of the fastest-growing segments of our national obsession with incarceration, with more than 65,000 immigrants being held against their will in private and public facilities in 2007.[80] That same year, according to the Pew Research Center, Latinos became the largest ethnic/racial group in federal prisons, making up one-third of the inmate population, despite comprising only 13 percent of the U.S. population.[81] This increase was due largely to tougher enforcement of immigration laws.

According to Davis and Moctezuma, there is also a "third border," the boundary that regulates the daily interactions between communities, including Latinos with U.S. citizenship. This particular border consists of efforts by governments and individuals to regulate immigrants' mobility and access through exclusion from certain public areas, neighborhoods, parks, pools, and other recreational facilities through legal or extralegal (i.e., violent) means. This includes the resolutions and ordinances of city councils from Escondido, California, to Hazelton, Pennsylvania, enacted to regulate and control Latino populations.

Davis and Moctezuma discuss the way in which whites in San Marino, California, pushed their city council to introduce weekend user fees for non-residents who seek access to the bucolic space of Lacy Park. This $12 charge limited working-class Latino families' access, while local wealthy whites easily secured entry to this coveted space. Similarly, San Marino's world-famous Huntington Library and Gardens is an ecological and architectural gem of Southern California. Recently, a new entry fee was introduced there (replacing the previous practice of a "suggested donation"), also aimed at restricting access to this space. Arcadia, California's gorgeous Wilderness Park, was the site of another such struggle. As more Latinos began using the park, whites protested. A leader of the neighboring Highland Oaks Homeowner's Association stated, "I've seen their graffiti. I've heard their ghetto blasters. I don't want any riffraff coming into our city." The mayor and city council agreed and renamed the park a "wilderness center" with public access limited to one eight-hour period on Fridays. This amounts to a privatization of public space, a corporatization of the commons. While the first and second borders are meant to exclude Latinos from the nation, the third border serves to produce racial segregation within the domestic interior. Davis and Moctezuma write, "This crabgrass apartheid, represented by blockaded streets and off-limits parks, should be as intolerable as Jim Crow drinking fountains or segregated schools were in the 1960s."[82] In our view, the third border reflects and facilitates environmental privilege, and is a core part of the complex of factors that produce environmental racism. Elites enjoy clean environments at the expense of the "commoners" who face pollution and low-wage jobs. And in Aspen, those commoners are blamed for polluting elites' protected space, literally and symbolically.

The third-border strategy, as we have seen, is powerful because it is amorphous and can manifest itself in many ways. It seeks to control the bodies and livelihoods of the country's immigrants, sometimes through blatant means and other times in much more subtle ways. One of today's most common manifestations of the third border is the passage of laws and ordinances that restrict the number of occupants per household. Since many new immigrants are low-wage workers in high-cost areas, they often save money by housing many people into a single domicile. The message these laws send is clear: you are only as free as we say you are.[83]

Carbondale, Colorado was perhaps the last town in the Roaring Fork Valley to pass a maximum occupancy regulation. By the late 1990s, Aspen,

Glenwood Springs, Snowmass, and Pitkin County all created rules limiting the number of unrelated adults living in a single-family dwelling. Carbondale's mayor Randy Vanderhurst felt it was time to consider a similar ordinance in his town, due to the perception that certain social ills were highly concentrated in the Latino community and spilling over into Anglo areas:

> If you look at the police blotter in Carbondale and the mid valley you'll find a disproportionate number of Latino surnames connected to everything from DUI's to drug dealing . . . I'm not saying because you live with ten other people that that forces you to go to a bar, have too many beers, then get in a car. But the stress when you live with that many people is probably greater than if you don't.[84]

Subsequently, Carbondale passed an ordinance setting strict limits on the number of people who could occupy a single dwelling.

Criminalizing people of color and immigrants is nothing new. The use of a maximum occupancy ordinance, however, is a good example of the "new racism"—racist practices that are less overt in their targeting of people of color. There is nothing in most of these regulations that is specific or direct about the populations at which they are aimed. That way, it is difficult to argue that they are explicitly racist. But the intent and impact are racist, as evident in Vanderhurst's quote.

More recently, however, the "old racism" reared its ugly head as towns across America boldly passed laws that explicitly made it a criminal act to hire or rent a home to undocumented persons. These laws strongly echo the restrictive covenants of a previous era, which forbade white residents from selling or renting their properties to African Americans and other undesirable elements in the suburbs and white urban neighborhoods.[85] Even a federal law proposed in 2005 by House of Representatives member James Sensenbrenner adopted similar language. Most of these proposed laws have been challenged and many struck down as unconstitutional, but unlike the more subtle expressions of "new racism," this racist anti-immigrant message remains increasingly bold and public.[86] These kinds of policies are excellent examples of how racism directly impacts both the victims and perpetrators; whites themselves experience a restriction of sorts since they are prohibited from selling or renting to whomever they please.

An age-old method of enforcing borders and white environmental privilege is interpersonal and vigilante violence. From the Texas Rangers to the Ku Klux Klan and the Minuteman Project, organized violence against immigrants and people of color in the United States has a deep history that continues to this day. On the eve of Independence Day, July 3, 2001, Steven Michael Stagner—a white man—shot and killed Angelica Toscano, Juan Hernandez, Mel-qui-des Medrano, and Juan Carlos Medrano. They were Mexican immigrants living in the Roaring Fork Valley town of Rifle. The rampage also left three other people wounded. Stagner began his shooting spree at the City Market grocery store before moving on to the Bookcliffs RV Park, a community of mostly Latino workers and their families.

The Mexican consulate in Denver was incensed at this crime and issued a statement that the four persons killed in the incident were indeed Mexican nationals. The consulate demanded "expeditious clarification" of the crime.[87] A series of public demonstrations followed, and while valley immigrants were fearful of continued violence, most of them would not be cowed by this hate crime.[88] Stagner was charged with first-degree murder but later found not guilty by reason of insanity. The immigrant community was outraged. The court ruled that Stagner be confined indefinitely at the Colorado Mental Health Institute, but that decision fell far short of the justice many activists and residents had hoped for. Colorado has a law against "ethnic intimidation," but that statute was not applied in this case.[89]

Shirley Otero, a Rifle resident, challenged the court's decision and reasoning. In a meeting of concerned residents and the local police and prosecutor, she stated:

> If he was insane, he would have randomly killed people. . . . But he didn't. He walked around and scoured the area. There were statements he made close to the time of the shootings that it was time that Mexicans get what they deserve because they are here illegally and feeding off the system.[90]

Scott Chaplin remembered:

> At the memorial . . . 2,000 people showed up and the governor showed up. There was a lot of beginning of healing and talking about the issues. We brought kids down from Rifle to talk on the radio station. When he

[Stagner] was found innocent, people were upset about that and said it definitely wouldn't have happened if he was Latino. There was one woman from Rifle who wrote a letter to the editor of the newspaper who said "Michael [the shooter] was right. These Latinos are taking over our Valley. Too bad he didn't shoot more." That was a letter to the editor.[91]

Georgi Aibner, a former teacher and friend of the victims' families, pledged to establish a memorial and scholarship to honor "los inocentes," the innocent victims of this tragedy. The fact that this hate crime occurred on the July 4 weekend, a time when the idea of American nationhood is on display and defended righteously by the state and millions of patriotic citizens, cannot pass without remark. Independence Day is a celebration built on the claim that the U.S. armed forces are the major reason for "our" freedom. In other words, our citizenship and rights as Americans are secured through violence deemed acceptable for the greater good.[92]

These kinds of experiences contribute to understanding why and how even a rumor of ICE raids in the valley can send shock waves through the community. The social terrain around immigration changed dramatically after 9/11 and the experience for people in communities throughout the United States became more stressful than ever.

Fear and Racism after 9/11

Since the attacks of September 11, 2001, and the development of the Department of Homeland Security, there has been a marked rise in the level of caution and anxiety among immigrant communities, and a corresponding increase in the day-to-day practice of state surveillance. Peter Jessup, a staff member of the local Catholic Charities organization stated, "I am concerned about it. I know a lot of organizations in the area that don't check people's papers, and I think they're going to be looked over a lot more. It's going to be harder for people without papers to find jobs."[93] Amy McTernan, the manager of the Aspen Temporary Labor Service, pointed out that there is always a "fear factor," even among local immigrants *with* documentation of legal residence: "Because some of these people, even if they're legal it's like, if you get stopped by a cop, you know what your heart does [it beats really fast]. Even if you've done nothing wrong . . . And they're all people with legal papers."[94]

The daily stress levels and surveillance practices that Jessup and Mc-Ternan discussed spiked as a result of the 9/11 attacks. Leticia Barraza, a student counselor at nearby Colorado Mountain College, spoke to the consequences of 9/11 for immigrant students in the valley:

> [A] lot happened after 9/11. I think we would have stood a better chance had 9/11 not changed the way people see immigrants in our country. . . . [A]nother issue that has come up is the driver's license. Before, through loopholes, they were able to get driver's licenses, but now it's nearly impossible to do. The Matricular Consular, the Mexican ID card, we were beginning to see them accepted as a form of IDs for immigrants here, but that's not accepted now. Those are the two main issues that have been affected, other than jobs and payment for some of these people. . . . A lot of it is just based on fear [and] the whole fear factor makes it difficult for our Latino communities and their families and students.[95]

The post-9/11 moment, though, was not just about nativist reactions to the fear of immigrant terrorists. There was also a significant financial downturn nationally. Pitkin County sheriff's deputy Marie Munday recalled many immigrants' responses to the economic slowdown in the valley: "After that, a lot of people left because the tourist industry was hurt as a result of 9/11. A lot of people left to Texas or the Midwest. Many called me to say goodbye. Others called me from places like Minnesota to get help getting their last paycheck, which may have been withheld."[96] Other area advocates like Scott Chaplin concurred: "A lot of Latinos went back home during that time."[97]

The Case of the ICE "Raids"

The Roaring Fork Valley was the site of a particularly tense moment in the aftermath of 9/11. It was the summer of 2004, and on a single day during the second week of July, the word on the street was that ICE was conducting raids throughout the valley. The raids were said to have

occurred at a gas station on Highway 82, at the shopping market in Carbondale, at an area hospital, and at various worksites. Agents were believed to have rounded up and detained numerous persons, including
men, women, and children. The news spread so rapidly that the next
day a large number of immigrants stayed home from work and school.
Many employers had few to no workers that day, and much of the valley
was silent, as immigrant families took no chances and remained behind
closed doors. The only problem was the "news" of ICE raids in the valley
was just a rumor.[98] While most of the public conversation during the following days was focused on how such a rumor could have started, the
more interesting question was *why* it had had such an extraordinary impact throughout the area.

Since we arrived for a field research visit just days after the reported
raids, numerous examples of the rumors came up during our interviews.
Marie Munday remembered getting a call from an immigration services
provider who stated, "a woman told me that the sheriff's department, the
Colorado state patrol, and Immigration are all doing roadblocks together."[99]
Munday called the captain of the state patrol: "And I said, 'now I know you
do roadblocks for DUIs. And you work with other agencies. Is Immigration
[ICE] over there?' And he goes, 'no, we don't do that.'" Munday also called
a colleague at ICE and stated, "they said you had roadblocks here, and I
named all the places, and that you did raids at all these companies. She
started laughing and she said 'that's pretty amazing for two guys [there are
only two ICE agents in the valley]! They did all that?' [laughter]"

Another person reported to an immigration services provider, "I got
chased down the highway by an immigration vehicle." There were similar
rumors of raids in Durango and Colorado Springs around the same time.
Munday told us, "I got this email from the Mexican Consulate that says
'There have been no raids, we went to the prisons to see if all these people
who were supposedly arrested were there and they're not there.'" Another
story claimed that fifty people were detained from the Aspen Temporary
Labor Service, but Amy McTernan and her staff confirmed that ICE never
showed up at their door.

There were as many theories about the source of the rumor as there
were stories of raids. However, there appears to be one plausible explana-
tion. The morning of the rumors, a person called in to a talk show on a
Spanish-language radio station in the valley who claimed to have seen vans

picking up Latinos and hauling them away. That phone call is believed to have set off the rumors throughout the area. While the claim turned out to be false, it may have been based on the observation that there were indeed roadblocks and police stopping cars and arresting people on various roadways at the time. These were routine sobriety checkpoints during the July 4 holiday. Marie Munday told us:

> State patrol always does a road block in Basalt for a DUI checkpoint. They said "we had cooperation of the local cops but no, Immigration did not come." This one Mexican man called me and asked about it. He was the first one to call me, when they had the DUI roadblock. He was in Aspen and afraid to go home to Basalt [just down the road] and he says "I can't go home to my children!" And his wife was there and they were both crying on the phone and I said "it's OK, just a DUI roadblock."[100]

Back at the Aspen Temporary Labor Service staff members recalled:

> [Staffer 1]: "coming to Aspen some mornings about a quarter to seven, and everyday you just see droves of people coming here, going up to the mountain towns. But this place was a ghost town, that Tuesday and Wednesday when it all happened."
> [Staffer 2]: "I know lots of people . . . still walking on eggshells, you know. They see someone who looks like they're official, they're wearing a uniform, they'll see them and they just take off running."[101]

Many observers anticipated negative lingering effects of the "raid" rumor on immigrant communities in the valley, despite it being an unsubstantiated story. Marie Munday mused:

> I'm guessing that it's just a matter of time before people start losing their jobs. People who had good—or I mean good *looking*—green cards, that's all an employer is required to look at. They're not required by law to be experts in fake documents. What I think that this has done is that a lot of people might have had a good green card, a decent-looking green card, and they got the job, and now because they're not showing up to work, the employer knows that they must be illegal, that that must have been a bad card. It has deeper implications.[102]

Peter Jessup of Catholic Charities connected the post-ICE raid sentiments back to September 11, 2001:

> So to me it was an aftershock of what happened after 9/11. That's how it played out in my mind. People were really afraid of being deported and were scared. I think immigration was going in the right direction right before 9/11, but when that happened, it created a lot more fear and segregation and a lot more problems . . . it just shows what level of fear there is in the community.[103]

A rumor, a false report, kicked off a community-wide panic that sent people running into the shadows, confined to their homes, or afraid to even try to return home for fear of being detained, deported, and separated from family, friends, and community. Just the mere threat of deportation is made very real in the everyday lives of immigrants. The seismic effect of the rumor reveals how tense relations are among the immigrant community, the Anglo community, and the state.

There is yet another view on the significance of the ICE raid rumor. Quino, a Mexican immigrant we spoke with about this issue, framed it for us as a response to the day-to-day racism he and other immigrants experienced at the hands of police:

> There's lots of discrimination in cars. It's terrible. They stop us with like three or four officers because they think we have drugs. It's just discrimination. Especially in Carbondale. They're very racist. We clean their houses, we take care of their dogs. What they don't want to do, we do. We need to be together to take the policemen away. We could stop traffic until they listen to us. We didn't go to work one day and the company lost a lot of money.[104]

Instead of seeing this episode purely as an example of a government crackdown, Anglo racism, and undocumented immigrants running scared, Quino urges us to also think of this case as a demonstration of the power of immigrants to conduct a general strike and withhold their labor. There are precious few instances where undocumented persons are able to exert such public power over employers, and this case might be re-examined as one such expression. That all of this could happen in and around the city of Aspen—a place of serenity, enlightenment, and breathtaking natural beauty—makes this struggle that much more interesting.

The Aspen Logic

The "Aspen Idea" was adopted by the Aspen Institute, an organization Walter Paepcke founded in the 1950s to boost the town's brand name and image. The idea was that Aspen was a place where the elite could rejuvenate and strengthen their minds and bodies through both intellectual stimulation (via Great Books seminars and lectures at the Aspen Institute) and physical exercise on the ski slopes and hiking trails. A local journalist offered his own view: "The [Aspen] Institute has from its inception been a bastion of corporate conservatism, just as Aspen is a favorite vacation retreat for many of the architects of monopoly capitalism and globalization."[105] The Aspen Institute commissioned Sidney Hyman, a University of Chicago professor, to write a book titled *The Aspen Idea*. This was a cultured, refined, and humanist approach to life that would allow the white-collar class to come to Aspen and return to their work refreshed and with renewed purpose.

We believe that the rarified, glorified notion of the Aspen idea often hides a whole mountain of ugly truths, both in the Rockies and in cities around the world. Peel back the ideals of the Aspen idea and you'll find the Aspen Logic—a way of seeing and shaping the world that preserves systems of inequality and injustice in a manner that allows one to justify and feel good about them. It is capitalism with a green facelift. And it's not found only in Aspen. Think of the "green wash" that occurs when the Dell corporation publicizes the fact that it plants trees, even as it uses tons of toxic waste to manufacture its computers;[106] or when Walmart sells low-energy fluorescent light bulbs while paying workers less-than-livable wages and sourcing materials from sweatshops in China. The Aspen Logic is not just corporate environmentalism or a green wash, though; it is also a *white* wash because it includes social, environmental, and economic claims to pureness and goodness, to *whiteness*. The Aspen Logic suggests that unfettered market capitalism is just fine as long as we give some of our profits to a charity for the downtrodden or to a fund for greening the city. As we pat ourselves on the back, we ignore inconvenient truths and the roots of innumerable social and environmental problems.

We can see the influence of the Aspen Logic spreading down valley. A councilmember from one of the valley's towns manages a corporation that works toward environmental solutions and is a classic illustration of the Aspen Logic. He told us:

> I run a company that is purely for making zero-emission, light-weight cars. Our company's goal is to make the car a much smaller player in the environmental pollution aspect. Part of the reason I'm an elected official is, you know, you can fix the car but still have suburbs, and they're still going to have issues. You can't have zero-emission cars without the environmental implications of everyone having two cars, etc. So keep going toward higher-density downtowns, rediscovering our downtowns, getting rid of our suburbs, it's going to take hundreds of years to do that, but I think that that trend needs to start as opposed to the "leave the city" mentality. I manufacture cars, so that doesn't exactly fall into environmentalism, but I think that's a dilemma that many people have with cars that they purchase. They want to be an environmentalists but then they need a sport utility vehicle to get to the mountains to go appreciate the environment.[107]

By his own admission, this council member's company might be a small step in the right direction, but it is not in any way a fundamental challenge to business-as-usual, and that's the point.

One of the many difficulties of the Aspen Logic is that it suggests that social change occurs only from the top down. In other words, the Aspen Logic suggests that in order to be a true environmentalist, one must be a millionaire or billionaire. Only then can you purchase guilt alleviation and truly have an impact on social change, despite the fact that your wealth likely originated in a socio-economic system that by its very nature produces social and environmental injustices. Within this logic, environmentalism and capitalism are natural allies—indeed, money is perhaps the only hope that our planet has! While radical ecology groups like EarthFirst! argue that the environment and the almighty dollar are diametrically opposed, the Aspen Logic takes for granted that we can achieve environmental sustainability only by supporting capitalism and the current social hierarchy. If Aspen is a defining space that embodies the best of environmentalism, then much of that movement becomes wed to the condition of the privileged. Thus, environmentalism is not progressive politics but a politics of the rich and comfortable that claims progressive ideals. Mainstream environmentalism thus becomes entirely consistent with—and a close cousin of—nativism and racially exclusionary politics, and has been since its beginnings, when environmental organizations defined themselves as part of America's white, affluent citizenry.[108] The Aspen Logic is merely today's manifestation of a centuries-old, deeply American, cultural dynamic.

Another difficulty of the Aspen Logic is the way it distorts our understanding of social realities. Still a force among America's intellectual Left today, the Aspen Institute funds scholars to study poverty, among other things. We find this emphasis curious, though perhaps not surprising. Poverty research in the United States tends to focus on the ghetto, the barrio, and black and brown women's reproductive behaviors, index crimes, and failing inner-city schools.[109] The Aspen Logic suggests that that is where the emphasis should be, and policymaking should focus on those problem "hot spots" in society, rather than examining the social system that produced such ills. We believe that in order to understand poverty we need to go not to the ghetto but to Aspen; in order to understand the Mexican border and immigration politics, we need to move beyond the barrios and instead go to Aspen; in order to understand the ugliness of racism and nativism, we need to go to Aspen. Scholars, journalists, politicians, and any of us wishing to understand social problems should stop focusing exclusively on poor communities—and turn our eyes toward the people and institutions that create poverty and environmental destruction in the first place: those places on the earth where the economically wealthy, the politically powerful, and the racially dominant live, work, and play.[110]

The Aspen Logic also serves as a very convenient mask. Much of what passes for environmentalism in the United States is not much more than people with wealth and privilege trying to mask that reality; power, and privilege "made over" to be something other than what it really is. Reading through reams of newspaper articles and personal letters from residents of Aspen from the nineteenth through the twenty-first centuries, it became abundantly clear that so much of the "news" from Aspen is actually boosterism, marketing designed to lure tourists and investors to the city. In that sense, Aspen feels quite artificial indeed. Imagine walking through a neighborhood in Aspen and realizing that the owners of many of the homes live there just two weeks each year, and that the immigrant workers who service the town are present but socially invisible and are being targeted for exclusion. This is a new kind of ghost town. Much of nature in Aspen is constructed. Like many ski resorts, they make fake snow when necessary; the trails are immaculately groomed; the streets and lawns in the town are manicured by a phalanx of immigrant workers. Nature is constructed in a more abstract sense as well: for most immigrant workers, the mountains are basically unreal because, for these workers, they have little or no access to them.

Through the privatization of nature—which is what a ski resort is, after all—the mountain becomes a product to consume, a replicable commodity, even for the wealthy who come to ski. Aspen is an "experience." When we privatize space and nature, we limit the kind of people who can enjoy it, and we limit our vision of the world in which we live. Capitalism, by its very nature, seeks to privatize everything with potential economic value. Superficiality is the result. In such a context it is difficult to build relationships and community. Aspen's local philanthropist George Stranahan noted, the community has become fragmented:

> [F]or most of the people, it wasn't bad having tourists here until about 1975 and then all of a sudden having tourists here wasn't really fun anymore. Now we had to get into the entertainment business. You can't chat with tourists. They send their maids to pick up the mail, to pick up the groceries. So I would say really a fragmentation of community is a lot of the change. It used to be a community because we all walked to the post office at the same time when we knew the mail was out. So there we all are, walking down the street for the purpose of getting our mail and that's when you did the little exchanges, you know, "did your sister have her baby yet?" "oh God! It was a boy!" "Really?" Yeah, that kind of thing. Socialization in the community. Without that kind of groove there is a fragmentation given that you're not talking to people who are on the East End, not talking to people who live on Pitkin Green. Not only geographical fragmentation, but a fragmentation of interest. [Tourists will say]: "Oh, I only care about the ballet;" "I only care about the art museum."[111]

The Aspen Institute was developed, in part, as a critique of the boom-bust, Old West, capitalist town embodied by the nineteenth-century Aspen and other mountain cities in the region. Unfortunately, any sense of humanistic community was destroyed when the Aspen idea gave way to the Aspen brand.

We All Live in Aspen

For those of us who do not own million-dollar second homes, or would not dream of driving an SUV, Aspen can seem as far away as it does for immigrant workers down valley. And yet none of us can avoid the consequences of what is happening in Aspen. The legal scholar Kevin Johnson, for example, reveals how the anti-immigrant agenda is almost always interwoven with broader racist politics directed at all citizens of color:[112]

> Rather than just a peculiar feature of U.S. public law, the differential treatment of citizens and noncitizens serves as a "magic mirror" revealing how dominant society might treat domestic minorities if legal constraints were lifted. Indeed, the harsh treatment of noncitizens of color reveals terrifying lessons about how society in fact views its citizens of color. It is no coincidence that anti-immigrant sentiment caught fire in tandem with the anti-minority backlash of the 1990s. . . . The connection between civil rights and immigration, and thus the struggles of noncitizens and citizens, has important implications for the quest for social justice. . . . Unless racial justice and immigrant rights activists work together, we can expect a "divide and conquer" strategy to the detriment of all people of color, immigrants and citizens alike.[113]

The way immigrants are treated via government policies and practices affects the political future of *all* people of color. But what about European Americans?

In our global world, for better and for worse, one's privilege and disadvantage is interconnected with others. The immigrant rights movement largely focuses on obtaining justice and legalization for undocumented persons, but without also paying sufficient attention to the ways in which citizenship for the rest of us has simultaneously come under fire and has been eroded. Consider the growth of the prison-industrial complex, the militarization of municipal police forces, the exponential rise in the use of surveillance technologies, the broader cultural transformation around civil liberties facilitated by the USA PATRIOT Act, and the weakening of existing protections and civil rights, all authorized by the federal government.[114] In other words, no matter your race, class, gender, sexuality, or citizenship status, we are all impacted by these changes and should have an interest in challenging the rapidly degenerating post-democracy in which we live.

Alongside our democratic ideals, there is perhaps one other thing that Americans hold sacred: our wallets. These too are in jeopardy. The best-selling author, columnist, Nobel Prize–winner, and economist Paul Krugman shares our concerns about the widening class inequalities in the United States. He contends that this country has entered a "new Gilded Age," with an economic hierarchy similar to that of the 1920s, as wealth is increasingly concentrated at the top of society's elite class. He writes, "Over the past thirty years most people have seen only modest salary increases . . .[but] the explosion in C.E.O. pay over the past thirty years is an amazing story."[115]

These national trends are also reflected globally. Both here and abroad, economic inequality is nothing less than a threat to basic democracy, since those with greater financial power tend to also enjoy disproportionate political power. Krugman is also worried about the problem of access to environmental amenities like public resources such as parks and open space. He tells the story of an attempt to secure environmental privileges during the first Gilded Age (as Mark Twain labeled the late nineteenth century):

> In 1924, the mansions of Long Island's North Shore were still in their full glory, as was the political power of the class that owned them. When Governor Al Smith of New York proposed building a system of parks on Long Island, the mansion owners were bitterly opposed. One baron— Horace Havemeyer, the "sultan of sugar"—warned that North Shore towns would be "overrun with rabble from the city." "Rabble?" Smith said. "That's me you're talking about." In the end New Yorkers got their parks, but it was close: the interests of a few hundred wealthy families nearly prevailed over those of New York City's middle class.[116]

Today, this penchant for what Mike Davis and Alessandra Moctezuma call "crabgrass apartheid" functions to make parks and other ecological amenities off-limits to the working and middle classes, and Aspen is only one site of the struggle.[117]

The consequences of the Aspen Logic are serious. An environmentalism that embraces market-based reformist tactics to solve the ecological crisis is doomed to fail. The point is, we are headed down a road where water-sheds, critical habitats, oceans, the air, land, and human health are deeply threatened by massive, human-induced changes. That road is Highway 82, and innumerable other roads both literal and metaphorical throughout the country.

The UN Millennium Environmental Assessment recently reported un-equivocally that the state of the world environment is worsening each year.[118] If efforts to combat these trends are not transformative and rev-olutionary, then they are simply neither serious nor worth our time and energy. The environmental movement will have to radically reorient and rethink its future, given its racist and nativist past and present, if it is to remain relevant.[119] Environmental justice movements offer a more plau-sible vision. But we cannot just consider the plight of the poor: if we are to truly challenge environmental racism and injustice, we must recognize the scourge of environmental privilege. We must confront the Aspen Logic wherever it appears. We must challenge crabgrass apartheid with grass-roots justice.

2

The Ultimate Elite Retreat

More than sixty years ago, an editorial in the *Aspen Times* summarized the challenge we face in this chapter: "To write a history of this famous old town in one newspaper article or even in one book, is a task which fails of accomplishment."[1] Instead of writing a history of this beguiling, maddening place, here we simply offer our own perspective on the crucial themes that are illustrative of the town's past and its legacy of environmental privilege. From these seeds, we can better understand the resource-destroying forest that Aspen has become. We begin with the lasting lure of Manifest Destiny in the American West. From this broad beginning, we gradually narrow our focus to the long and embattled relationship between those white settlers who were pursuing their manifest destiny and the various nonwhite peoples who either stood in the way or facilitated that goal. From these relationships we gain a new understanding of Aspen's evolution: for more than a century, this area has hosted extractive industry of one kind or another, and today's Aspen, and the people who both revel in it and service it, are the latest link in that long, environmentally and socially degrading, chain.

Stories from the American West

The histories of the American West are largely contained and shaped by the ideology of Manifest Destiny and the desire to conquer new frontiers. For more than a century and a half, individual citizens, the state, and innumerable industries have searched for storied wealth and riches in this region. The West was, and remains, a site of imperialism for the U.S. government, corporations, and a largely European American population; it is a resource colony because it facilitates the continued domination of both people and nature. This process is made easier by more than a century of permissive federal legislation, which essentially handed over public lands and ecosystem resources to prospectors, miners, and companies of all stripes, both domestic and foreign.[2] The historian Patricia Limerick put it this way:

> We now have a situation in which the resources of the United States' public lands are being mined by companies that are, many of them, foreign corporations—Canadian, northern European, and South African. Thanks to the 1872 Mining Law, these companies do not contribute revenue to the United States Treasury in return for the minerals taken from the public lands.[3]

Unlike *people* from particular global South nations, foreign *corporations* were welcome to come to the United States and, for a pittance, can mine or strip western land of its natural wealth and can use laborers from across the globe to perform this dangerous work. Those corporations that engage in hard-rock mining of gold and silver from public lands pay no royalties at all. Through the 1872 Mining Law, combined with earlier legislation, the federal government encouraged the exploitation of the land and its settlement by European Americans during the nineteenth century and after.[4] During the twentieth century, the U.S. Forest Service subsidized the timber industry by selling tracts of forests at huge discounts and building roads for that industry. Together with the federal Bureau of Land Management (BLM, part of the Department of Interior), these two agencies have largely viewed their role as facilitators of mining, oil and gas extraction, logging, and cattle-grazing operations in the West, particularly on public lands.[5]

The historian and conservationist Bernard DeVoto spoke and wrote adamantly against the use of the West as the East's resource colony. He fervently believed the western United States had a right to its own autonomy from the East Coast and that the nation had every obligation to protect its precious ecosystems. He described the situation in this way:

From 1860 on, the Western mountains have poured into the national wealth an unending stream of gold and silver and copper, a stream which was one of the basic forces in the national expansion. It has not made the West wealthy. It has, to be brief, made the East wealthy[6]. . . . Eastern capital has been able to monopolize oil and gas even more completely than it ever monopolized mining. In a striking analogy to eighteenth-century mercantilism, the East imposed economic colonialism on the West. The West is, for the East, a source of raw materials for manufacturing and a market for manufactured goods. Like the colonies before the Revolution the West is denied industry.[7]

Such voices among prominent scholars, however, are in the minority. For, as we know, much of U.S. history is built on the notion that such exploration and exploitation are essential aspects of our psyche and national identity. Unlike DeVoto, many historians have heralded such practices. Frederick Jackson Turner's famous 1893 paper "The Significance of the Frontier in American History" contended that the idea of the frontier was a looming—and positive—presence in the American mind because it contributed to the nation's cultural vitality and global exceptionalism. The 1890 Census declared that the frontier of the American West had been reached, populated, and closed; Turner's thesis thus gave support to those who anxiously believed that the United States must continue this process of infinite expansion (i.e., frontier seeking) beyond the West via overseas imperialism.[8] Turner's paper was deeply influential in shaping the popular imagination of the American West, but it was also problematic in that his perspective was contemptuous of people of color and women, if only in their glaring absence in the essay, and the notion that the western frontier itself was closed was just plain wrong. As Limerick argues,

> There was more homesteading *after* 1890 than before. A number of extractive industries—timber, oil, coal, and uranium—went through their principal booms and busts after 1890 . . . the nineteenth-century westward movement was the tiny, quiet prelude to the much more sizable movement of people into the West in the twentieth century.[9]

New frontiers—or, the term Limerick prefers, "conquests"—were continually unfolding in the West well after the Census and Turner declared its closure. The West is dotted with massive hydroelectric dams, oil, timber, and mining operations, and commercial farming and ranching; all of these industries are significantly larger today than they were in the nineteenth century. The continued and increasing reliance on extractive industries like oil, timber, mining, and hydropower also suggests that the term "Information Age" applies only to some sectors and puts to rest the notion that we have somehow entered a post-materialist economy.[10] We are as dependent upon the extraction of ecological wealth (or "natural resources") as we have ever been.

Our reliance on ecosystems is so great, in fact, that today these practices are often politically explosive and increasingly unpopular among affected communities, since they typically harm local ecologies and ensnare people into volatile economic cycles.[11] Towns across the American West—certainly in the Rocky Mountain region—have seen their fortunes rise and fall based on a close reliance on a single ecological resource, tapped for export—the environmental consequences be damned—which has rendered much of the West a supply depot for the rest of the nation.[12] As one historian put it, the "drive for economic development of the West was often a ruthless assault on nature, and it has left behind much . . . depletion and ruin."[13] It is also a heavily militarized region, with many parts of the area used for bombing ranges, testing sites, and nuclear waste dumping grounds.[14]

Many scholars argue that the West is also a site where movements for environmental conservation and preservation have taken hold and where environmental ethics run deep. We agree, but we must also qualify that claim. As we look more closely, we can see that most of these efforts have long been and continue to be aimed at the protection of open space and ecosystems *for* affluent or white populations and *from* people of color and indigenous peoples.[15] That quest for white environmental privilege has been a defining feature of environmentalism and cultural politics in the West, just as it has been in the rest of the United States.

We should not forget that the American West is where many of the largest Indian reservations are located and where Mexico lost major territory through the Treaty of Guadalupe Hidalgo in 1848. This is also where some of the nation's most impressive and vast national parks are located, which were produced in the name of patriotic conservation and preservation, but which also involved the displacement and exclusion of Native peoples who first lived in these spaces.[16] Patricia Limerick reminds us that multiple groups have been marginalized and oppressed in western history, not just the

working classes, women, and people of color. She explains how religious minorities and labor radicals are often forgotten members of oppressed populations in the region. "Judging by the written record alone, a historian blind to
actual physical characteristics might think that there were at least eight oppressed races in the West: Indians, Hispanics, Chinese, Japanese, blacks, Mor-
mons, strikers, and radicals."[17] The West is a landscape charged with politics,
violence, and righteous ideologies of who belongs and who does not, and
who should and shouldn't have access to the land and its ecological wealth.

What Frederick Jackson Turner *did* get right was his observation that
the idea, the myth, of the frontier is one of the most important stories in
the American imagination. The frontier was and is a site of conquest—of
both nature and the people who inhabit it. The frontier, in his words, has
"been the means to our achievement of a national identity, a democratic
polity, an ever-expanding economy, and a phenomenally dynamic and
'progressive' civilization."[18] Across the twentieth century, even as the literal
"frontier" became more and more settled, the potency of the metaphoric
frontier remained. John F. Kennedy's use of the imagery and symbolism
of the "new frontier" after his presidential nomination by the Democratic
Party in 1960, was a linguistic technique he employed to justify his use of
power. Just seven years later, U.S. forces would be heard talking about Viet
Nam as "Indian Country" and describing war tactics there as a game of
"Cowboys and Indians."[19] Decades later, U.S. troops would refer to places
like Iraq and other spaces around the globe as "Indian Country."[20]

Today's American West, like the West of the late nineteenth and early
twentieth centuries, remains ensconced in this mythical narrative. Alongside
mining and ranching and other extractive industries, a powerful new economy has emerged: tourism. In addition to utilizing the land's material wealth,
now a different group of corporations utilizes a more ethereal resource—the
land's beauty, and its capacity for entertainment and adventure.[21]

The Peoples of Colorado

Colorado's state seal features a pick and shovel, highlighting the fact that
mining and ecological wealth extraction are at the core of the state's history and anticipated future. Paralleling that history and continuing legacy

of environmental domination, are long-standing practices and polices of racial exclusion, violence, and control.

It seems Colorado has been the site of more than its fair share of right-wing causes since it began as a mining state. In the 1990s alone, this state spawned several right-leaning initiatives, including the anti-gay Amendment 2, the Aspen and Pitkin County resolutions on population stabilization, and legislative efforts by the "English only" movement to maintain the dominance of a single language in Colorado's public institutions. It is also home to notoriously powerful conservative Christian groups like Focus on the Family. Also located in southern Colorado is the U.S. Air Force Academy, contributing official respectability to militarism. Even so, it is important to acknowledge the constant presence of countervailing progressive forces, including environmental, labor, peace, indigenous, and racial justice movements in Colorado. This would include the Chicano Movement organization known as the Crusade for Justice, led by Rodolfo "Corky" Gonzales (who also helped found the La Raza Unida Party), the Colorado Chapter of the American Indian Movement (AIM), and environmental justice and human rights groups like the Colorado Peoples Environmental and Economic Network, Global Response, and the Rocky Mountain Peace and Justice Center. But long before these organizations were born, the state's cultural and ecological terrain was under a full-scale assault from the military, settlers, and corporations.

The first U.S. official to fully explore the mountains of Colorado was Zebulon Pike who, during his travels to the area in 1810, came upon numerous Spanish and Indian settlements that had been thriving for years.[22] The U.S. military continued to survey and map the area for decades afterward. In the late 1850s there was a Gold Rush in the Colorado Territory that triggered a reverse migration, as many of the '49ers in California returned East to seek fortune in the mountains and streambeds of the Rockies. By the 1870s, white settlers had built several small towns in the Rockies where they routinely expressed fear of Indian attacks and frequently called on the government and military to control Native populations.

One of the most horrific chapters in Colorado's history was the 1864 Sand Creek Massacre of a band of the Cheyenne and Arapaho people. With the movement of federal troops from the West to fight in the Civil War, white citizens and the press felt vulnerable and urged Governor John Evans to solve the "Indian Problem." Tensions increased as Indians resisted their confinement to reservations, and Anglos continued their incursions onto Indian lands. In response, Evans authorized citizen militias to exterminate any "hostiles" who refused to give up their arms and return to lands agreed upon in an 1861 treaty.[23] These social dynamics and Evans's authorization contributed to the Sand Creek massacre, in which at least 165 Cheyenne and Arapaho were killed in an early morning surprise attack by U.S. troops on November 29, 1864. A special investigation of the incident concluded that the army unit involved had perpetrated "gross and wanton outrages" against a peaceful people.[24]

Tribes from what whites called the Colorado Territory (statehood came in 1876) were targeted for reservations or extermination. But the Utes were the last to retain any claims to lands in the state. Silver prospectors first called the town that would become Aspen "Ute City" because the Utes were the main Native population in the area. The growing numbers of white miners on the Utes' hunting grounds was the beginning of a long struggle over what would become a playground for the ultra rich.

The Utes signed their first treaty with settlers in 1863, which reduced their land base to acreage in the Colorado Territory west of the Continental Divide. But, as whites sought more gold and silver, those boundaries were seen as threats to progress. An 1868 treaty between the Utes and the federal government pushed the tribe onto reservation lands in southwestern Colorado to ensure Anglo access to minerals and lands fertile for agriculture. A major loophole in the treaty was that Anglos and the government could drive railroads and highways through Ute land in perpetuity to gain access to other territories. This was guaranteed to produce further conflict and did, when, in the summer of 1879, whites discovered silver in Colorado's Roaring Fork Valley. There, they staked claims and built camps, including in a place that, in 1881, would become the city of Aspen.[25]

That year, an Indian agent, Nathan Meeker, plowed the White River Ute's lands, without their permission, in an effort to force them to take up Anglo farming methods. A conflict ensued, escalated, and ended in Meeker's murder, which in turn spawned the Ute War of 1879. The "Meeker Massacre," as it became known, provided a justification for moving the Utes farther West, so as to make the Roaring Fork Valley available for white settlement. Colorado's governor Frederick W. Pitkin adopted the slogan "the Utes must go!" and fully supported tribal displacement and genocide.[26] In a statement he made before the Colorado legislature, Pitkin made the case for Indian removal and exclusive environmental privilege for whites:

Along the western borders of the State, and on the Pacific Slope, lies a vast tract occupied by the tribe of Ute Indians, as their reservation. It contains about twelve million acres and is nearly three times as large as the State of Massachusetts. It is watered by large streams and rivers, and contains many rich valleys, and a large number of fertile plains. The climate is milder than in most localities of the same altitude on the Atlantic slope. Grasses grow there in great luxuriance, and nearly every kind of grain and vegetables can be raised without difficulty. This tract contains nearly one-third of the arable land of Colorado, and no portion of the State is better adapted for agricultural and grazing purposes than many portions of this reservation. Within its limits are large mountains, from most of which explorers have been excluded by Indians. Prospectors, however, have explored some portions of the country, and found valuable lode and placer claims, and there is reason to believe that it contains great mineral wealth. The number of Indians who occupy this reservation is about three thousand. . . . If this reservation could be extinguished, and the land thrown open to settlers, it will furnish homes to thousands of the people of the state who desire homes.[27]

The governor's words made it clear that vigilantes and frontier extremists were not the ones driving Indian removal and extermination; this was a process being spearheaded by state and corporate interests.

Still another treaty the following year reduced the tribes' land base even more. In a racist dehumanization that typically supports such moves, a local newspaper front-page story read: "Colorado's Governor has declared it to be the duty of frontier settlers to treat as wild beasts all Indians found away from the reservation."[28] One year later, in 1881, most of the Utes in Colorado were moved to reservations in Utah.[29] This case was just one of many in which indigenous peoples in the United States were living on lands that contained ecological wealth, which whites saw as their God-given entitlement.[30] The displacement of natives from mineral-rich lands and their relegation to reservations is a time-honored example of the use of borders and violence to maintain white supremacy and environmental privilege.

Even after being removed and sent to Utah, the Utes were required to have a special pass to travel off the reservation, and such a pass could be granted only by an Indian agent or well-placed public official. The following pass was found in a raid on a Ute camp in Utah:

Ouray Indian Agency, Utah, May 15, 1886. To whom it may concern: The bearer of this is Uncompaghre Colorow, who asks for a paper as he intends visiting Meeker [reservation]. I request kind treatment for him from all citizens he may meet and forbearance so long as he remains peaceable and friendly to the whites. He asks me to say that he feels friendly to all Americans. Signed, Edward L. Carson. U.S. Indian Agent.[31]

Troubles continued well into the late 1880s as Native uprisings occurred periodically, but the Utes were soon overwhelmed militarily, and the Rocky Mountains were secured for white exploitation and enjoyment.[32]

In 1993 an historic powwow took place in the Roaring Fork Valley. This event united the three Colorado Ute tribes for the first time in one hundred years. They came together for this occasion because the U.S. Forest Service and other federal agencies wanted them to sign a Memorandum of Understanding, which would allow the agencies to consult with tribes to make sure that sacred sites and artifacts would be preserved in the face of future development.[33] In other words, the primary driver for this agreement was—and is—to guarantee the rights of developers. This agreement actually allowed these agencies to prevent legal liabilities by securing tribal agreement to the consultations and still allow ski area and commercial and residential developments to go forward. The U.S. economy's thirst for land and other ecological resources was so strong that even seemingly positive developments like consulting with Native nations in order to preserve their sacred spaces actually revealed other motives.

At the same time, in places like Aspen, Native American culture is appropriated and sold mercilessly. In 1992—the year of the five hundredth anniversary of Columbus's genocidal voyage to the New World—the Windstar Foundation in Aspen hosted an event called "Living the Sacred Circle: Healing Time." According to the brochure, the theme was "the Native American way of life" and participants paid up to $500 for admission to hear the wisdom of the Natives, none of whom were Utes, despite the fact that they were the first people in Aspen. Luke Duncan, chairman of Uintah-Ouray tribe (an Ute band) commented to reporters:

I've seen so many times across Indian country how other people . . . have picked up on the ways of the Indians, only to turn around and sell that ceremony to someone who lives in the urban areas. And it happens

Cigar-store Indian statue next to a furrier. Photo by L. S. Park

right here in Aspen. That is a form of disrespect to Indian people, since that ceremony belongs to the Native Americans and we do that with respect. . . . The healing process we go through, it is not a game to us and it should not be used for monetary gain by anyone, including Native Americans.[34]

Throughout the Roaring Fork Valley today, disturbing signs of the appropriation of Native history and culture abound.

Walking the streets of Aspen and other Roaring Fork Valley towns, you pass cigar-store Indian statues, and you can buy a dream catcher to hang in your window or an "authentic" Indian blanket to keep you warm. You can even experience the "Happy Hunting Ground" of the Sioux Villa Curio in Glenwood Springs.[35] Native Americans, just like the minerals in the land itself, have become one of Colorado's most valuable and most exploited resources.

Historically, as Native Americans grappled with the growing stream of new arrivals on their land, more and more of the faces they encountered were not white. Since the mid-nineteenth century, Colorado has always had a significant immigrant population. By 1870 around 17 percent of the population was foreign born.[36] Most of these immigrants were from northern Europe or spoke English (Germans, Canadians, Swiss, French, Britons, Scandinavians). By 1910 the immigrant population in Colorado was increasingly from other parts of Europe or from countries where English was not the primary language (Slovenia, Hungary, Croatia, Serbia, Russia, Poland, Greece, Mexico, Japan, China, the Netherlands, and Finland). These groups faced a great deal of hostility at the hands of Anglo and native-born white Coloradans, attributed to nativist anxieties over ethnic, religious, and linguistic differences. Not surprisingly, environmental injustice was common. Many of these groups were packed into segregated communities like Globeville and other Denver neighborhoods where living and working conditions were dirty and hazardous. The American Smelting and Refining Company (later renamed ASARCO) operated a refinery that polluted many neighborhoods in the Denver area, the majority of them populated by ethnic minorities. In Leadville, immigrants were the hardest hit during a typhoid outbreak in 1903 that claimed five hundred victims. And while European immigrants were allowed to enter the formal political arena, like most of the country, African Americans and Asians in Colorado were "totally excluded from politics" in the late nineteenth and early twentieth centuries.[37]

Many whites in the American West at this time seemed to reserve a particular contempt for Chinese immigrants, reflecting the national mood at the time, which was punctuated by the 1882 Chinese Exclusion Act, barring most Chinese immigrants from entering the United States. A sign posted at the Leadville city limits summed up the sentiment rather bluntly: "All Chinamen will be shot."[38] Chinese people were also barred from setting foot in the city of Aspen during the town's early years, beginning in the 1880s.[39] A group of Chinese men was run out of Caribou,

Colorado, in the early 1880s, and a newspaper in Boulder praised this action.[40] Denver was also the site of an anti-Chinese riot in 1880, in which
homes and businesses were burned and looted, and many people were
assaulted, including an elderly Chinese man who was hanged from a
lamppost on the corner of Lawrence and Nineteenth streets.[41] This, of
course, was part of a much broader rash of anti-Chinese violence and riots occurring throughout the American West from the 1870s to the turn
of the century.[42]

Mexican immigrants and Mexican Americans in the state fared no better. Mexicans have been in western Colorado since the time that land was
owned by Mexico. After the Treaty of Guadalupe Hidalgo (1848) and the
subsequent founding of the state of Colorado (1876), Mexican Americans
and Mexicans migrated from nearby states and from Mexico for work.
There was a spike in Mexican immigration to the U.S. Southwest during
and after World War I to fill jobs in steel plants, agriculture, and other
key industries. For them, school and residential segregation in Colorado
were the order of the day. In rural Weld County, the school superintendent
made it clear that education would remain segregated for as long as he
was in office: "the respectable people of Weld County do not want their
children to sit along side of dirty, filthy, diseased, infested Mexicans."[43] And
while the Colorado Fuel and Iron Corporation, the Great Western Sugar
Company, the Holly Sugar Company, and the American Beet Company all
heavily recruited Mexican immigrants to work in their southern Colorado
facilities, many Anglo residents despised these newcomers, often making
little distinction between them and Hispano Coloradans who had lived
there for generations and faced similar hardships. During the Great Depression, there was such anxiety about job security in the state that in
April 1936, Colorado governor Ed Johnson declared martial law on the
U.S.–Mexico border and ordered the Colorado National Guard to prevent
Mexicans from entering the state.

Colorado was a hotbed of nativism and religious and racial intolerance,
stemming in part from its embrace of the doctrine of Manifest Destiny,
which assumed a white birthright to the land. People of color, immigrants,
and Native peoples continued to experience displacement and discrimination in terms of property, politics, housing, and labor markets throughout
the twentieth century.

The Rise and Fall and Rise of Aspen

A group of silver miners founded Ute City in 1879, ignoring the governor's pleas that they leave the area during an Ute uprising. A year later the businessman, promoter, and publisher B. Clark Wheeler incorporated the Aspen Town and Land Company, on behalf of eastern investors looking for silver wealth in the Rockies, and renamed the town Aspen. Many of Aspen's founders and first residents came from other nations, such as East Prussia (Henry P. Cowenhoven), New Brunswick, Canada (David R. C. Brown) and Bavaria, (David Hyman).[44] As a result, like the goldfields of California, Aspen was largely under the control of absentee corporations.[45] The Aspen Mining and Smelting Company was headquartered at 54 Wall Street, in Manhattan. The historian Malcolm Rohrbough wrote, "the single most powerful economic force in Aspen in 1888 was a corporation with its headquarters on Wall Street in New York City. . . . Aspen had become simply another part of industrial America."[46]

As with many western towns, Aspen quickly experienced boom and bust cycles. In 1892 the city was producing one-sixth of the total volume of silver mined in the United States. By 1893 Aspen had grown to become Colorado's third largest city, but with significant accompanying ecological costs. As early as 1881, official reports emerged that pollution from the town's sawmill was befouling the nearby rivers and streams, posing health risks to wildlife and to the residents who depended on the rivers for fish and drinking water.[47] Moreover, timber cutting for use in the mines reduced nearby forested areas to dust within a short time. In nearby Garfield County, even after President Benjamin Harrison established the White River Plateau Timberland Reserve in 1891 (later renamed the White River National Forest by FDR), hunters wiped out animals for food and profit, driving many species to extinction. In 1895, a hunter killed the last native elk in the area, the final chapter in a short twenty-year span of time in which the animals were mercilessly slaughtered without regard for preservation.[48] Deer, bears, grouse, mountain sheep, and fish nearly met the same fate, until local newspapers campaigned against such destruction.[49]

The social landscape of the Aspen area was also an exciting and dynamic space. The town soon became a site of intense class divides, with mine company investors and their socialite families on the West End of town, and mine workers living in cramped, makeshift housing in the East End. Moreover, the work of mining silver was as difficult, unrewarding, and lethal as anywhere in the West. Miners' consumption, or silicosis (caused by inhaling silica dust), afflicted many workers in the mines around Aspen. The miners experienced shortness of breath and coughing along the road to a slow death. Near the turn of the last century at the Union-Smuggler Mine in Aspen, an underground fire took the lives of fourteen miners. For many years, tragedies like these were not followed by industrial reform because, legally, miners were responsible for their own health and well-being on the job, until modern occupational safety and health regulations were instituted in the twentieth century.[50]

Aspen developed a strong tradition of working-class populism and labor-union militancy in the late nineteenth century, partly because of the low wages and high risks associated with the work.[51] Regrettably, as was the case elsewhere, such unionism often took on an anti-immigrant flavor because mine owners frequently pitted these groups against each other. During strikes in 1892 and 1893, for example, foreign workers were brought in to fill jobs at lower pay. The city also had a policy of placing indigent people on a train with a one-way ticket out of town, so there was little in the way of a social welfare ethic in this place of vast riches and hard luck. At the same time, a group of wealthy women in town started organizations such as the Women's Home Missionary Society, St. Mary's Guild, the Women's Assembly of the Knights of Labor, the Women's Literary Club, and the Ladies Aid Society. These groups raised funds for charity, for a lecture series, and for the general elevation of refined culture in Aspen.[52]

Aspen was not exactly a melting pot but had its share of ethnic and racial diversity.[53] According to the 1885 Census, African Americans made up just 1 percent of the city's population, and they generally worked in the service sector. An early newspaper laundry advertisement may have reflected their role in the community: "Mr. Pearce's African can change soiled clothes to garments as white as snow."[54] The town's population of thirty-two African Americans was, like many African Americans today, highly segregated from whites, even in church. An article in the *Aspen Times* reported that the "colored people, headed by Brother Jones," held prayer services every week on Deane Street."[55] In nearby Glenwood Springs at the time, many of the professional servants were African Americans, several of whom were former slaves.[56] There was one Mexican in Aspen, and not a single Chinese, as they were banned from the town. The local newspaper described Chinese as "surly, treacherous, and careless, and indifferent workmen."[57] Nearly one-quarter of the city's population in 1885 was comprised of immigrants, the vast majority of them northern European.[58] A great percentage of the persons living in Pitkin County, Colorado, (of which Aspen is the county seat) were from nations such as Ireland, England, Scotland, Canada, Russia, Wales, Denmark, Poland, Germany, and France. Some of the occupations they held were listed in the 1885 Census as miner, housewife, teamster, grocer, laundress, student, baker, restaurant cook, carpenter, laborer, dressmaker, freighter, blacksmith, butcher, bartender, civil engineer, mine foreman, saloon keeper, salesman, and lawyer.[59] This was indeed a prosperous city during those heady economic times.

Then, with the Panic of 1893, everything changed. That year President Grover Cleveland overturned the Silver Purchase Act of 1890, which had provided price supports for silver producers. The repeal of the act drove the price of the precious metal down, dooming silver mines and all those whose fates were tied to them. Many workers and investors organized to stop this onslaught, calling the newspapers (such as the *Denver Republican*, the *Denver Post*, and the *Rocky Mountain Sun*) that embraced the demonetization "vile and contemptible."[60] Their efforts fell on deaf ears, however, and hundreds of thousands of people were thrown out of work almost overnight as mines across the West suddenly closed. There was some good news that year, however. In 1893, Colorado became the first state to approve women's suffrage by popular vote. The Aspen papers supported this effort as well.[61] But with the collapse of silver, the booster brigade had to step up to the plate and either market the town or watch it die.

Marketing the Mountains

Many towns in the nineteenth-century West were literally promoted into existence. Newspapers published advertisements and personal stories, while business organizations, railroads, and traveling salesmen were critical to getting the word out and getting investors and workers in. In 1872, the same year the Mining Act was passed (opening up public lands to private companies), the Colorado Territory set up a Board of

Immigration—an agency whose purpose was to recruit immigrants to live and work in Colorado. The plan was to increase investment, improve the tax base, and make a successful bid for statehood, which they did in 1876.[62] This was the first wave of the "sell Colorado" campaign that continues to the present day. Some of the many features of the territory that were emphasized in advertisements were its mild climate, ecological beauty, and mountain ranges, earning Colorado the label of "The Switzerland of America."[63] Another popular phrase in the booster lexicon was Colorado's "champagne air," which, along with its many hot springs, had a purported medicinal effect on visitors. Racism and Anglo supremacy were often coupled with these campaigns. One promotional venture for the town of Colorado Springs came with a description that the city was "a fine place to live because so few Irish polluted its refined atmosphere."[64]

Published personal dictations of Aspen residents were an effective way to publicize a vision of prosperity. Newspaper editors and journalists (whose economic interests were tied to promoting the town to outsiders) would seek out and publish these accounts. Consider the dictation of Harvey Young, who spoke about his exploits in the Crystal City, as Aspen was known then: "Mr. Young took the Emma lode [a mine], something that was generally supposed to be worthless, sunk a shaft, and took out $75,000 in a month. Made several other good strikes. Regards Aspen today as the most promising mining camp in the state."[65]

Continuing this tradition into the early years of the twentieth century—which was important, since those were the "quiet years" of economic recession in Aspen—the Colorado Board of Immigration published the following description of Pitkin County in 1916:

Why Come to Colorado? They who seek for wealth by delving into the bowels of the earth, may know that within the accessible fastnesses of our mountains lie buried, and awaiting development, untold millions which can be had by energy and well directed toil. . . . They who fancy the charms of unsurpassed scenery, varying with every light and shade, yet ever the same, come and look upon the lofty crags which lift their "awful forms" around, and crown our everlasting mountains. They who fear that the rigors of a variable climate will shorten their days, come to Colorado and take a new lease of life, by breathing the invigorating air which gives life and health to declining invalids.[66]

It is interesting that within this booster call, the Board of Immigration saw no conflict between promoting mining and maintaining the natural beauty and ecological charm of the area. This reflects a long-simmering tension in the American West wherein boosters and residents have emphasized the aesthetic attractions of the region, while also embracing a laissez-faire approach to tapping ecosystems for financial wealth.

Marketing the Mountains . . . again

The period between the Panic of 1893 and the late 1930s is commonly known as Aspen's "quiet years." It was a sleepy town, where some old-timers hung on to a dream that had long since faded in the shadow of the silver collapse. But even amid the inactivity and silence, changes loomed.

With the emergence of corporate capitalism, the completion of the transcontinental railroad, and the advent of new communications technology, one of the West's now-permanent features bloomed: tourism. The notion of traveling in order to see something of interest was developed as an elite practice and promoted as a patriotic duty. Until that point in time, nearly all tourism in the United States centered on the East Coast. As the American West opened up, however, ancient ruins, natural wonders, and other sites became marketed under the government's "See America First" campaign. This was an effort to build a new national identity that reinforced imperialist ventures across physical and cultural frontiers.

In the 1930s, when investors turned their eyes on the Crystal City once again, they had money, snow, and tourism on their minds. Aspen's ski slopes first opened in 1936, but the dream was deferred when World War II broke out, and the nascent resorts closed down until the war was over. At that time, Walter Paepcke, an industrialist from Chicago, like the boosters of old, once again promoted this town into a renewed existence. Beginning with a nationally lauded celebration of the famed scholar Johann Wolfgang von Goethe's Bicentennial in 1949, Paepcke inaugurated Aspen's rebirth as a city where great ideas, culture, and the enjoyment of nature could thrive and intermingle. With his Aspen Skiing Company, the Aspen Institute for Humanistic Studies, the Aspen Music Festival, and the

International Design Conference, Paepcke created an exclusive space for the elite business class to network, hear lectures and music, and rejuvenate their minds, bodies, and spirits. The Aspen Institute's lectures soon morphed into "the Executive Seminar," specifically created for leading corporate executives who could attend conferences, take in a concert, and rest far away from the fast-paced life of the cities.[67]

Paepcke's vision reveals the heart of contemporary Aspen. He sought to create a getaway for those executives who could enjoy nature while relaxing from hectic jobs; then they could return to those jobs refreshed and resume their corporate activities with renewed vigor. This is central to the Aspen Logic—that what is good for the executives is good for society, that a top-down approach to social planning and politics is best for all, and that capitalism, environmental sustainability, and democracy are intimately compatible.

The highbrow facelift promoted by Paepcke and other boosters did not sit well with many old-timers, who would have appreciated some acknowledgement of Aspen's proud mining history and working class presence. As one former miner put it, "Gallons of printer's ink to lure the tourist! And not a drop of ink to tell the world where we stood, back in the Eighties,"[68] exhibiting the pride that many locals feel about Aspen's boom town days in the 1880s. But the plan to build the "American Salzburg" would not be sidetracked by working-class nostalgia. Paepcke was a genius at bringing media coverage to this mile-high town. One national magazine boldly proclaimed that as of 1950, Aspen was the nation's "intellectual center."[69] Another magazine declared, "Accommodations in Aspen are suited to all tastes and pocketbooks. . . . Today the old-timers and the visitors agree that Aspen has never been a ghost town and that now it's the melting pot on top of the nation—in Colorado."[70] Despite such generous proclamations, however, Paepcke's plans were always more socially specific: to create a place where white, elite, ecological privilege reigned supreme. In October 1950, the *Saturday Evening Post* reported:

> The rise in property values that accompanied Paepcke's development in Aspen was welcomed by some and feared by others who became priced out of the market. And an unfortunate rumor went around at one time that Paepcke no longer wanted the "local peasants" to make a social center of the Jerome Hotel.[71]

Aspen was to become a town for the rich, while working-class folks, people of color, and immigrants by necessity had to live down valley and work in a support capacity in the service of that fantasy. As one reporter stated around the time of Aspen's rebirth, "One of the nicer things about the capitalistic system is that it permits enough private money to accumulate now and then to make possible a venture like Aspen, Colorado."[72] Therefore, despite claims that the marketing of Aspen was a mass advertising campaign, it was a targeted promotional effort aimed at a limited demographic group.

Aspen's Growing Pains

Back during Aspen's quiet years, the town leaders and would-be boosters carried on a continuous chatter about how to recapture the magic and return the town to its former greatness. In a typical 1913 newspaper article, the author lambasted Aspenites for behaving like "mossbacks"—lazy and unwilling to get the word out to tourists and "sell" the town.[73] Apparently, with Paepcke's help three decades later, they eventually did. So much so that by the 1960s, Aspen's marketing "problem" was that they had been *too* successful, as evidenced by the growth in population and development in the area, and by the presence of some new undesirable social elements—hippies.

A place like Aspen was heaven on earth for hippies, or at least, hippies with money. Known variously as flower children or, today's term of choice, "trustafarians,"[74] these free spirits by choice are said to have taken over cities like Berkeley, Portland, San Francisco, and Boulder. Aspen was also on that list; in the 1960s and early 1970s those long-haired nature lovers were flocking to town. According to one report, Aspen was so popular among this set that one hippie reportedly hijacked a blimp in California and attempted to fly it to the Crystal City.[75] The hippie "problem" rubbed Aspen's elite the wrong way, and they pushed the city leaders to pass a vagrancy ordinance, which led to many instances of harassment and arrests. The *Aspen Times* sided with the cause of civil liberties and took a huge hit when advertisers organized a boycott of the paper (business leaders were, after all, the main force behind the vagrancy ordinance). Eventually, the ACLU brought a class-action lawsuit against the town in 1968. Even though a federal judge in Denver refused to rule on the issue, three months later the city repealed the vagrancy ordinance. Soon after, the Colorado Supreme Court ruled such laws unconstitutional, including a similar one on the books in Denver.[76] Aspen has, since its founding, had both prominent progressive and reactionary elements among its denizens. The following two editorials illustrate this divide:

> Aspen is tourist oriented and must do all it can to attract and satisfy tourists if it is to exist and prosper . . . the hippie movement is as radical and undesirable to the essence of Aspen as can be produced by any group or individual. This conglomeration of disenchanted misfits who are unable and unwilling to meet the competition which prevails under the long-established concept of society in America would foster their level of existence upon others, dragging down everything with them. Some methods of control must be put into use in Aspen.[77]

> One cannot compare Aspen to Germany during World War II. But certain similarities exist between the condition in Aspen today and the early years of Nazi rule. There are the brown-shirted bully-boy police who seem to delight in harassing and apprehending those people who appear poor, ill-dressed, ill-shaved or ill coiffed. . . . It is time for the City Council to recognize the evil it has created and to take steps to end this reign of evil and injustice.[78]

The controversy over hippies was part of the larger and ongoing conflict over Aspen's future. While everyone wanted a prosperous Aspen, many people felt that commercial and residential growth had gotten out of hand. Anti-growth or growth-control sentiment gained support during the 1960s. One resident at a town hall meeting at the time suggested placing a sign with the word "FULL" on it at the city limits.[79] This might be thought of as the more respectable version of the "All Chinamen will be shot" sign that appeared outside Leadville in the previous century. Today, Coloradans defiantly sport bumper stickers on their SUVs and Subarus bearing the message "No Vacancy."

Aspenites wanted growth control and open-space preservation, and over the years they tried to institutionalize these goals, with varying degrees of success. Nongovernmental organizations sprang to life and stepped up to fight developers and urge the city council forward on these issues. Groups that formed on short notice in the late 1960s for this purpose included Citizens for a Better Aspen, the Pitkin County Park Association, the Aspen Valley Improvement Association, the Roaring Fork Foundation, and the Aspen Liberation Front.[80] People were troubled about threats to their enjoyment of a peaceful and exclusive environment, including a development plan that might add 45,000 new people to the valley; Texas International Petroleum's plan to purchase a green space just to the west of Aspen for a megadevelopment; and a proposed widening of Highway 82 to four lanes.[81] Joe Edwards, an Aspen attorney, and several other local activists formed yet another group called Citizens for Community Action. Edwards told a newspaper reporter, "We cannot stop all growth, but we can regulate it to ensure open space and the preservation of our ecology."[82]

The city responded and produced the "Aspen Area General Plan" in 1966. This growth-management plan was an effort to accommodate future economic development in a way that would "retain the fine balance between man and his environment, the essence of Aspen's character."[83] In 1970 the city council approved a 1 percent sales tax to be used toward the purchase and maintenance of open space. The council hired a full-time planner, bought up a prime half-block near the base of the mountain to stave off further development there, and in 1974 the council approved a law protecting mountain views from downtown Aspen so that no new construction would be allowed if it blocked the scenery.[84] It soon became evident that the earlier growth-management plan was having limited success because it was designed to channel the "right kind of growth," not limit growth altogether.

In 1977 the city put forth an updated plan. Only a 3.47 percent growth rate would be allowed annually, and this was enforced via the issuance of building permits through a quota system resembling the plans that Petaluma, California, and Boulder, Colorado, had already adopted (these two cities are also excellent examples of white environmental privilege in action). Aspen took the quota system an additional step forward by extending it to the main business district.[85] For those who wanted to visit or live in Aspen and whose salaries placed them below the ranks of the upper economic class, the town was becoming increasingly unaffordable. Aspen's plan, like many growth-management plans based on limiting growth, created a housing scarcity that rapidly increased prices and reduced the supply of affordable places to live. These growth-management plans were multifaceted, and contained potentially important and beneficial ecological elements to them, but they also produced greater social inequalities. The anti-growth ethic in Aspen was tested again and again during the 1970s and 1980s, and was slowly being chipped away as the power and reach of the town's elite became clear. As one plaintiff stated, regarding a lawsuit brought to allow him to develop 115 acres in Aspen during the early 1980s, "There has been a change in the general public mood and the law from the early '70s 'no growth' to 'reasonable growth.'"[86]

Aspen is a complex place, and city leaders, residents, and activists must be credited with being progressive and socially open-minded from time to time. Consider the passage, in 1977, of a pioneering anti-discrimination law by the city council. The law prohibits discrimination in employment, housing, public services, and accommodations. It makes unlawful:

> any act or attempted act, which because of race, color, creed, religion, ancestry, national origin, sex, age, marital status, physical handicaps, affectional or sexual orientation, personal appearance, family responsibility, political affiliation, source of income, place of residence or business which results in the unequal treatment or separation of any person, or denies, prevents, limits, or otherwise adversely affects, the benefit or employment, ownership or occupancy of real property or public services or accommodations.[87]

This is an expansive, far-reaching, and generous law, way ahead of its time. Of course, it is not difficult to abide by a law that prohibits discrimination against groups that cannot even afford to visit—let alone live or work in—the town.

Similarly, there have been attempts at building affordable housing in Aspen, but nearly everyone we asked about it had the same reaction: loud, throaty, and therapeutic laughter.[88] The point was that affordable housing in Aspen is a contradiction in terms. Moreover, the symbolism of *real* affordable housing in the imaginations of many wealthy white Aspenites is similar to that of many whites and middle-class communities nationally: it is unwanted and associated with people of color and the working classes. One Carbondale City trustee Alice Hubbard Laird put it this way:

So I think there's a lot of basic sympathy for wanting to keep the air clean, but also varying levels of hypocrisy at the same time. Aspen has been really great and progressive on arts, transportation, energy, and open space. At the same time there's this big brouhaha around an affordable housing development up there, with people complaining about sprawl. So you're going to complain about *that* sprawl, but not complain about sprawl down valley and the long commutes?! . . . there's that odd hypocrisy where they're saying "we want our little corner of the world to be very pristine" and then a development less than two miles outside of town, where people wouldn't have to drive forty miles to work, to some of these staunch environmentalists it's horrible.[89]

Colorado's Growing Pains

By the early 1960s, Colorado's economy shifted from mining and extractive industries to one based primarily on tourism. The silver mining economy had hit rock bottom decades before, so this was a chance for a rebirth. State boosters successfully marketed the natural beauty that had, in a previous era, netted billions of dollars in mineral wealth, to attract visitors from out of state.[90] Ironically, the resulting nature-loving activities have taken a great toll on the West. Tourism, hiking, camping, and skiing have grown in ways that the Sierra Club founder John Muir could never have anticipated. Outdoor recreation has become one of the most significant activities impacting the ecological integrity of Western lands.[91] Skiing in particular has damaged the West's ecology, despite its eco-friendly image. One author writes about the faux snow that is used on so many ski slopes in the West:

> Snowmaking isn't a zero-pollution activity; it's an elsewhere-pollution activity. . . . In the West, where most electricity is produced by coal-burning power plants that release significant quantities of sulfur dioxide, the precursor to acid rain, the air pollution impacts of snowmaking are exponentially greater. Here, snowmaking is a form of alchemy, of turning coal into snow. In Colorado, 94 percent of electricity is generated by coal-burning power plants. If a ski area pays a million dollars

over the course of a winter for electricity to run its snowmaking com-
pressors—not an unreasonable amount by today's standards—it has
paid its utility company to burn fourteen million pounds of coal, which
produced thirty million pounds of airborne carbon dioxide, the leading
greenhouse gas that causes global warming, and, by extension, may be
altering weather patterns in ways that will make commercial skiing in
the United States a thing of the past during the twenty-first century.
Much of the power for ski resorts in Colorado comes from the Hayden
power plant in northwest Colorado. This plant, the region's largest pro-
ducer of sulfur dioxide, was found by a federal court to have violated
clean air regulations 19,000 times in five years.[92]

Contributing further to ecological woes associated with skiing are the
air and automobile traffic that comes with ski tourism, and the machine
grading of mountain slopes and artificial snow produced at many resorts,
both of which cause long-term damage to the vegetation and can take
decades to recover.[93]

In response to these kinds of allegations, the National Ski Areas Association recently published a report titled "Sustainable Slopes: The Environmental Charter for Ski Areas." The report declared skiing a pro-environ-
ment activity and, through voluntary principles that it hopes ski resort
operators will choose to follow, predicted that the industry will soon reach
a state of sustainability. The resort association's president, Michael Berry,
stated, "Resorts across the country are well on their way to implement-
ing environmental practices and programs that will ensure a sustainable
future."[94] Vera Smith, the conservation director for the Colorado Mountain
Club, critiqued this report as an example of self-monitoring that ignores
the larger ecological footprint of ski resorts. Concurring with a number
of respected experts, Smith declared, "The real impact of ski areas today is expansions and the commercial development in and around the
ski areas. . . . It's the condos and the strip malls and everything else that
comes along in the valley and by the river, which is the ribbon of life for
that area. The "Sustainable Slopes" [report] deliberately did not address
those issues."[95] Or as the activist Nicole Rosmarino put it so succinctly: "I
see skiing as just another extractive industry."[96]

But the ski industry would not be half what it is today if not for the
subsidies that resort developers enjoy through their privileged access to

public lands. The U.S. government gives ski resort developers rights to build and expand on federal land all over the western United States, in a way that parallels the subsidies given to mining and other extractive industries operating on public lands.

Perhaps a predictable outcome of this control over land and nature by the ski industry is *ecotage*—the deliberate sabotage of machines or other symbols of industrialization by activists who believe these instruments do great harm to ecosystems. In October 1998, the Earth Liberation Front (ELF) took credit for torching the Two Elks Lodge on Vail Mountain, apparently in response to the planned expansion of the resort and the possible threat that move would have posed to the habitat of the endangered lynx. The federal government labeled this action the costliest act of "eco-terrorism" in U.S. history.[97] The incident called into question developers' and skiers' self-proclaimed roles as environmentalists and avid nature lovers. The ELF may have spoken a dirty truth by calling these elites the primary threat to sustainability. In response, it seems that some of those who enjoy and benefit from these ski resorts have found a convenient scapegoat in order to distract people's attention from their immense contribution to environmental degradation.

There were efforts to rein in growth decades earlier at the local and state level. California was the gold standard for urban sprawl and out-of-control growth. Accordingly, one bumper sticker popular among Colorado anti-sprawl advocates in the early 1970s read "Don't Californicate Colorado." And, while the present day spike in anti-immigration politics has a long history in Colorado, it is also part of the broader anti-growth politics evident in that state since the 1960s.

Many laws were passed and numerous officials elected on growth-control platforms in the late 1960s and 1970s in Colorado. The statewide Land Use Act of 1970 required all sixty-three counties to develop plans to control growth, particularly the increase in housing subdivisions in the rural and mountain areas. Evidently, this law had little impact on deterring growth because the housing and tourism boom continued. Richard Lamm ran for governor of Colorado in 1974 and placed environmental issues at the top of his campaign. He, Gary Hart, and Timothy Wirth all ran for elected positions and prominently stressed environmental protection themes that year. The election was buttressed by the recent memories of Lamm's 1972 campaign to challenge Denver's bid for the 1976 Winter

Olympics on the grounds that it would only exacerbate future growth. Lamm successfully ran the Olympics out of town and was elected Colorado's new governor.[98] He billed himself as new blood in a state where the establishment politicians promoted a "sell Colorado" mentality to the outside world in order to secure capital investment for the state's economic stability.

Lamm and others were publicly more concerned about quality-of-life indicators, and Lamm specifically noted that overpopulation and immigration were part of the problem.[99] Lamm, a longtime nativist, ran an unsuccessful campaign for election to the Sierra Club board of directors on an anti-immigrant and population-control platform in the 1990s. George Stranahan told us that in Aspen, "We have the Dick Lamm Syndrome, which is overpopulation will be the death of all of us and tourism too and immigrants are a large part of creating overpopulation issues."[100] Aspen activist Rebecca Doane agreed with Stranahan when she told us "he's [Lamm] a fairly radical—in my opinion—right-winger who, if it were up to him he'd close the borders. So he occasionally shows up around here trying to get the INS to run people out of here."[101] Lamm has served as chair of the Advisory Board of the Federation for American Immigration Reform (FAIR)—one of the most prominent and respectable nativist groups in the United States—and became infamous for giving a speech in which he argued that bilingualism and multiculturalism will "destroy America."[102]

But Lamm also exhibits a populist and anti-corporate streak. He once vowed, "We're not going to let exploiters rip us up and rip us off . . . I know that just as soon as some Eastern politician's constituents get cold in the winter, he's going to say 'screw Colorado.'"[103] Colorado has vast coal, crude oil, and natural gas deposits that are exploited for energy consumption, and the animosity toward eastern capitalists who habitually and historically use the state as a resource colony remains strong to this day. After becoming governor, Lamm once cautioned, "We don't want to be a national sacrifice area."[104]

No-growth politicians and propositions continued gaining ground in Colorado during the 1970s. The cities of Fort Collins and Colorado Springs elected anti-growth city council members, and Boulder passed a measure that limited new housing construction to four hundred units per year, while also buying up large tracts of rural land to create a "greenbelt" around the city. But eventually, the call of the beautiful Rockies, the bucolic meadows, and open space were too strong for tourists and retir-ees to resist. The magnetic force that Colorado's natural wealth has long had on investors was also too powerful to ignore. The state's growth trend continued upward. Figures from the 2000 Census show that since 1990, there was growth in every county in Colorado's Western Slope but one. Eight counties experienced growth rates higher than 50 percent, and five of them grew by more than 80 percent. With the state's established his-tory of anti-growth sentiment, such jumps were troubling. In the minds of nativists, the source of this growth was clear. But was immigration from south of the border the primary culprit? The Colorado state demographer Jim Westkott stated, "The second homes are the driver (of population increases), more than anything. . . . We've had seven, eight years of very strong second-home development in some of those counties, and it looks like it's going to stay pretty strong."[105] It is unlikely that many of the immi-grants coming to work in Colorado's service and construction industries are these second-home owners. In fact, according to one custom home-builder on the Western Slope, typical buyers are semi-retired or retired en-gineers, stockbrokers, and dentists.[106]

The growing divide between the have-mores and have-nots in America has been called "the Aspen effect" because that city is an excellent, ready-made, localized example of how capitalism in the late twentieth and early twenty-first centuries has culminated in shocking extremes of wealth and poverty, of riches and rags, of profit and misery.[107] Ski resorts across Amer-ica reflect this pattern of social violence, which is also mirrored nationally in virtually every city and state. The writer Harlan Clifford may have said it best when he wrote, "The lesson from Europe and from our own destruc-tion of communities in the name of progress is that the time has come for Americans to set aside the concept of manifest destiny."[108]

3

Living in Someone Else's Paradise

> You call me wetback because I
> crossed a river, so what can I call you?
> You crossed an ocean.
>
> —Carlos Loya, Roaring
> Fork Valley resident[1]

While there may not be such a thing as a typical day in the life of an immigrant family in the Roaring Fork Valley, Luisa's story may come close:

> A normal day for me, it's different in the summer from the winter of course because the children are on vacation. On a normal day, I get up at five, make breakfast for my husband, at six o'clock, make the bed, do all the chores. Wake up the kids, ask and organize all the activities for the kids for the day. At eight we leave to clean houses. Ten houses. Tuesday evenings I have English classes with a volunteer from the library. I always like to be home by four, because the children are just getting home then and I don't like to leave them alone. And then my husband gets home, and we talk, talk about our days. Eat dinner. We go to bed at ten thirty and get up again at five.[2]

During our many visits to Aspen, we spoke to dozens of immigrants in the Valley; some of them longtime residents of the area, others were recent arrivals. We spoke with immigrant men and women in churches, day-care centers, schools, social service offices, and community organizations during the evenings and weekends when they were able to take time off from work. The stories they told us were numerous and revealed great variation, yet they shared many common themes.

Many newcomers to the valley face difficult living conditions, as they are frequently crammed into apartments or mobile homes on the side of highways or tucked away into residential enclaves out of sight down valley. One Carbondale activist described his brother's home:

> [T]here's about eight people living in there and they're all from different parts of Central America. My brother, being from Puerto Rico . . . he's probably the only legal fellow in that house, the one that signs the bills and pays the rent . . . the house is about to fall down to the ground, it's kind of sketchy. But nobody speaks up about those things, they're just happy to have a roof over their heads and not being evicted by the landlord. It makes me a little mad because, as a white Anglo Saxon, you probably wouldn't even consider living there or you would tell your landlord to fix the leaking roof and the toilet . . . the place is a mess. Not very nice.[3]

A number of people we spoke to were employed sporadically. The nature of work in a tourist economy is unstable, seasonal, and largely informal. This is true during both the winter and the summer, depending on one's employment networks and skills. One man we spoke with, Jorge, was out of work at the time and living in an apartment with six other people, some of whom were not family members.

> I'm from near Puerta Vallarta [Mexico] where I used to be a taxi driver and a waiter. The best thing about this area is the work because that's what we're here for. And it's still better even if there's not a lot of work because the wages are better than in Mexico. The worst thing is when there's no work. Everything is fine, the snow, the winter, as long as there's work.[4]

Veronica is from El Salvador and struggles to make ends meet. She told us:

I live in an apartment. They ask for a lot, I don't have any rights. The rent is very expensive. So are the bills. Catholic Charities helped me find a place. They've been helping me financially. It's difficult to live here. If I could get an ID, I could use my driver's license. Sometimes we are forced to get IDs from Mexico even though we're not from Mexico.[5]

Renaldo Menjívar, from Costa Rica, is a landscaper who lives in Carbondale. He emphasized that although there is plenty of poverty, there is also significant class diversity within the valley's Latino community that should not be overlooked:

There are different classes of Latinos here. So there is a lot of wealth, there is money. And you can see that in the living conditions—they have a nice flat. And the opposite is also true. There are people that live two to three families in a small trailer and very poor conditions and they just have the basics. So there is a whole range.[6]

In our interviews, some people indicated that they were content with the opportunities they saw ahead of them, while others sought to move up and out of their living situations, which they defined as undesirable and often unsafe. The national fixation on whether immigrants themselves are here legally likely contributes to the fact that employers, landlords, and the police treat so many undocumented persons in ways that violate the laws of this country. Racial profiling, neglect of housing stock, wage violations, and health and safety risks on the job are routine insults facing these populations.

The Struggle for Affordable Housing

Most of what passes for "affordable housing" in the valley are mobile home trailer parks where the residents are working class and mostly Latino. In this area, these are the least desirable places not only because of the stigma of living in a trailer park but because they are viewed as inherently unstable habitations. There are some exceptions, however. For example, in Aspen, there are middle-class professionals who live in trailers that cost more than $300,000. The general rule, though, is that these are not the most sought-after living arrangements. There is a wide range in the quality of mobile homes throughout the valley, and those deemed "affordable" are at the bottom of the quality scale. The working-class trailer parks are unstable for at least three reasons: (1) many residents view them as transitional housing, which people hope to pass through only temporarily on their way up the socio-economic ladder (which reflects and creates a built-in disincentive for trailer-park managers to practice good upkeep and maintenance, and it lends the perception that these communities matter less than others); (2) many of the trailer parks are located in flood-plains or on the edge of highways—a classic example of environmental racism because such proximity produces greater risks to residents' health and well-being; and (3) many of these communities have been threatened with displacement by developers who wish to build more profitable businesses at these locations.

The trailer parks in the valley (outside the city of Aspen) are mostly Latino, but they also include some professionals (for example, Scott Chaplin, a Carbondale city councilmember) and middle-class Latinos and Anglos who have simply been priced out of the traditional housing market in the area.[7] Even so, these are not places that people would choose to live if they had options. *La Unión's* Luis Polar noted that the entire valley is dotted with trailer-park communities, from just below Aspen all the way down to Rifle:

> They also have some enormous trailer parks down there that are really run down. You go in there and there's kids running around and there's no roads. It's a dirt road, and you think how can this be happening in a town that's such a beautiful town? But they have these little sections that are hidden from the main road.[8]

Marie Munday spoke with us about two trailer parks in the valley and how these communities have taken on ethnic identities over time:

> We have a place called the Aspen Mine Dumps, which are just old beat-down shacks that used to be where all the ski bums used to live, but now it's almost all Latino. Once I was interviewing a person and asked them where they lived and he said "I live in Tijuanita." That's the name

they gave it because everyone there was from Tijuana, but none of us cops knew that's what it was called. There's another trailer park in Carbondale they call Chihuahuita for the same reason: it's all people from Chihuahua, Mexico.[9]

We asked Munday about the living conditions in some of these trailer courts. She replied:

> The living conditions . . . there's one really really bad trailer park down in Glenwood Springs that another cop had asked me to look into. He said half the time they don't have electricity, so he asked me if I could get Latinos Unidos [an advocacy group] involved. . . . They're paying really high prices to live in these trailers and the landlords don't give a damn, and the place looks like hell, and it's open sewage. I know where this trailer park is. So I talked to a few Latinos before I walked over there, which is something I do out of respect as an outsider. They told me that that's mostly where all the newcomers live. It's real horrible conditions there.[10]

There was widespread agreement that some of these trailer parks were one step up from a town dump.

Many of those we spoke with concurred with Munday that these communities are places seen only as temporary living arrangements, which residents hope to leave for better housing as they increase their savings and move up and into better jobs. Scott Chaplin stated that trailers are a "real place that Latinos could afford to get into. . . . So, it's the kind of housing that Latinos would be more likely to get into because it's much cheaper to get into a trailer than into a real house."[11] The temporary nature of residential life in these communities can intensify the tendency for many Latinos in the area to shy away from participating in public life and community politics. There are already more than a few reasons for this guarded stance, including the fear—among undocumented persons—of employer retaliation and ICE detention and deportation. Compounding that dynamic is the external perception that these mobile home communities are less stable and less important than others.

Not only is there poor waste management (in the form of open sewage) documented in some of these communities, they are often at a higher risk of exposure to ecological dangers such as flooding. The *Denver Post* reported that "[i]n Basalt . . . two of the parks are in the floodplain of the Roaring Fork River."[12] Jessica Dove, who works in Basalt, confirmed this claim. She explained that there were limited options for alternative sites for those in need of affordable housing. To its credit, the town wanted to move people out of the floodplain without simply shifting people downstream and out of the community altogether.[13] Unfortunately, like so many communities, the situation remains stalled until a better idea is presented or disaster strikes.

As Hurricane Katrina and other tragedies around the world have revealed in recent years, the environmental injustices associated with politically and culturally marginalized peoples living in floodplains is not only unfortunate but exceedingly common.[14] What is also evident from these tragedies is that moments of crisis are perhaps the worst time to device long-term solutions. Instead, ad-hoc temporary measures many times create greater future problems. And environmental problems require long-range thinking.

In the late 1990s and early 2000s, a conflict erupted in Carbondale's Bonanza Trailer Park. The residents there were scheduled for eviction because a developer had purchased the property and was preparing to build a more profitable operation on the space. Most of the trailer park residents owned their homes, but not the ground beneath them. So they were paying a monthly lease to stay on the property. There were twenty families living in the trailer park (one of six such parks in Carbondale) and 80 percent of the residents were Latino. They were given a nine-month eviction notice when the Texas-based developers reached a deal with the property owners. The notice included six months free rent and a three-month grace period, which would cushion the blow of displacement, but residents were deeply upset at being forced out. In response, they organized themselves into a group called the Bonanza Families Secure Homes Project.[15] One of the first items of business was to request that the town trustees pass a replacement housing ordinance.[16] The neighboring town of Basalt had passed such legislation the year before, guaranteeing that 100 percent of all homes displaced by development projects would be replaced. Simultaneously, the Bonanza Families group tried several other strategies: they offered to purchase the land from the property owner, and they asked the city to buy the property and lease it back to the residents.[17] Neither proposal got very far because the offers were for $1 million while the property had a market value of $2 million. The low offer was understandable, considering that the Bonanza residents held down jobs at which they typically earned between $8 and $12 per hour.[18] At that point, the Bonanza Families sent an open letter to lawyers in the area requesting legal aid to support their case. Scott Chaplin was a resident of the trailer park and was among the public voices representing his community. He wrote, "We have begun collecting money from each household for legal expenses and other assistance."[19] Chaplin also conducted a survey of the Bonanza residents and found that the average monthly salary was $2,000 (which amounts to an annual salary of $24,000, a poverty wage in the Roaring Fork Valley) with 40 percent of residents bringing in less than $1,300 each month. The survey also found that the majority of the trailer park's residents work in Aspen, followed by Carbondale and Snowmass; the typical residents' occupations include carpenter, house painter, cook, landscaper, construction worker, stone mason, housekeeper, and ranch worker; and the average adult had lived in the trailer park for six years.[20] Chaplin and Bonanza Families used this information to make the case that they were hardworking members of the valley community who simply needed assistance in keeping their homes.

In addition to collecting money from the trailer-court residents, the Bonanza Families Secure Home Project organized public benefits to raise funds for the cause, including a dance party complete with a band. The flyer for the occasion reads: "Dance to the Norteña rhythms of Los Brillantes del Valle. Funds will be used to help pay legal and planning fees for the group's effort to create a new affordable housing project."[21] A note written on the flyer after the event took place states "we made over $5,000!" Latinos Unidos was the sponsoring organization, but despite this outpouring of local support, the fund-raising effort fell significantly short of its goal.

With no success in sight and in a moment of desperation, the group's allies on the Carbondale and Basalt town councils asked their richer brethren—the Aspen and Pitkin County officials—to assist with the relocation of the Bonanza residents. Unfortunately, this effort failed.[22] The situation became particularly tense when it was discovered that the Carbondale Council on Arts and Humanities (CCAH) was considering a "land carrot" offered by the developer interested in placing a three-story, mixed-use commercial and residential facility on the property where the Bonanza Mobile Home Park was located. A press release stated, "This location would enable CCAH to play an active role in supporting and continuing the vitality of downtown Carbondale. Bringing gallery openings, art shows, and frequent performances to downtown could be mutually beneficial to CCAH and the commercial core businesses."[23] In other words, the deal with CCAH and the developer was that the arts council would receive a new space in return for the eviction of the families from the Bonanza Trailer Court. At this announcement, two prominent members of the arts council board resigned in protest.[24]

The trailer park was eventually torn down and the residents evicted. Speaking about the legacy of this struggle, Scott Chaplin recalled, "Some of the families were able to find new places in town. They knew about a year in advance that they would have to start saving money. Some of them have been able to buy houses, others are renting. Some moved to Rifle, others left the state, and one family moved back to Mexico."[25] Chaplin remains friends with some of the former residents, but the fact remains that the community was destroyed.

The problem of marginalized immigrant communities scraping by to make a living in mobile home parks in the valley is common. We spoke to Simon Silva, a Mexican immigrant and resident in a similar community, which was on the developers' chopping block as well. He told us that the trailer park owner sold the property without consulting the residents. The new owner planned on building condominiums and a retail village on the site, and the residents had limited time to leave and find new housing. Silva said there were more than one hundred families in the community:

> [T]hey don't think about the families, the children. Where are we going to live? They're not going to relocate somebody, they're not going to do it. Why? Because nobody's going to make a big loud noise, you know? They only make the business, between the owners and the new owners. Everybody wait and see what happens. We need the place, we need to make noise. What happened, what happened with these kinds of people is really amazing, it's really bad because we pay taxes, we work, we are a hundred people in Aspen and Snowmass. We make money for these guys! Somebody has to do something. Because it's really bad for us.[26]

Mr. Silva makes clear the reality that immigrants in mobile homes simply do not count socially, and this devaluation is reinforced by the absence of significant public political participation on the part of these communities. This is why the most powerful and positive legacy of the Bonanza Trailer Court struggle—despite losing the battle with the developers—was that a previously inactive group of people became politicized and vocal, contributing to a public discourse around affordable housing and equitable development in the valley, where virtually none had existed before the incident.

Documented, Undocumented, and Brown

In interview after interview, virtually every immigrant and immigrant advocate we spoke with underscored the importance of legal status in shaping the quality of people's lives in the valley. This comes as no surprise. Legal status determines whether you can feel safe driving a car, coming and going to and from work, to the supermarket, or to your child's school. And considering the ever-present threat of ICE raids on businesses and communities, legal status determines whether you can feel safe at work and in the privacy of your own home. The activist Felicia Trevor remarked, "I think legal status is the most pressing issue. How to get it."[27] Luis Polar seconded her point: "I'd have to agree. Because if you are an illegal individual, you know that your paperwork is corrupted, or whatever . . . that if you are driving down the road and you get pulled over, there's a chance that they might find that paperwork being illegal and you're going to find yourself in the Garfield county jail, or find yourself back in the country where you came from."

Julio Soto, a Latino immigrant we spoke with declared, "Cops will just be on my tail and they'll just follow me around, they won't turn their lights on sometimes, just following. Especially, we have two Hispanic officers and they are the most notorious [laughter]." Scott Chaplin chimed in, "Those are . . . forms of harassment, driving while Latino, like driving while black." Renaldo Menjívar added, "I remember one year there was a guy that got his car stolen so he called the police and he ended up in jail because he didn't have papers." Such incidents serve as a serious deterrent to undocumented persons cooperating with law enforcement, which immigrant advocates argue ultimately harms everyone.

Many interviewees linked the rise in official immigration surveillance and harassment to the fear and loathing of foreigners that gripped the nation in the wake of September 11, 2001. Marisa is a Mexicana and has full documentation, but that has not protected her from regular monitoring by the authorities:

> In my case, now to go to the airport—I had to go register at the airport, when I go in and picked up my boss there. And before, it was not like that. Now they are asking for IDs, you have to fill out forms—you just get checked more, you know? We never saw that before. And now it's like people around here I hear that they have to travel with their legal papers or else police will turn you over to the INS. All that has gotten worse after September 11.

The job-related stress for undocumented Latinos has also increased lately, as the national nativist sentiment remains high. Lorenzo Vera works on construction sites in the Valley and has seen this more and more:

> You can see the pressure in the work, the employees . . . it's harder to get a job because they're getting more interested in if you're legal or illegal. Now it's "no good papers, no pay." I have an employee that's getting legal papers and he hasn't gotten social security to be able to work. And my boss said if he doesn't get a social he's not going to get paid. And I said "what do you mean? You owe him like a month now." And he said "sorry, if we don't get a good social, he's not getting paid at all." So he [the employee] was kind of worried because he said, "well, what if I never get my social? I'm not going to get paid." And I said "well, don't worry, I'm going to start looking around for some information and see what we can do." But I don't think they can keep your money if you already worked. And the question is, don't they think that he has to pay rent, he has to pay his way of living here? It's getting really tough.[28]

Many other immigrants we interviewed confirmed these claims. Melinda is from Mexico and works as a housekeeper in an Aspen home. Unfortunately, like many of her friends, she is dealing with an abusive employer:

My employers didn't pay me and I'm still trying to get my money back. And that's the difficulty that I've been having here. I've been getting jobs, but not getting paid. I've been working for this person for three months and she didn't pay me anything in three months . . . it's very difficult to get an American, to force them to pay an immigrant.[29]

Legal status also serves as a dividing line within Latino communities, as some documented and native-born Latinos discriminate against and harbor real contempt for those who are *recién llegados* ("recent arrivals") or those *sin papeles* ("without papers"). One of the most difficult realities facing undocumented persons in the valley and around the United States is the treatment they receive at the hands of some documented and U.S.–born Latinos. There is a long and simmering relationship between these groups, which adds complexity and pain to the white racism many *indocumentados* experience. This discrimination along the lines of citizenship status, generation, and language adds salt to collective social wounds.[30] Much of the contempt stems from anxieties that undocumented persons drive down wages and contribute to harmful stereotypes that many Anglos have of all persons of Mexican descent.[31] Javier, a recently arrived Mexican immigrant, spoke about these tensions:

I don't feel safe here. Some people are really nice, and some people are not. There is racism here. But the immigrants are worse than the non-immigrants. I mean the other Latinos in the valley. The other immigrants who get here first get frustrated with the new immigrants, because they feel like they're taking their work away. Sometimes when people have papers, they're the ones that treat the undocumented worse.[32]

Celia, a Mexicana immigrant, concurs: "Basically the ones who are documented are sometimes more racist than Americans. That's what I see happening."[33]

Leticia Barraza, of the Colorado Mountain College Office of Student Access, knows this dynamic well, personally and through her children, revealing some of the complexities and nuances of race and citizenship in the United States today. As native-born Latinos in an environment increasingly characterized by new immigrants, her children have to negotiate a difficult path through their teen years:

My kids are kind of in-between, they don't fit in either world. They have to deal with three groups: the Anglos, their generation that's been here, and the newcomers. I've raised my kids to be themselves, who they are and to be proud of that, so they're very outspoken. My son wants nothing to do with Anglos, especially Anglo teachers. But he doesn't know enough about his Mexican and Latino culture, so he really can't identify himself in that position either, although he leans more toward the Latino/Mexican culture. But that's the major conflict and I'm constantly at school talking to teachers and they say "Your son has no work ethic, he doesn't want to be at school." And I bring up the issue that "He feels you're racist, he feels you're doing this" and they say "Oh no, we're not doing that." It's very confrontational.[34]

Laura is a college graduate from Mexico City with a degree in political science and public administration. She came to the valley in 1997 and has done very well for herself, working at a bank. While she agrees that legal status is a major concern within the community, she notes that language is also a serious issue:

I think that more than the legal status issue it's the language. You can have a better communication with the culture here, it can open doors, and give you the opportunity to work in a different environment, and learn more about the culture and the problems around you. So I worked in different nonprofit organizations like Stepstone, Latinos Unidos, and La Misión, which opened my mind and eyes to see how important it is to support the people who are not legal. And how you can support something to make this valley a better place to live. So learning English would be the priority. There are a lot of people in this valley who are legal, but they don't speak English. In my work environment I see a lot of people doing labor work because they don't speak English. Sometimes people who are workers are being mistreated by somebody because they have a heavier accent than me, and they are laughing at them and that really makes me pissed off.[35]

David, a Honduran immigrant, echoes Laura's analysis more bluntly: "Yes, the language is most difficult. If you don't learn English, you don't work."[36] Or at least you do not get respectable work. Leticia Barraza concurs and links the language issue to Latino youth experiences in the valley, particularly the divide between native born and immigrants:

> There is a big gap, because those who have *been* here feel that they are *from* here. Those that are coming in, come in with a sense of "I don't want to be here, and I don't know why you brought me here." And they do get at each other because they say "Oh you think you're so good because you talk good English." So they do get at each other, especially at the middle school level.[37]

All of the above issues—discrimination, legal status, and language skills—intersect to create hardship and opportunities for immigrants in the Roaring Fork Valley. Those immigrants without papers and with poor English skills tend to face the greatest stress in terms of risk of harassment and discrimination by law enforcement, Anglos, and other Latinos (especially those with documentation). But the list would not be complete without a consideration of working conditions and health care.

Work

Coming to the United States is often a trial. Most of those crossing the border without papers are forced to pay exorbitant sums of money to *coyotes* (those who smuggle people over the U.S./Mexico border), and they are frequently robbed, raped, and dehydrated while moving through rugged, inhospitable terrain like the Sonora Desert (located in parts of Mexico, California, and Arizona). They come to the United States for jobs that are in short supply back home, where wages are depressed, agricultural economies destabilized, and land systems altered to drive up prices to benefit investors, making life difficult for working-class people. The North American Free Trade Agreement (NAFTA) ushered in many of these changes, intensifying unemployment and social and environmental inequalities throughout Mexico, increasing the appeal for people from rural areas to migrate to work in border *maquiladora* factories or to continue northward to the United States.[38] Countless other immigrants come from throughout Latin America for similar reasons.

Work is the singular reason for migration into the Roaring Fork Valley. In our focus group interviews, the list of occupations people held was long, some of which included housekeeper, landscaper, child-care provider, banker, electrician, sheet rocker, maid, nanny, cook, carpenter, and non-profit staff member. Amy McTernan, the manager of Aspen's Temporary Labor Service, described the range of jobs in which she places people (mostly immigrants):

> We do house cleaning, we do snow removal, we do all kinds of secretarial, bookkeeping, a lot of construction labor. In this part of the county there's events all the time, so we do a lot of events. The workers, they are probably two-thirds men, and they do construction mostly. The women tend to do secretarial, housekeeping, landscaping, property management. And the pay's good up here for them. In Loveland they were paying six bucks an hour and up here the lowest pay is ten dollars an hour. And the Ski Club . . . some of those jobs are $9.50 an hour, but I've never paid anybody less than that. The popular jobs are the jobs where they're going to be there long term. As far as the least popular jobs, you know, to me, digging trenches would be the worst.[39]

Gloria is an immigrant who works as a housekeeper. She described her schedule to us:

> I clean houses, for the eight years that I've been here. I work in Aspen, Snowmass, and the Rancho Roaring Fork [residential community] in Carbondale. Everyday is the same, I get up at five thirty, make lunch for my husband, pick the house up a little bit. I work maybe six or eight hours a day, Monday–Saturday, it's the same routine.[40]

While her work is hard and monotonous, Gloria is fortunate to have a steady job. Jorge Carillo explains that, because of his limited language skills, his employment opportunities are limited. He says that back in Mexico,

> I used to be a heavy machinery operator—that is my passion. But unfortunately here in the States with my lack of English—I don't speak much English—at the ranch that I work on I do mostly maintenance. Keeping

the grass, cutting the grass, doing posts, cutting trees, keeping the land-scape in proper shape. I also paint. So all sorts of manual labor.[41]

While many workers face extraordinary hardships, some enjoy more privileges than others. Rosalinda works in an upscale hotel in downtown Aspen:

> I've been working . . . for ten years. I work in the lobby. I get up every morning at five, take a six o'clock bus, and then I finish at three thirty. In the lobby I make sure that everything's in its right place—you know, this is a very fancy hotel—that the furniture is in its right place. I make sure that it's all clean, so I vacuum the carpet. I work forty hours in a week and get medical and dental benefits, personal days and a holiday bonus.[42]

One of Rosalinda's co-workers proudly adds, "And she was the employee of the year. Two times! In 2003, employee of the month, and in 2004, employee of the year."

Many of the folks we spoke with emphasized that, despite the hardships, they also worked hard to ensure family stability and contributed to the lives of others in various ways. Carla stated, "I have been working in Snowmass at the hotel. I'm a housekeeper, for two years. I work five days there, and on my extra day, I clean houses. I get up at 6 a.m. I finish at 7 p.m. And every other Friday I volunteer at the Aspen thrift shop."[43] Federico, a longtime resident of the valley, leads a full life, which integrates different opportunities in the area. He and his family have been able to enjoy an existence that is beyond the labor of survival. Federico proudly tells us:

> I'm a carpenter. I also work in Aspen. I remodel houses, very big houses. I work eight hours a day, 7 to 3. Tuesday and Thursday evenings, I go to the Colorado Mountain College in Carbondale for classes. I also help my kids with homework, to help them with their Spanish because they speak more English than Spanish and we want our kids to maintain both languages. Two of my youngest sons dance for the city of Aspen ballet. We go to church on Saturdays—the Spanish masses—because it's very important for us to maintain our religion, pass it on to our children. Another routine is that I referee soccer.[44]

Rosalinda and Federico are documented immigrants, and it is likely that this legal status is part of what makes their relative success possible. As remarkable as Rosalinda and Federico's stories are, they are eclipsed by the painful daily encounters with racism and nativism that so many other immigrants—particularly the newcomers—face. Lupe spoke to us about her difficulties getting paid a decent wage, when she got paid at all:

> It's been twelve years since I arrived in the United States. I am from Honduras. I heard stories from people who used to come here for work. Financially, they were paid more here than other places. But when I arrived here, it was a different issue. I came here and I was having trouble finding a place to live, finding a job. For the reason of being undocumented, it's been difficult. They don't pay what they said sometimes. Instead, they would pay you how much they want to pay. I've been in Glenwood Springs for five years now. We have to do a lot of work and we don't get paid very well.[45]

Seasons Change

The nature and availability of work can change dramatically, depending on the season and one's social networks and work experience. For some, winter is a time of abundant employment opportunities, while for others it is a lean season during which work is rare and one waits for summer. For temporary labor contractors, however, it is always busy. Amy McTernan of the Aspen Labor Service told us:

> Yes, well, this time of year [summer], is the "slow season" or what they call the "off season," but I'm nuts because they're fixing everything, they're building everything. And then in the "on season" you're nuts because I get up ordinarily around 4:30 a.m. or 5 a.m. and I don't usually get home until around 6p.m. or 7 p.m. at night. So mostly in the summer it's construction and in the winter it's work for the ski resorts and property management.[46]

Juanita, a staff member at Catholic Charities, explained why the seasonal changes can play havoc on people's lives:

> In winter it's very difficult to pay the bills and rent because a lot of people get laid off. In the winter it's only the people who work in the hotels or restaurants in Aspen that have work. Other than that a lot of people are laid off. That's the worst part of the year.[47]

Magdalena and Corazon, two Mexicanas, confirmed Juanita's assessment. Magdalena stated, "The winter is better because the hotel is full in winter." On the other hand, Corazon noted, "for my husband the summer is better. When there's snow, there's no construction."[48]

Evita Salinas is Amy McTernan's counterpart at another temporary labor contractor in the valley. She offers more details on the difference between seasons, particularly in terms of how the work varies by gender:

> Most of the guys here are doing construction labor—about 80 percent of them. It all depends on the season. During the summer time you can have like 60 percent working construction and the other 40 percent are landscaping. During the winter it's very tough and there's not a lot to do, so many people are getting out and working in hotels and restaurants. There is a little bit of construction. And snow shoveling. For women, during winter time there is the hotel. You can do piece rate and you do as many units as you can—they pay you per unit—or you can work on shifts at hotels. That's tough for women because there's not a lot, just cleaning and landscaping. Or on the golf course the girls are doing some restaurant work. And it's tough because most of the girls in this town have kids. There is no real childcare here. There is a lot of childcare for gringos, but you need to pay a lot of money and you cannot afford it. So what we do is to have one friend take care of ten kids, but it's awful, it's tough. It's like a system. Somebody will take care of the babies and they will get maybe $10 per baby, but its very difficult. That's why I don't have babies [laughter].[49]

As with many tourist economies, services like affordable childcare for the manual workforce are rare or nonexistent. The available choices for the care of children of immigrants are extremely limited. We interviewed

Gustavo, a grandfather in his late sixties, who, for the second time, crossed the treacherous Sonoran desert. He did so at the request of his daughter who asked him to come to the States in order to care for his ill young grandson. Like many immigrants, Gustavo had worked for much of his adult life in the United States, sending his paychecks to his family in Mexico with the intent of building a house and retiring there. After many years of hard labor, Gustavo achieved his goal only to find that his grown children needed his help while they struggled in Colorado. Now, he spends his days inside a trailer home that he shares with his daughter's family of four, looking after a grandchild with special needs and who requires round-the-clock care, while his daughter and son-in-law work as janitors in Aspen. His deeply lined face, marked from years of labor in construction sites and agricultural fields, showed little emotion as he cracked a polite smile and said with a shrug, "Of course I'm here. My grandson needs me. Who else is going to take care of him?"[50]

In addition to challenging the notion that ski resorts are lucrative for everyone during the winter, these stories offer insights into how resort economies are fickle and unforgiving for those who live there year-round with family responsibilities. Healthcare is also a constant concern for these residents.

Health and Healthcare

Healthcare is often a struggle for native-born U.S. citizens, more than 46 million of whom currently have little or no coverage.[51] Given the scope of the problem for people *with* citizenship, one can imagine what it must be like for undocumented immigrants from another nation. We spoke to one young couple—Josefa and Tomas—who had arrived from Mexico just a few months prior to our visit. Tomas had a chronic health condition related to a perforated liver, and Josefa was seven months pregnant. She told us:

> We are worried about the healthcare because everything here's pretty expensive. We tried to sign up for some services and couldn't get them here. They told us that we have to pay four hundred dollars up front, and it's a cost between seven and eight thousand dollars to have the baby in the hospital.

Given that child labor and delivery are covered under emergency healthcare and therefore available for everyone—including undocumented immigrants—we asked if the clinic and hospitals Josefa visited had enrolled her in the public health insurance program.[52] She said, "I already went for one office visit and had an ultrasound and it was eight hundred dollars. And I haven't been able to pay, and now I have another appointment on the 29th, but if I don't bring four hundred dollars they won't see me."[53] Already in her third trimester, Josefa had only had one prenatal care visit and did not expect to go back to the hospital until the labor.[54] Another interviewee experienced similar treatment. She said, "I paid six thousand dollars for my birth. I gave four hundred the first visit, eight hundred the next, and now I'm making payments." However, in an earlier focus group, we spoke with another Latina who had just given birth a few weeks ago at the same clinic that Josefa visited. She was judged to be indigent and was not charged for her delivery. There appear to be significant inconsistencies in the cost and quality of healthcare in the valley. For low-income immigrants, whether they receive health care for which they are eligible seems to be at the whim of clinic administrators, sheer luck, or divine intervention.

Other immigrants and advocates we spoke with related similar stories. Juanita, a staff member at Catholic Charities in Glenwood Springs, told us, "There's a clinic in Rifle, but we've been receiving a lot of complaints that they are being really racist—the people who work up there—they don't tell clients that there's a low-income service up there. So even people from Rifle are coming up here for services."[55] Jasmine, another immigrant valley resident, stated, "Healthcare is a huge issue. We don't have health care. I had to pay $600 for $100 worth of insurance. It's really bad here. There are programs to help Latinos for health care, but I don't know which ones they are. There is Medicaid, but in order to qualify, you have to make *no* money. We don't get health insurance through the job."

Most Latino immigrants working in the valley do not have employment-based, healthcare benefits. Instead, immigrant residents have found ways to maintain their health through other means. Jasmine's uncle added, "I don't have insurance. None of the members of the family have insurance here. We get medicine from Mexico and try to stay away from the doctors here." Renaldo agreed and also linked the issue of healthcare to work:

I don't have any insurance either. I had pinkeye and went to a pharmacy, but you have to have a prescription. So I couldn't do it, so I treated it myself. We all medicate ourselves. I had a friend who got shot with a nail gun on the job. He has some doctor but he can't go back to work because he is injured all the way to the bone. His boss doesn't care. Employers will fire him. They don't understand about health.

We asked Renaldo, "Do you worry about your health and what you'll do if you get sick and need serious healthcare?" He responded, "No. It's just in the hands of the Lord. It's something that you just put aside, and focus on another thing . . . I don't think about that. I just hope nothing happens."

Questioning Racism, Resisting Invisibility

Many of the people we interviewed expressed frustration with the sense of collective impotence, a general feeling of powerlessness and invisibility within the immigrant and Latino communities. These individuals work to confront these issues everyday. Echoing Simon Silva's earlier comments, Renaldo Menjívar also spoke to the lack of political participation among many immigrants in the valley and how undocumented status simply exacerbates that problem:

I would say it's almost 80 percent of the population that is just surviving. And they get, they don't get involved in anything because they know that they don't have papers. So this is why they don't get involved in the community, politics, anything, they don't even organize themselves. They take whatever, nine dollars, ten dollars, eleven dollars [per hour]; they take it because that's the way it is. And that's a big concern and people are afraid so they don't get involved in anything.

Laura, the college graduate from Mexico City, agrees with this assessment and intends to be a part of the effort to change things. She describes the political environment today as tough largely because of what she views as the federal government's harassment of immigrants:

Immigration [Service] is like a crazy government organization that takes forever. They charge you a lot of money. They're always trying to scare people, asking "What is your criminal record?" A lot of harassment, even though you show them that you're a good person and have a good record and don't want to do anything wrong. Plus, they kill a lot of hope in people, because if you try to do the right thing, then it's not enough. It's not right! We need to do something. That's one of my goals. I need to get citizenship and that way I can vote and I can support my people.

Immigrant residents of the valley may not always be visible and public with their politics, but this does not mean they do not have strong feelings about the way they are treated. What emerged from most of these interviews was a distinct sense of not being wanted or appreciated by the dominant culture around them. Or perhaps more accurately, many immigrants expressed the sense that they were wanted in Aspen and the surrounding towns only for their ability to do the work no one else was willing to do. Aside from that, they felt as if Anglos just wanted them to disappear. For example, Marisa lives in a mostly Anglo neighborhood in Carbondale and has never felt entirely comfortable there, despite her being middle class:

I've had some neighbors that are Anglos and I got the feeling that when I moved to the neighborhood they kind of said, "Oh, more Latinos are coming in here," like if we were going to come and destroy the neighborhood or something. And I said well, why can't they just see us as, we're here for the same reason that they're here. We're here to work and to make a living. We have to work harder to be able to show the rest of the population that we're not as bad as they think. If something looks bad it always goes to the Latino people. They say "Oh, it was them" or "Oh, it was probably Mexicans that did it." And we have to work harder to demonstrate that it's not that way.[56]

Statements like Marisa's deepen our understanding of the broader ramifications of environmental privilege because it is not just reflective of the ways that Anglos secure greater access to ecological amenities and exclusive social spaces; it is also about the ways other groups are restricted from that world but whose labor is required for it to function.

Marisa and many other Latina/o immigrants understand the unequal scrutiny under which they are judged. This makes them cautious and self-conscious about what they do and how they do it. They must work against negative assumptions regarding who they are and why they are here. This kind of self-monitoring and discipline works to maintain environmental privilege by marking particular people as unwanted or a burden upon someone else's space. The needs and desires of a wealthy tourist who visits his or her second or third home for two weeks out of the year are unquestioned. Marisa, on the other hand, is made to constantly account for her existence.

This scrutiny is pervasive and exists on a daily basis, not only with regard to housing, work, and health care but also in almost every other institution immigrants encounter, including local law enforcement. Luis Polar of *La Unión* newspaper voices a critique of local police harassment: "People are afraid when they see a police officer. People are scared, people don't trust police officers. They'd rather somebody get something stolen from their house rather than calling the cops. They're not going to do it, because they might get searched or harassed or something like that. So it definitely has a negative effect."[57]

Many immigrant advocates and law enforcement officials note that these dynamics between undocumented persons and police often create a crisis for both citizens and noncitizens. The lack of cooperation with police in many situations can endanger the lives of those in serious need of protection or emergency services. Additionally, local law enforcement's disproportionate attention to immigration policy issues may have a similar effect.[58]

We repeatedly saw how people lived with the fact that federal authorities could swoop in on their homes or places of employment and detain them at any moment, day or night, yet they continued on with their lives in spite of these real threats to their future. When we asked Amelia what she thought about the proposed ICE office in Glenwood Springs, she told us "I'm worried because if I saw Immigration [ICE] I would have to say I don't have papers, I don't have nothing." We asked her "Does that keep you from doing certain things?" and she responded, simply, "No".[59] We view this response as evidence of resistance and resilience to continue building a life undeterred by these terrifying possibilities.

Karina works at an insurance company in the valley and offered a critique of racism, patriarchy, and other forms of social inequality in the United States. She stated:

> I think the United States is a joke because I don't think there's equal opportunity of anything. Working at an insurance place, I learn that there is a lot of discrimination issues with Americans: if you're black, white, if you're old, or young, there is a lot of things. And being a woman, I don't get the same pay as the guys that I work with. Plus I'm Hispanic, but they look good as a business because they have a Hispanic working there. At the insurance place, a woman's license will never make the same amount of money as a guy. I can't understand that. I'm very disappointed because I had to pay more taxes because I'm single, I don't have babies. I think there's a lot of things that are not fair between men and girls.[60]

Carlos Loya works as a laborer throughout the valley and has had plenty of experience with racism. Sometimes when whites yell epithets at him, he responds in one of two ways. He might tell Anglos, "My ancestors were here in Aspen long before you got here. This land used to be our land." Or he poses a question: "You call me wetback because I crossed a river, so what can I call you? You crossed an ocean." Loya stated, "Without knowing it, they are making us tough and giving us patience and strength when they do this. We have a strong shell."[61]

Many of the parents and youth in the valley resist racism in multiple ways. One of the primary sites of confrontation over institutional racism in the area is the school system. In January 2004, a group of Latino parents secured a meeting with Roaring Fork School District officials to discuss concerns over state educational testing, substandard English as a Second Language (ESL) offerings, overcrowded classrooms, and racial discrimination directed at Latino students at Basalt High School and Carbondale Elementary.[62]

And after the July 4, 2001, murder of four Mexican immigrants in Rifle, Colorado, concerned parents there organized in the schools specifically around racism and nativism. A flyer announcing a meeting of "Parent Issues at Rifle Schools" stated that one of the primary issues of concern was

"No more tolerance of racist actions such as racial slurs and not helping when asked." Under the heading "Possible solutions" the flyer read, "Rules regarding discriminatory or racist language. . . . Teachers enforcing the rules . . . Training on what is a 'slur.'" Other proposed actions included greater resources for ESL and bilingual teaching and staff at the town schools. Spurred by violence and growing hostility, parents in the valley organized to confront the racism facing their children in the school system and in the broader community.[63]

For their part, Latino students in the valley express their discontent with the system of inequality in often subtle ways. Leticia Barraza from Colorado Mountain College's Office of Student Access told us:

> A lot of the kids do have jobs. Once they reach a certain age, it's expected that they are here to help the family. And if they need to quit school, then that's what they are expected to do. When we surveyed Latino kids in all three of our high schools, the number one reason they left was to work to support their families; the number two reason was the racism they felt from their teachers and from the administrators of the school.[64]

Numerous Latino immigrants and other people of color paint a portrait of the Roaring Fork Valley as a place where opportunities for advancement and success exist for some newcomers, but for the vast majority of folks from south of the border, the road to opportunity is paved with everyday insults and assaults in the form of institutional racism and violence. And while many undocumented Latinos feel compelled to remain under the public radar, others are able to engage in private and public expressions of protest and demand change.

Challenging Environmental Privilege

We asked José Cordova, a local resident, worker, and activist, what he thought about the claim that immigrants harm local ecosystems. With a degree in environmental sciences from a university in Central America, Cordova was very critical of such arguments. He stated, "I think that's a misperception because I've been working with construction companies and the mess that they do with that stuff! There's no ecological preserva-tion. They just throw away everything. I don't think it's the Latinos affect-ing the environment."⁶⁵ Cordova then became more specific about the re-lationship between population growth and environmental harm, and how that debate masks important power relations:

> My position is that that the concept of overpopulation is not that accu-rate. That's one of the arguments of groups to justify policies, to say there is poverty because of overpopulation. But if we go into details about wealth and the lands that are available, we see that maybe we may all fit in the world. I don't think the problem is overpopulation; the problem is redistribution of the wealth and the redistribution of knowledge.⁶⁶

Cordova offers a critique of the general orientation of environmental policy in this nation. He contends that the focus is never on the point of produc-tion, but rather on what to do *after* we have produced or consumed goods. Like the population-environment debate, the post-production and post-consumer recycling fixation of U.S. environmental policy and environmen-tal movements benefits powerful institutions that remain unchallenged:

> I understand all these programs of recycling, reuse, rethinking. It's OK, it's nice. But that's not the problem. The problem is from the begin-ning—how you produce those goods. You can produce something and make something new out of this, but the problem is that they are pro-ducing it in the first place, so the problem is conceptual and ideologi-cal. The forest and all the resources will suffer because you have not changed the approach to nature. . . . So we produce more and we are working in this [consumer] phase of the production cycle, so they say we can recycle and reuse, but the problem is the same. And from that perspective you cannot say or argue that the foreigners or immigrants are the cause of the environmental problems. The companies are drilling for oil right now, it's right here, these companies need natural gas and money, so it's not the foreigners. It's how you use nature.⁶⁷

Finally, Cordova issues a criticism of the United States in terms of its lack of commitment to global environmental agreements, implying that the immigration-environment debate benefits not only corporate polluters but also the federal government, which will not seriously address its environmental responsibilities within and beyond its national borders.

> The United States has not signed the Kyoto Protocol [on climate change] and all those agreements that are well accepted all over Europe, and other countries have accepted it. I understand that they say that it's not economically sound to change all the production systems. But all these other countries are doing it. Germany has changed legislation to change the way the companies work.[68]

Cordova's analysis and assessment of U.S. environmental politics coincides with what progressive scholars, policymakers, business leaders, and activists here and in other nations have been arguing for years.[69] His appraisal of the population-environment debate speaks directly to the overarching quest for environmental privilege in the Roaring Fork Valley and elsewhere. Environmental privilege is not just about maintaining exclusive access to ecological amenities (mountains, rivers, lakes, beaches, parks, trails, etc); it is also about maintaining access and belonging to broader social spaces, of which both ecological and non-ecological amenities are a part. In other words, environmental privilege is part and parcel of the larger problem of social privilege. The dominance over social space in the valley is as real as the mountains that mark the landscape. Many Latinos feel it when they walk around places like Aspen. Karina is a Mexicana and works in hotels in the valley. She explained:

> You don't fit in Aspen. It's like I don't feel comfortable to even be walking on the streets in Aspen because people look at you like you got out of the sack or something, you know, "go back!" You get that feeling. People look at you different. They're very scared to see a lot of Hispanic or Latino people around because it's very exclusive. So I think that the main point is that they are being concerned about, you know, losing the exclusive part of this area.[70]

The kind of control over social space that Karina spoke of is at the heart of white environmental privilege. Lorena is a co-worker and friend of Karina's. She told us:

You just feel that you're not wanted around those rich people other than to do their housekeeping and work for them, you know? At one point I got stopped by a police officer in Snowmass Village. And he told me I was speeding and I said, "I'm sorry. I wasn't paying attention," and I gave him all my information, my license and registration, everything. And then when he came back [from his car], he said, "Everything's fine, just take it easy." And I said "Oh thank you sir," and he said, "Don't thank me. Even if I charged you, you wouldn't have enough to pay me." And I was like, "Oh okay." You know? Yeah. That's what he said. It got me mad at that point, but I said oh, Aspen people, just let it go. You get that, treated like that all the time up there. In stores and when I have to go into town and do errands for my boss, I feel bad because people look at me like "What are you doing?" You don't fit with the Aspen people.[71]

Aura works as a housekeeper in the valley and concurs with Lorena and Karina in their characterization of social space in Aspen:

I had an experience like a couple of years ago, when I went with one of my best friends to buy a sweater—a very expensive one. So when we get in there [the store], we were looking, and the lady told us, "Oh, that sweater is like eight hundred bucks. Do you have enough money to pay for that?" You don't see people like us in that kind of stores. I mean you can see Hispanic people in the Gap or some other kinds of stores, but you will never see them in Gucci or some other [fancy] places. They always think that they don't have enough money to spend in those stores, or just they don't deserve to buy whatever stuff they have.[72]

Aura added that some other places are much more welcoming than Aspen: "I think Carbondale is a very friendly town." However, she noted, "But if you go farther south, like the lower cities like Rifle, they look at you like 'What are you doing here?'"

White environmental privilege is apparently enforced from one end of the valley to the other, with a few notable exceptions. Karina continued with an analysis of how the changing cultural and political dynamics reveal threats to white environmental and spatial privilege:

The problem is when the Hispanic community are getting businesses and they're interacting more with the organizations, and they're getting more involved with the important issues in this valley. That is when it pops up as a problem. That is my experience. More than, "I don't like you because you're Mexican."[73]

In other words, structural or institutional racism, not just interpersonal racism, is at the core of the struggle for white environmental privilege—the most important and troubling response to the growing Latino and immigrant presence in the area. As José, Lorena, Karina, Aura, and so many others can attest, environmental privilege is ultimately an exertion of power; it is what happens when the dominant culture employs nativism and its racist logic to demarcate where particular people belong.

Where We Live and Work . . . where Other People Play

This phrase is a twist on the popular reframing of the way "the environment" is defined by many environmental justice activists as those spaces "where we live, work, and play." One thing that struck us in many of our interviews with immigrants in the Valley was how few of them ever had a chance to enjoy the one thing that attracts Anglos and other tourists to the area: *nature*. While a few immigrants were able to ski from time to time, they were the exception to this social rule.

We asked Marisa what kinds of recreational activities she and her family enjoy, and whether they ever ski. She responded:

Not in my case because it's so expensive to do that. In our case everything was going to our mortgage, so I haven't been able to take my kids. They really want to go skiing. My daughter, she's already ten years old, and every year she's like "Mom, when are you going to take me to ski, I want to learn." We just keep saying every year, "we'll go so that you guys can start taking advantage of what's around this area." It's funny because when we go to Mexico or we go out to other states, they think that we come from Aspen and that we take advantage of everything that's out there, when we don't even know what it's about. For us, it's "no, we just do the work, we just do the cleaning" and that's it. We don't even know the mountains out there.[74]

Juliana added, "We'd like to ski here but we've never done that. We don't ski or even know the mountains. When we visit Mexico, people think we're doing skiing here, but we're not."[75] Most of our interviewees echoed this point. There are multiple Aspens—depending upon who you are. For Latino immigrants, this life generally entails little to no engagement with the area's natural landscapes.

We stated earlier that immigrants are often socially and politically invisible, since they form the backdrop of the local economy in the valley and are forcibly socially segregated. Julio's story is yet another illustration of this practice. He and his wife live half the year in Mexico and the other half in a trailer park in the valley with his adult daughter and her family. The trailer park manager knows he is undocumented and will not allow him and his wife to live there even though his daughter is a resident. Julio said,

I have to go in, sneaking in. The manager is always watching. But if the manager finds out that I'm there with my daughter, he will just tell her to move out of the park. I have to park like a mile away and just walk home, sneaking, you know. So that's why we don't even go out, we don't even enjoy the garden, we have to be in the house. My wife doesn't work, so she's in the house twenty-four hours a day. Even though we have good salaries out here, with the rent and things they have to pay, you don't get to enjoy, you don't get any extra time or money to go bowling, to do fun stuff with your family. We don't get to have fun stuff like most people do.[76]

Julio and his family live in constant fear and enforced invisibility, and the isolation under these conditions is severe. Other immigrants who are more privileged in their ability to move about the valley have made efforts to find ways to develop friendships and build meaningful community connections. For example, José Cordova stated,

I go to church, you know? And usually we have Mass and a little youth group. And I'm involved in that, in helping teenagers. On weekends, we have retreats and . . . we've become friends with the youth and we go sometimes to camping or we play football, soccer and stuff like that.

Even just sitting around and talking about different topics, that's what we do usually.[77]

Others find or make time to relax after work, in ways that would be familiar to most people. Javier said, "After work sometimes we have a beer and play soccer, here in Carbondale. Behind the middle school there's a basketball court, and we organize there to play soccer in the field."[78] Josefa is also involved in a church group and works hard to carve out a space there for the Latino community. She explains, "We can't do skiing and other things that are expensive sports that the Aspen people do. We do baseball, though. The whole Latino community reads *La Unión*—that's our paper. And we also listen to radio."[79]

Still, it must be said that the Aspen Ski and Snow Club is bucking the trend by offering discounts and scholarships to a modest number of low-income families in the valley. This special deal allows children like Carlos and Isabel Loya's sons access to ski lessons and a chance at the slopes during the season.[80] This practice is acknowledged and commended, but it is not likely to seriously alter the reality of environmental privilege. For the great majority of immigrants and people of color in the valley, they are there to work and make a living so that the wealthy of the world can play, relax, unwind, and enjoy nature, unsullied by the hordes of brown folks who must remain off the social radar but always be available for a good housecleaning, a hot meal, condo construction, or a landscaping touch up.

Nuestro Futuro, Nuestros Sueños

For everyone who articulates a critique of nativism, racism, and environmental privilege, that person also offers a vision of a hopeful future—"our future, our dreams"—for themselves and their communities in Colorado and their countries of origin. Carla and Roberto spoke of their trials, aspirations, and successes as new immigrants. Roberto said,

We took four planes from the capital to the border. I learned the English vocabulary for the orchards, apples, and tomatoes, in the hotel and on different jobs. My English grew. In carpentry, my English grew. That's when I went to school so I could speak a little better. We have the desire to have the opportunity to grow, to improve. All the Latinos do. We just came looking for opportunity. We all have the capacity, all the talent that we're bringing from our country and we're just looking for an opportunity.

Carla continued the story:

It's really hard when you first get here. It's not all rose colored. When you get here your house isn't waiting for you [laughter]. We don't know English, we don't have a house, we don't have anything. When we arrived here, we had a house in Mexico. When he arrived here, it was like, there's your little corner. We did not come to slave for somebody, we came to work. We rented an apartment for half of one year in Carbondale and we got an opportunity to buy a mobile home in Carbondale. And we are finishing to pay this December [everyone present cheers and claps].[81]

Eva, an undocumented immigrant from Mexico, spoke to us about her hopes for the future: "to improve our lives a little bit more, economically. The most important thing would be to buy a house. A car isn't as important as a house." We asked Eva where that house would be, and she responded "in Mexico." We queried about the rest of her family—her children in particular. She told us,

My husband and I have a plan that the kids will study English for five years and learn it really well and then we're going to go back to Mexico. They'll really be able to get good jobs in Mexico if they know English well, like telephone operator or something like that. That's all we care that they learn English. By the grace of God we have enough money to feed our kids. It's really difficult to raise kids in Mexico right now. So we're just really happy to have this opportunity to come here to make a better life for them to go back to Mexico to.[82]

While Eva and her husband spoke of their children's future here and in Mexico, others dreamed of contributing to the lives of others, beyond their immediate families. Elena told us of her plans to complete her degree at Colorado Mountain College, not for personal advancement but for community building:

I want to get that degree and get back to Mexico to use that knowledge to help people. In this country, they have a lot of organizations that can help people . . . they give some help. In my country they don't have these organizations period! So my goal will be to start something . . . to help people on the streets. That will be my goal.[83]

We return to José Cordova, who clearly is an inspiration to many people in the valley. Cordova is a carpenter and works as an activist and youth mentor during what little free time he has. Like Elena, he spoke about his hopes for a better future by sharing his energies and skills with a broader network of people:

I actually work down valley and up valley. I do carpentry. And I like it because I think it's an opportunity for me to learn. It's not just about the money, the money's good, you know? But I'm learning. I'm learning the base, how to build houses and stuff like that. And one of my main goals is to go and maybe work for a development organization. One day, you know? Maybe building small houses for poor people.[84]

During our time in Aspen, the power and strength of people like Carla, Roberto, Eva, Elena, and José was clear. The depth of the challenges that these men and women face every day move us to believe that a socially, economically, and ecologically sustainable and just future is possible. Like them, we also believe that people from different national, racial, ethnic, linguistic, and cultural walks of life can communicate, collaborate, and cooperate to build such a future, pursuing a social carpentry of justice. However, the barriers to justice are formidable given the extent to which nativist logic has pervaded our public discourse, and shaped the ways people in the United States see each other and their environment.

4

Nativism and the Environmental Movement

> Demography drives human destiny.
> —Meredith Burke, Negative
> Population Growth.[1]

The call of immigrants to America's shores is one of our country's most foundational stories. But if we are indeed a great melting pot, many of us have been burned along the way. Since at least the eighteenth century, every wave of people immigrating to the United States has had to deal with the antagonism of those who immigrated before. The result has been a vicious cycle of "quality-of-life" nativism, by the white Anglo-Saxon Protestant community in particular and by successive groups of European Americans in general.[2] This includes nativism directed at Austro-Hungarians, Chinese, Filipinos, Germans, Indian immigrants, the Irish, Italians, Japanese, Jews, Mexicans, Poles, Russians, Scandinavians, and people from all over Latin America and the Caribbean. Nativist movements today are not fundamentally different from those of the past. The claims of threats to "quality of life," "American culture," and the anxiety over "limited resources" continue to animate and motivate these groups, and the quest for environmental privilege has always fit nicely into that model of racism.[3]

If the peoples of America make up one half of our triumphant national saga, then the land itself is the other half. Ours is a country that glories in its majestic landscapes and great natural riches, "from sea to shining sea." But that glory is not without its downside. Our environmentalist history does not just harbor strains of nativism here and there; rather nativism is embedded throughout.

As an effort to protect the finite resources of the earth, the idea of controlling the world's population seems like an excellent one. Many who support the ideas of family planning and an awareness of our ecological impact are motivated by genuine concern for our planet. But there is also a dark side to such efforts. Many of the organizations and governments that have made attempts to control human reproduction have had other goals in mind.

The conquest of Native lands and peoples was supported by U.S. federal law and several Supreme Court decisions, all of which relied on the view that such actions were just and moral because of the inherent superiority of European American culture and people.[4] Native peoples were viewed as foreigners in their own land and were judged incompetent stewards of nature.[5] In the early twentieth century, many European American elites turned their sights on newcomers and identified immigrants as a primary cause of ecological woes in the cities. Specifically, immigrants were blamed for the rise in urban pollution, when in fact, these populations were associated with polluted spaces because they had to live and work in smoke-choked neighborhoods and occupationally hazardous factories and sweatshops.[6] Many leaders of environmental preservationist groups at the time—including William Hornaday, Madison Grant, and Henry Fairfield Osborn—decried the influx of Jewish immigrants and other newcomers from Italy, China, and Japan as a threat to American values concerning the sanctity of wild places. In some locations, tensions arose between members of the upper classes who hunted for sport and trophies, while many Italian immigrants hunted for food sources. Prominent environmentalists in the early 1900s worked with the eugenics movement in the United States, viewing immigrants and people of color as naturally inferior to Anglos, and voicing approval of reproductive restrictions on these groups.[7] In fact, the noted preservationist and eugenicist Madison Grant collaborated with Margaret Sanger, the early U.S. women's movement leader and supporter of birth-control technologies, on parallel agendas, revealing how gender and women's reproductive capacity underpin ideological battles over immigration and population growth.

Despite our enormous advances at the beginning of the twenty-first century, the power of racism continually presents itself in both environmentalist and nativist movements. At the 1987 Round River Rendezvous gathering of environmentalists, the EarthFirst! founder Dave Foreman and his fellow EF! activist and author Edward Abbey insulted the peoples of Latin America and the Caribbean by describing them as backward and primitive.[8] Abbey's 1988 book, *One Life at a Time, Please*, featured his favorite essay—"Immigration and Liberal Taboos." Abbey, who has inspired innumerable radical ecologists the world over, wrote in that essay that "it might be wise for us as American citizens to consider calling a halt to the mass influx of even more millions of hungry, ignorant, unskilled and culturally-morally-genetically impoverished people."[9]

There are many possible explanations for the persistence of nativist environmentalism. Historically, nativist scholars, politicians, and activists in the United States have often harbored concerns about the prospect of "race suicide" that might result from either a lack of white population growth or from being "overrun" and outpaced reproductively by non-whites.[10] More recently, since the 2000 Census, several states now have "majority minority" populations (collectively, the African American, Latino, Arab, and Asian American populations in these cities are larger than the white populations), predictions that the United States as a nation will one day follow suit with a white minority have generated some anxiety. According to that Census, almost half of the one hundred largest cities in the United States are, for the first time, "majority minority" cities.[11] This is largely the result of white flight to the suburbs and increasing Latino and Asian immigration. California, Hawai'i, New Mexico, and Texas have already reached "majority minority" status, and more states are expected to join the ranks in the coming years. Reports of these demographic shifts have produced fear and worry among native-born whites concerned that it is not just "their jobs," but now "their *country*" that is in danger of being taken over by foreigners. This anxiety is directed mostly toward immigrants as whites and other citizens try to restrict access to education, health and social services, decent jobs, housing, and a broad range of environmental amenities. Those are long-standing and continuing nativist concerns.

Because the U.S. electorate is so deeply divided on the issue of undocumented immigration, none of the recent federal proposals to address "the
immigration problem" is finding traction with the majority. One divide in
this battle is between nativist conservatives who seek to increase "border
security" and prevent "amnesty" for immigrants versus more liberal politicians who wish to allow some undocumented persons to eventually gain
citizenship—but only after a stringent series of language, labor market,
residential, financial, and other requirements are met. Another set of major players in this drama are leaders of the business community who seek
lower wage labor in the context of a highly competitive global economy.
Virtually none of the major proposals put forth in recent years addresses
concerns over living wages, human, civil, and labor rights for immigrant
workers who desire regularization. This debate will continue, and intensify, given the failure of NAFTA to alleviate migration pressures.[12]

These long-standing debates are now tinged with even greater consequences. The dangerous coupling of the nativist and environmental movements, what we term "nativist environmentalism," is today all the more
potent because our planet's ecological systems are in peril and many conservationists believe that the vast interior spaces in the United States are
relatively pristine and are capable of being "saved" from humankind's rav-
ages. The western European idea of the "virgin land" or "empty land" is also
critical in this regard. This concept stems from a centuries-old doctrine
concerning the protocols that early European explorers were directed to
follow. The idea was that the only foreign lands that Europeans could mor-
ally and legally inhabit were those that were either devoid of people or
where the existing natives entered into treaty-making and negotiations to
allow such activity. Of course, there were few places on the planet where
Europeans ventured that actually had no people, so colonizers produced
a logic that placed these indigenous peoples outside of the realm of law
and history. Since they were subhuman they had no rights to the territory
on which they lived; thus, Europeans could rightfully and conveniently inhabit these lands after all.[13] This myth of the virgin or empty land and the
accompanying notion of European entitlement to foreign lands—indeed
any lands they saw fit to explore and occupy—was operative in the founding and conquest of the Americas, Australia, and elsewhere.[14] We contend,
though, that the myth of the empty land is at the root of what undergirds
nativist environmentalism in the United States today. It is what authorizes

European Americans to continue occupying Native American land, and it is precisely that which facilitates the exclusive access to spaces of environmental privilege throughout this country.

Too Many Brown People

The Federation for American Immigration Reform (FAIR) is the largest and most influential immigration control organization in the United States and one of the most active groups maintaining the links between immigration and environmental politics. Since 2003, FAIR has worked to intervene in the national debates over guest worker programs for undocumented persons. John Tanton, who served as a past president of the Sierra Club, founded FAIR in 1978. This organization claims that undocumented immigration is diminishing jobs and other critical resources for native-born U.S. citizens. One of the main forces behind the 1994 passage of California's Proposition 187, FAIR targeted undocumented immigrants in order to deny them public services.

The organization's leadership is a Who's Who of American eugenicists and respectable racists. The late Dr. Garrett Hardin was a founding board member. Hardin was a biologist who enjoyed fame for his 1968 essay "The Tragedy of the Commons," in which he argued against the idea of shared public resources and in favor of a Darwinian-Hobbesian struggle, a ringing endorsement of public policy organized around the idea of survival of the fittest. Hardin used a "lifeboat" metaphor to describe the relationship among the earth, its ecosystems, and human populations. On a lifeboat, there simply are "not enough resources for everyone to share," so some people will have to be thrown off.[15] Hardin was a longtime supporter of eugenics and publicly opposed sending food relief to poor nations on the grounds that their populations were threatening the planet's "carrying capacity."[16] Not surprisingly, he proposed population control via abortion, sterilization, and family size limitation, all of which have strong racial implications.[17] Hardin was once quoted in a magazine interview arguing that "[I]t would be better to encourage the breeding of more intelligent people rather than the less intelligent."[18] He was a Eugenics Society fellow in 1977 and went on to become a founding member of FAIR and Californians for

Population Stabilization (CAPS). Hardin and his wife, both of whom committed suicide in 2003, had their deaths memorialized by Linda Thom of the white nationalist group VDare (the name of this organization refers to Virginia Dare, the first white person born of English immigrants in the Virginia colony). Thom stated, "I have never met such environmentally conscious people."[19]

John Tanton became infamous for a memo, which he wrote to members of another organization he founded, that stated "As whites see their power and control over their lives declining, will they simply go quietly into the night? Or will there be an explosion?"[20] Tanton also owns a publishing house, the Social Contract Press, which has published such books as *Immigration Invasion* and many others by prominent nativists like Garrett Hardin, Roy Beck, Samuel Huntington, Richard Lamm (former Democratic governor of Colorado and former president of Zero Population Growth), and Michelle Malkin. The press's editor, Wayne Lutton, has been affiliated with the Council of Conservative Citizens (the contemporary successor to the White Citizens Councils of the 1950s and 1960s, which fought racial desegregation efforts), and refers to himself as a "right wing green."[21] Tanton also helped found the U.S. English organization that spearheaded many "English only" campaigns attacking bilingual education programs around the nation (and counted former Labor Secretary Linda Chavez and legendary television broadcaster Walter Cronkite among its board members). This group has fought to pass laws that would mandate that English be the exclusive and official language used for communications in all U.S. institutions.[22]

Tanton is also a past president of Zero Population Growth (ZPG), an organization whose mission statement declared "Overpopulation threatens the quality of life for people everywhere."[23] The organization officially changed its name to Population Connection in 2002. Taking a seemingly broader view on immigration, Population Connection states that they are a "national grassroots population organization that educates young people and advocates progressive action to stabilize world population at a level that can be sustained by Earth's resources."[24]

According to the Southern Poverty Law Center (SPLC), organizations like FAIR and Population Connection "skirt the line between right-wing immigrant reform organizations and racist, nativist hate groups."[25] John Tanton also founded U.S. Inc., which serves as an umbrella organization for many of these groups. With Tanton as its chairperson, U.S. Inc. "undertake[s] a variety of projects related to the conservation of natural resources, population, immigration, and language policy."[26] Although primarily identified for his anti-immigration politics, Tanton has always been on record that he is first and foremost an environmentalist, which only underscores our contention that there has frequently been a convergence between nativism and environmentalism in this country.

The alleged scientific basis for most arguments that immigrants threaten "our" carrying capacity is derived from a mathematical formula (I=PAT), which Paul Ehrlich and John Holdren developed in the 1970s, and which Garrett Hardin and many respected academics have used for years. The formula states that the environmental *I*mpact of human groups equals *P*opulation size, multiplied by *A*ffluence (or the average volume of goods consumed per person), multiplied by *T*echnology (or the pollution that results when goods are consumed). There are many problems with this model, such as its blind spot concerning the political and financial institutions that shape consumption patterns and that wealthy populations consume far more than do the poor. But that has not stopped some of the most distinguished scientists from using this model to declare doom and gloom at the hint of another immigrant crossing or, indeed, even giving birth.

Organizations like NumbersUSA and the Center for Immigration Studies have effectively taken the basic IPAT equation and translated it into language that is more accessible and digestible for the average person. Consider the text from an immigration control organization's pamphlet: "Sick of the traffic sprawl and congestion? You can do something about it." The pamphlet features a photo of a white man in his car in the middle of a traffic jam, wearing a suit and throwing up his hands in exasperation. The pamphlet goes on to state "The evidence is clear: sprawl cannot be tamed unless Congress stops forcing U.S. population growth!" This message is accompanied by a statement that reads "sprawl worsens dramatically the more a city grows in population."[27]

NumbersUSA is a Washington, DC–based organization that produces literature, statistics, and other data about the alleged impacts of current immigration numbers on "the American people." Roy Beck, the director of NumbersUSA, is a tireless immigration control campaigner and has given countless presentations of his film *By the Numbers* to communities and government bodies around the country. He often serves as the major consultant to municipalities crafting nativist legislation. Beck was credited as one of the primary influences behind the nativist environmental resolution passed in Aspen, Colorado in 1999.[28] Like some of the more respectable Beltway nativist lobbyists, Beck goes to great pains to convince people that he is not a racist and harbors no anti-immigrant sentiments.[29] Despite its solid budget and soaring membership, NumbersUSA practices the frugality that it preaches: the organization shares an office with the groups ProEnglish and Evangelicals for Immigration Reform.[30] Further evidence of the integration between nativism and environmentalism is that NumbersUSA receives most of its $3 million budget from sources that strongly identify with environmental conservation.[31]

The Center for Immigration Studies (CIS) produces reports, congressional testimonies, and op-eds that build on the same message. Steven Camarota is the CIS director of research and offered the following statement to a congressional committee:

> [I]mmigration will add 76 million people to the population over the next fifty years [which] means that we will have to build something like 30 million more housing units than would otherwise have been necessary. . . . This must have some implications for worsening the problems of sprawl, congestion, and *loss of open spaces*, even if one makes optimistic assumptions about successful urban planning and "smart growth." A nation simply cannot add nearly 80 million people to the population and not have to develop *a great deal of undeveloped land.*[32]

The CIS proudly bills itself as "the nation's only think tank devoted exclusively to research and policy analysis of the economic, social, demographic, fiscal, and other impacts of immigration on the United States."[33] In a recent *Los Angeles Times* editorial, the CIS executive director Mark Krikorian says it all: "Fewer Migrants Mean More Benefits."[34]

NumbersUSA, CIS, and many other nativist groups contributed to the demise of the comprehensive immigration bill that George W. Bush proposed in June 2007. This bill was a difficult compromise, which created major hurdles to citizenship for undocumented persons and gave considerable influence to politicians anxious about threats of terrorists crossing the border. The bill would have offered legal status and a path to citizenship to millions of undocumented immigrants and launched a new temporary worker program while building up militarized security measures on the Mexico–U.S. border. Conservative pundits and talk show hosts on AM radio stirred up millions of people, repeatedly referring to the bill as an "amnesty" proposal, and worked with nativist groups to bring the bill to a halt through a massive phone and Internet campaign. This successful effort garnered many new supporters for nativist-environmental organizations. Rosemary Jenks, a NumbersUSA staffer, reported that the group added seven thousand new members in a single day during the height of the debate.[35]

Frank Sharry, the executive director of the National Immigration Forum (a pro-immigrant advocacy group) states "Roy Beck takes people who are upset about illegal immigration for different reasons, including hostility to Latino immigrants, and disciplines them so their message is based on policy rather than race-based arguments or xenophobia."[36] This is a pattern we have noticed repeatedly among many contemporary nativist groups, especially those that are insiders in lobbying circles in the nation's capital. They go to considerable lengths to declare that they are not racist and are only interested in "preserving a way of life." Excluding others is simply a crude way of ensuring that goal. Other activists echo this "new racism" of kind words and harsh deeds. A former meatpackers' union steward who opposed the 2007 immigration bill told a reporter "We are not racists, nor are we bigots. . . . We are not interested in doing anything other than preserving a way of life."[37] That same year, a suburban, white, Michigan woman told a newspaper reporter, "These people came in the wrong way, so they don't belong here, period. . . . This hit home with me because I knew it was taking away from our people. . . . What happened to taking care of our own people first?"[38] This language gives cause for concern because it is exactly what many white southerners (and whites everywhere) said when they opposed racial equality in the 1950s, 1960s, and 1970s. To underscore this point, David Duke, the former Ku Klux Klan leader, has been particularly active around the contemporary immigration debate.[39]

Barbara Coe and Glenn Spencer are nativist organizers who enjoy a national following. They are often credited with authoring California's Proposition 187 and are openly racist, unlike some Beltway activists. Spencer once commented that "the Mexican culture is based on deceit," and he has never denied making this statement when confronted by pro-immigrant activists or the media. Coe has described immigrants as "the people who take our jobs, trash our environment, rob, rape, and murder us and then demand we reward them for sharing their drugs and disease with us."[40]

Gender Politics

One cannot understand nativist-environmentalist politics without grasping how deeply certain ideas concerning gender permeate the movement, from the university and the cities to the rural communities and from Aspen to the U.S. Congress. Immigrant women are blamed for producing children who then become the public burden, the cultural contaminant, and the driving force of ecological decline.

The environmentalist slogan "Love Your Mother—Don't Become One" deftly places accountability for ecological harm on women's reproduction. This kind of ideological bent might be expected from right-wing nativist groups, but some EarthFirst! activists and other radical environmentalists have given voice to this framing of the problem for years. At the 2009 EarthFirst! Round River Rendezvous, a young Chicana told us that an activist friend of hers decided not to attend the event out of fear that she would be chastised for being a mother and therefore responsible for adding an additional ecological burden (i.e., a baby) to the planet with finite resources. It becomes evident then, that white racism and patriarchy work together to reinforce nativist-environmentalism. Sara Diamond, a critic of right-wing movements, notes that "Two staples of anti-immigrant literature are the obligatory photos of Mexican 'illegal aliens' running perilously from INS agents across traffic on San Diego freeways, and the requisite folklore about 'legions' of pregnant Mexican women arriving in Texas just in time to suck up free childbirth services and 'instant citizenship' for their newborns."[41]

This linkage among gender, immigration, and population is central in the ideology that blames immigrant women's fertility for the problems of global ecological degradation, for which corporations, militaries, and governments are arguably largely responsible, according to many progressive scholars.[42] The feminist scholar Betsy Hartmann calls this the "degradation narrative" or the idea that poor women around the globe produce too many children, which drives up population numbers, causing environmental harm and poverty. Under this model—which Hartmann rejects—the poor are to blame for their own poverty and for the environmental crisis that affects the rest of us, including the rich.[43]

An example of the degradation narrative was a full-page advertisement in the *New York Times,* paid for by the Population Institute. It reads: "Stop: Denying poor women protection from unintended pregnancies. Grinding Poverty, Hunger, Resource Depletion, Environmental Degradation. Civil Unrest."[44] The photograph accompanying this message is of a group of women and children, presumably from South or Southeast Asia. The advertisement decries the Bush administration's freezing of $34 million that Congress had approved for the UN Population Fund that would go to family planning in the global South. The advertisement claims that U.S. funding for this work is now $100 million less than what it was in the 1990s because of the right-wing anti-abortion agenda of the Bush regime. While that critique of the pro-life lobby is warranted, this advertisement is sponsored by an organization that encourages population control and could all too easily reinforce the agenda of eugenicists and population control advocates who care less about people and more about having fewer of them on their planet. Considering how powerfully destructive economic globalization is of ecosystems and how it consistently produces increasing economic inequalities, the degradation narrative reflects a selective viewpoint on environmental politics.

Nativist-Environmentalism and the American Way of Life

The desire to "preserve our way of life" and to protect "American" culture, language, borders, and jobs through restrictive immigration policies is also a desire to preserve environmental privilege; such policies mark certain spaces as the birthright for some groups and off-limits to others. At the forefront of promoting the immigration-environment nexus, FAIR's website argues:

> Protecting the environment requires opposing immigration-driven population growth. Reigning in American's rapid population growth

is necessary for the sake of the environment and for the preservation of the quality of life for future generations. As a prime factor
in the demand for new housing, construction, urban sprawl, and the
consumption of natural resources, immigration must be significantly
reduced.[45]

Within this quote is a convenient amnesia that allows European Americans to ignore the fact that they were once immigrants to this land. A
major difference between today's immigrants and the British migration of
the seventeenth century is that the latter were part of a violent coloniza-
tion and conquest of the land and its peoples. However, FAIR is not about
to let history get in the way; they are more worried about their future. A
similar pamphlet from NumbersUSA reads, "The environmental choice is
yours: a sustainable future with a stabilizing U.S. population or never-end-
ing U.S. population growth."[46]

To the contrary, much of urban sprawl occurs because of "white flight"
from urban centers to the edges of metropolitan areas, combined with the
work of developers who build bedroom communities there, pushing these
boundaries into previously rural and ecologically sensitive spaces.[47] This is
nothing new. For instance, General Motors, Firestone, Mack Truck, Phillips
Petroleum, and Standard Oil bought up and dismantled the electric trol-
ley systems in Los Angeles and one hundred other cities during the 1930s
and 1940s in order to create a consumer demand for the automobile, tires,
and gasoline.[48] This action contributed immensely to the massive sprawl
we see across the United States today. In other words, white residents, developers, the government, and corporations have contributed massively to
environmental degradation in this country. And they did that with little
help from immigrants from south of the border.

Border-crossing itself has become a controversial issue for ecologists
who worry that migrants have a negative impact on natural habitats on
the border. People have raised concerns that undocumented persons
harm fragile and endangered plants during their journey from Mexico
to the United States. Additionally, there are claims that migrants sometimes damage the nests of endangered birds and even eat their eggs.[49] This
may all be true, but it misses the larger point that a focus on immigration
ignores a host of other major causes of ecological decline in the United
States and around the world.

Some nativist-environmentalists put forth a critique of American consumerism as a cause of environmental degradation. They argue that instead of reducing our own consumption here at home, we should simply keep immigrants out so that there will ultimately be fewer Americans voraciously consuming the planet's resources. The Carrying Capacity Network offers a typical example of this tortured logic:

[W]e need to recognize the simple fact that the last thing this world needs is more Americans. The world just cannot afford what Americans do to the earth, air, and water. And it does not matter whether these Americans are Americans by birth or by border crossing. It does not matter what color their skin is. It does not matter what language they speak or which God they worship. What matters is that they will live like Americans. We need to accept the fact that the environmental community's admirable efforts to reduce our consumption and pollution have largely failed.[50]

According to this quote, environmentalism is dead, and we should surrender to nativist policies in order to "preserve *our* way of life," as problematic as it is. Certainly, Americans *do* consume more resources than most everybody else: "The United States is home to 5 percent of the world's population yet consumes 30 percent of the world's resources."[51] Given this reality, it seems the targets of environmental initiatives should be the wealthiest communities. There is far greater benefit for everyone if the privileged few consume less. The position of the Carrying Capacity Network and other similar organizations works against environmentalism in their capitulation of gross unequal consumption as inevitable. We (the authors of this book), on the other hand, have a more optimistic view of the environmental movement and believe that social justice is still possible through the equitable care of global ecosystems. However, it seems the lure of nativist policies that favor anti-immigration legislation and population control is too powerful for many environmental organizations to ignore. It is far easier to target segments of vulnerable populations than to focus on the extremely privileged few.

Nativism was recently at the center of an intense debate within the nation's largest environmental organization—the Sierra Club. That struggle provides a useful lesson with regard not only to the ways these sensitive issues are approached by politically liberal organizations but also what the implications might be for environmental justice politics.

The Sierra Club Case

The Sierra Club recently published a pamphlet "Family Planning and Women's Empowerment: Saving Lives and the Environment." The publication contains photos of African and Latin American women and their children. The text declares "nearly 600,000 women die in pregnancy or childbirth each year" and continues with the following statement:

> Many of these deaths could have been averted if women had access to reproductive health care. A growing population places pressure on the environment by depleting vital resources. Empowerment of women and universal access to family planning and reproductive health services are integral to curbing global population growth and improving the quality of life for families throughout the world. In 1994, 180 nations agreed to this approach, but since 1995 the United States has cut funding for family-planning programs and projects that empower women. Urge your senators to save women's lives and protect the environment by increasing funds for these projects.

Under pressure from pro-life organizations that felt that women the world over should be shielded from the "sin" of abortion, President George W. Bush further cut funding for international family planning. Most women's rights advocates condemned this action.[52] The Sierra Club's response, however, was a standard "degradation narrative" of white environmentalists from the United States seeking to "rescue" poor women in the global South—indeed saving these women from themselves. Bush's policy was no more offensive than the thinly veiled conclusion in the Sierra Club pamphlet that one of the major environmental problems is the fertility and reproductive behavior of women of color around the globe. The environmental movement will fall short of its goals if it continues to blame women of color for the world's ecological crises, and the Sierra Club pushes that unfortunate message just as much as any other group.

In the 1990s, the Sierra Club was the target of two attempted takeovers by nativists who wished to convert the nation's largest environmental organization into a much more open advocate for immigration control. With a membership of more than 700,000 people and a budget hovering around

$100,000,000, the organization is an attractive mark. The symbolic value of taking over the Sierra Club would be irresistible to "outside" forces seeking to influence the U.S. environmental movement.

Although the fireworks did not start until the mid-1990s, the Sierra Club takeover began in the 1980s. In 1986, in a series of strategy memos at the FAIR organization, mentions were made of a possible move against the club. In one such memo, John Tanton wrote, "The Sierra Club may not want to touch the immigration issue, but the immigration issue is going to touch the Sierra Club!" He also rhetorically asked in the memo, "Will the present majority peaceably hand over its political power to a group that is simply more fertile?"[53]

Then in 1996 and 1998, the Sierra Club weathered attempts to put ballots to the membership that would embrace an explicitly anti-immigration stance. The 1998 measure received endorsements from Gaylord Nelson, the retired Wisconsin senator and Earth Day co-founder, the World Watch Institute co-founder Lester Brown, and the Harvard professor and sociobiologist E. O. Wilson. The measures were defeated, but they cost the club in public relations and in the high-profile defection of key supporters. Shortly afterward, the legendary environmentalist David Brower resigned from the board "with no regret and a bit of desperation."[54] Brower belongs in the pantheon of ecologists in U.S. history, so his resignation was no small matter. He joined the organization back in 1933, served as its first executive director during the 1950s and 1960s, and brought the Sierra Club into the modern era. One of his stated reasons for leaving was the club's leadership's stance on immigration. He said, "the planet is being trashed, but the board has no real sense of urgency. . . . Overpopulation is perhaps the biggest problem facing us, and immigration is part of the problem. It has to be addressed."[55]

The battles of the 1990s raged on into the 2000s. On April 21, 2004, the Sierra Club's membership voted in new board members. This event is not normally newsworthy to the public, but prior to the vote, the SPLC publicly announced word of an impending "hostile takeover" by openly nativist candidates. The candidates with anti-immigration agendas included Richard Lamm, Frank Morris, and David Pimentel, who, if voted into office, would give the existing nativist board members—Ben Zuckerman, Paul Watson, and Doug LaFollette—a majority vote on the club's board of directors. Paul Watson declared, "I'm not here to represent people, people are well represented. . . . I don't allow any human politics to influence my decisions . . . I'm here to represent non-human species and ecosystems."[56] According to Watson, immigration brings too many people into the nation, threatening the species and environments he wishes to protect. Another insider—a club member, not a director—was Brenda Walker, who urged supporters of the VDare white nationalist group to join the club and vote for the new candidates. Walker had raised eyebrows in an earlier essay she had written on VDare's website in reference to Southeast Asian Hmong immigrants coming to the United States: "So will thousands of drug-addicted polygamists be welcomed into America in another escalation of multiculturalism against American values?"[57] The SPLC charged that this takeover was being orchestrated by FAIR, CIS, U.S. English, NumbersUSA, and CAPS, which allegedly sought to infiltrate the Sierra Club with a new board that would shift the mission to focus on anti-immigration concerns. The SPLC also pointed out that the founder and major supporter of those groups was John H. Tanton, a known nativist. The news created such an alarm that progressive members of the Sierra Club formed a group called Groundswell Sierra, which launched a publicity campaign and website aimed at defeating the "outsider" candidates.

Countering the Groundswell Sierra group, another new group formed within the Sierra Club, calling themselves Sierrans for U.S. Population Stabilization (SUSPS). In the run-up to the board election, SUSPS sent out a mass mailing to the entire Sierra Club membership and launched a website and publicity campaign supporting the anti-immigration initiative. In that mailing, they advocated a return to pre-1965 immigration levels established by the overtly racist Immigration Act of 1924, which imposed strict ethnic quotas to ensure that most immigrants allowed into the United States were from northern and western Europe.[58] The SUSPS website declared:

> As a result of our country's immigration policies coupled with birth rates, the U.S. has the highest population growth of all developed countries. SUSPS demands that the Sierra Club stop placing political sensitivities ahead of the environment and begin addressing migration levels and birthrates in the U.S. . . . While we support the Sierra Club's current global policies designed to stabilize world population, we urge the Sierra Club to return to the roots of the environmental movement that encompass U.S. overpopulation—to also preserve and protect our own environment for the benefit of future generations.[59]

This last statement is a quintessential example of the quest for white environmental privilege. Again, the responsibility for the global environmental crisis is placed squarely at the doorstep of the people of the global South while the United States is cast as the victim.

The fight got even uglier when it was alleged that David Gelbaum, a liberal wealthy donor, was heavily influencing the Sierra Club's policy on immigration. Gelbaum allegedly made it clear that he would not support the club financially if they adopted an anti-immigration policy. Gelbaum is a reclusive, retired mathematician and Wall Street whiz, and was uncommonly generous in his giving to environmental and social causes, including donations in support of the efforts to defeat Proposition 187. Gelbaum's wife is Mexican American and his grandfather was a Ukrainian Jewish immigrant, perhaps shaping his views of this issue. He stood firm in his opposition to nativist policies, and in a *Los Angeles Times* interview he stated for the record, "I did tell Carl Pope [the Sierra Club's executive director] in 1994 or 1995 that if they ever came out anti-immigration, they would never get a dollar from me."[60] After the club enacted its neutrality policy on immigration in 1996 and successfully opposed a referendum to overturn that policy in 1998, Gelbaum seemed to reward them. In 2000 and 2001 he gave the Sierra Club more than a whopping $100 million in donations. Sierrans for U.S. Population Stabilization justifiably asked whether it was appropriate for the club's leadership to adopt certain policies based on a single "super rich" donor while much of its membership felt differently.[61]

Ultimately the 2004 "takeover" was stopped by a record voter turnout, but this stands out as yet another major wound the club will have to nurse. Moreover, it is unlikely that this issue will die anytime soon among the club's leadership or membership.

A Reality Check

The history of the Sierra Club's positions on immigration reveals that the situation is in fact much more complicated and less flattering than the progressives of the Groundswell Sierra group would have us believe. The Groundswell Sierra members like Carl Pope and Adam Werbach paint a portrait of the Sierra Club, which gives the sense that its core membership and history are basically free of nativism and that they were the unfortunate victims of an attempted hostile takeover by outsiders. Our interpretation is otherwise. First, many of these takeover participants have currently or previously held leadership positions (or simply been members) in the club, so it is difficult and disingenuous to argue that these individuals are "outsiders." Second, it would be incorrect and impossible to try to distinguish between the nativist or "anti-immigrant" faction and the rest of the club: the Sierra Club has a long-standing love for people-less nature, including its long-term relationship with photographer Ansel Adams. Adams sometimes deliberately removed people from the landscape scenes he photographed, and even the club's founder, the Scottish immigrant John Muir, helped to create the national parks system, which required Indian removal. Therefore, the club's roots were perhaps "pro-immigrant" only in the sense that the founder celebrated and facilitated the migration of *white* people onto Native land.

In addition, the Sierra Club's population fixation has been present since at least the 1960s, and it remains today, with some modifications. Consider the following text from a resolution, adopted by its board of directors on March 13, 1965, just months before President Johnson signed the Immigration and Nationality Act into law, abolishing the racist quotas codified by the National Origins Act of 1924:

> The "population explosion" has severely disturbed the ecological relationships between human beings and the environment. It has caused an increasing scarcity of wilderness and wildlife and has impaired the beauty of whole regions, as well as *reducing the standards and the quality of living.* In recognition of the growing magnitude of this conservation issue, the Sierra Club supports a greatly increased program of education on the need for population control.[62]

A year later, another resolution stated "The Sierra Club endorses the objectives of legislation to establish federal machinery to deal with the problems of rapid human population growth."[63] Three years after that, in May 1969, the board of directors passed the following resolution:

> The Sierra Club urges the people of the United States to abandon population growth as a pattern and goal; to commit themselves to limit the

total population of the United States in order to achieve balance between population and resources; and to achieve a stable population no later than the year 1990.[64]

The following year, in June of 1970, another resolution stated, "The Sierra Club endorses [the following] resolution from the organization Zero Population Growth concerning measures to inhibit population growth. In essence, the resolution parallels an earlier Sierra Club statement of policy"[65] regarding a call for the United States to pass state and federal laws that would encourage limiting family size and birth control to reduce population size through humane and voluntary measures. We should not forget that ZPG was an organization that John Tanton led for many years (as did Richard Lamm, one of the so-called "outsiders" seeking to take over the club's Board in 2004), so the connections to other nativist groups run much deeper than Groundswell Sierra Club leaders would like to admit.

At that time, the Sierra Club was largely divided between members who urged the organization to "actively involve itself in the conservation problems . . . of the urban poor and the ethnic minorities" (as the text of a 1971 referendum measure stated), and members who thought that social justice work would displace the more important goal of natural preservation.[66]

Many other resolutions were debated and passed in the ensuing years and, when the issue became more heavily politicized in 1996, the board adopted a resolution that it "[would] take no position on immigration levels or on policies governing immigration into the United States." The resolution astutely added, "The Club remains committed to environmental rights and protections for all within our borders, without discrimination based on immigration status."[67] That resolution was adopted, after an amendment, by the membership in 1998 and, after amendment, by the board again in 2003.

After the 1998 battle, Carl Pope waxed eloquently while breathing a guarded sigh of relief at the vote's outcome:

This Spring the members of the Sierra Club made a historic decision. On this year's Club ballot, they were asked whether we should address the problem of overpopulation by limiting immigration or by dealing with its root causes. Six out of ten voted to defeat the immigration initiative. . . . Taking responsibility for their own resource use, they refused to blame newcomers to our country for our own overconsumption. . . .

Immigration restrictions don't solve environmental problems, they merely shift them elsewhere. Proponents of the immigration-restriction initiative argued that we need to protect our own backyard, or 'lifeboat,' in environmental philosopher Garrett Hardin's metaphor.. . . . Instead of a lifeboat, the Sierra Club chose Buckminster Fuller's vision of "Spaceship Earth" . . . Rather than slamming the door, members directed the Club to devote its energies to global stewardship, to mitigating the conditions that drive people from their homes.[68]

Given the 2004 battle over the same issue, Pope seems to have spoken too soon. Ultimately, this "takeover" attempt was, in large part, of the club's own making, given its history of supporting population control. We should not forget that perhaps the most influential book on population hysteria in U.S. history was Paul Erhlich's *Population Bomb*, published by the Sierra Club. The "victory" in which those coup attempts were stifled reveals the entrenchment of nativism in the U.S. environmental movement.

We cannot overstate the importance of the Sierra Club case. The club is not only the nation's largest and most influential environmental organization, it is also a group in which nativism and population control politics have run deep since its founding. This organization sets the tone and standard for the U.S. environmental movement and remains a space in which nativist-environmentalism exerts influence on the nation's civic culture.

Nativist Environmentalism

Colorado is a place where immigration and environmental politics have come to a head many times. From Aspen to Boulder and Denver, from the Eastern Slope to the Western Slope, the Rocky Mountain state has struggled with how to maintain its labor force for ecological wealth extraction and tourism, while protecting the ecosystems threatened by those industries.

This struggle is evident in public discourse among Roaring Fork Valley residents. One long-running argument evident in these debates is that the United States is the most generous nation in the world with regard to its immigration policy. Other debates focused on the risks that immigration posed to quality of life, public health, safety, and security.

The theme of America's beneficence and that anyone here should "love it or leave it" was prevalent in letters to valley newspaper editors. Mike McGarry, a vocal Roaring Fork Valley resident and leading nativist environmental activist, expressed these ideas in the following colorful language:

> Editor: I just read your October 16 article ("English-only opponents gather") where one Mr. Juan Antonio Garcia, who recently "came from Mexico," was quoted as saying the motives of the supporters of Amendment 31 [the English-only ballot proposition] are "probably racist." Mr. Editor, can you imagine someone moving to Colorado from a junk country and retrograde culture and within two years of his being in the state he is badmouthing the people of Colorado while he leaches off their generosities? Señor Garcia, haul your arrogant, slanderous behind back to Crapville until you develop some gratitude and humility and until you are reminded just how much you already owe the citizens of the most tolerant society you will ever experience. And Mr. Editor, even more insulting, although expected, is that apparently not one of the losers at that Stepstone Center-sponsored, typically one-sided "forum" had enough self-respect to give Mr. Garcia—as I would have had I been there—the wedgie of that punk's piss-poor life.[69]

We also find scores of letters to editors invoking the "quality of life" argument that we see articulated on a national scale. One resident wrote: "The regulatory power of our government was granted by us, the citizens . . . and we need to ensure that our standard of living does not decline further. The INS is a beneficial agency to our standard of living."[70]

Health risks and the fear of epidemics have been a traditional concern among nativists and governments regarding foreigners entering the country. At Ellis and Angel Islands during earlier waves of migration, physicians were on hand to check each person coming off the boats for communicable diseases that could spread among the majority population. In recent years, U.S. consulate offices in other nations have handled this kind of health screening. These fears of contamination have periodically reached hysteria and have contributed to the perception that poor hygiene and disease are inherent in many immigrant populations.[71] One Roaring Fork Valley resident wrote a letter to the newspaper editor:

I have issues with tuberculosis. I was exposed to that by an illegal alien who coughed near me and it required medical treatment. Remind me that eating out isn't worth the souvenir of hepatitis A either. . . . Hepatitis A is also spread by hand and mouth contact. And something all illegal aliens are not screened for.[72]

Another letter-writer publicly supported the Aspen City Council's decision to pass the "population stabilization" resolution in December 1999. The writer referred to ecological threats from immigration as well: "I applaud Aspen City Council's passage of the resolution on immigration control . . . it's just not that much fun to live here anymore and our beauty is fast evaporating. My thanks to the Aspen City Council for speaking up."[73]

The following letter was brutally honest in its contempt but also reveals how some valley residents view immigrants as a threat to the peace, security, and lives of Anglos in the community:

[B]because we can't make our own beds, do our own landscaping, wash our own dishes, and cook our own food, we'll trash a nice little town like Carbondale. We'll stuff it to the brim with illegals. We'll stand by as they jam fifteen or twenty men in a three-bedroom apartment. We'll tolerate gang graffiti, we'll listen to ultra-loud stereos, we'll wink as they deal drugs to our kids. We'll clean up bloodstained highways after they drive drunk with no driver's license, insurance, or registration. We'll pay the hospital bill for a *coyote* who crashes a van crowded with a dozen or more immigrants."[74]

Complicating this debate is the fact that some Latinos also harbor strong anti-immigrant feelings for a range of reasons. Although these sentiments may reflect patriotism, a desire to be law abiding and to assimilate (as well as generational, class, and other divides between Latinos and Latin Americans), it ultimately also contributes to the maintenance of white supremacy.[75] Consider the following letter from a Latina:

If I read another illegal-alien sob story I am going to vomit! These illegal creeps give all Hispanics a bad name because Americans tend to believe that all Hispanics are cheering for this criminal invasion. . . . I may be Latina, but if it were up to me, every one of these illegal creeps would be the hell out of here. They are destroying the United States![76]

These strong nativist sentiments were supported and reinforced by individuals and groups involved in political organizing for immigration control across in the state of Colorado in the 1990s and 2000s. We also want to emphasize that the letters to editors we have quoted from were representative of the general nativist rhetoric and messages found regularly in the valley's newspapers during moments of heightened tension around immigration politics.

Organizing in Aspen

In June 1999 the Valley Alliance for Social and Environmental Responsibility formed, spearheaded by two Aspenites who have been vocal nativist environmentalists for many years.[77] Terry Paulson moved to Aspen in 1982 and has served on the city council since 1993. He is an outdoor enthusiast who loves downhill skiing, has taught cross-country skiing for many years, and is a licensed paraglider pilot. Paulson was instrumental in getting the Population Stabilization resolution passed in the Aspen City Council and at the Pitkin County Commission. Mike McGarry is the other driving force behind the Alliance. He has devoted considerable time and effort in fighting immigration as a member of a number of organizations including the Colorado Alliance for Immigration Reform (CAIR) and the Minuteman Project. He is a unique and boisterous man who lives in Aspen and works as a maintenance technician and custodian. In 1995 he filed a federal lawsuit charging that the Pitkin County government exercised bias in favor of people of color whom it hired for three different maintenance jobs instead of him. Challenging the county's affirmative action policy, McGarry (who is white) alleged that he had been the victim of "reverse discrimination," and he sued for what he claimed were lost wages. The case eventually made it to federal court and he won a $50,000 settlement. He rightly took credit for being the impetus behind the county's elimination of its Equal Employment Opportunities policy. In 2001 McGarry joined the race for a city council seat (he lost), and as he filed his petition he stated, "If elected I will make it part of my every decision to consider the greater geographic and demographic picture."[78] Together, McGarry and Paulson have made immigration the number one villain of environmental sustainability in the valley—and they have support from high places.

The same week that the Valley Alliance was launched, the former Colorado governor Dick Lamm spoke at a Men's Club luncheon in Aspen. He warned his audience about the social and environmental degradation such as urban sprawl that he claimed results from continuing immigration into the United States. Lamm has a second home in Aspen and is adamant about wanting to protect Colorado's ecosystems from population growth and other threats.[79] Lamm considers Paulson and McGarry his colleagues and offered public support for their efforts. In fact, Mike McGarry joined Lamm during the luncheon presentation to offer his own thoughts on the matter. A Democrat, Lamm has been a longtime immigration critic. He became a populist environmental hero in Colorado in the 1970s when he was instrumental in preventing the Olympic Games from coming to the state on the grounds that it would produce an enormous negative ecological footprint. He has taken a stand on environmental issues ever since. He also stands firmly in the nativist camp. He is a board member of FAIR, and has written extensively on immigration and population growth as ecological threats. He was also one of the nativist candidates running for election to the Sierra Club board of directors in 2004.

During the 1960s Lamm and his wife spent time in India. That experience left a profound impact on his thinking about population growth. He recalled, "We came back from there really believing very strongly that the world ought to stabilize its population and so should the United States."[80] Later that same year (October 1999), Lamm returned to Aspen to deliver a keynote address at a Valley Alliance conference: "The Myth of Sustainable Growth: Population, Immigration, Environmental Degradation." Lamm proposed that the United States decrease legal immigration levels by 80 percent. Referring to this event, Mike McGarry declared, "Population is the No.1 factor in the encroachment of environmental degradation—immigration is the No. 1 factor contributing to population growth."[81] All of this work was done prior to the December 1999 population stabilization resolution by the Aspen City Council, as part of an organizing campaign that eventually built up to that outcome. Lamm continued to work with the Alliance, using troubling metaphors to describe immigration's effect on the country: "Cheap foreign workers are like heroin: they're addictions, you get hooked on them."[82]

The Valley Alliance also counts the outspoken nativist Republican congressman Tom Tancredo among its supporters.[83] Tancredo is virulently anti-immigrant, Islamophobic, and pro-war.[84] He has repeatedly placed himself on the fringe of the Republican Party and has earned the respect of many racists across the country for his uncompromising stances on these issues. The Alliance is one of many well-networked nativist groups in the state of Colorado and in the Rocky Mountain Region and has friends and supporters in Congress, FAIR, NumbersUSA, and other nationally active nativist groups.[85]

At the Myth of Sustainable Growth Conference held in Aspen in 1999, many nativist leaders spoke to a packed audience. Jonette Christian, the founder of Mainers for Immigration Reform, gave a speech at the conference that was very well received and got straight to the point from an unapologetic nativist perspective. Christian's presentation made two key nativist claims. The first is that the culture of the U.S. Anglo majority is superior to that of any other nation:

> Culture is fundamental in understanding poverty and high growth. Authoritarian cultures, not surprisingly, produce authoritarian governments, and these nations are especially vulnerable to economic domination from outsiders. The ruling elites of Latin America have had little interest in protecting the welfare of their own people. But the problem lies within the culture. In Latin societies there is no code of conduct that calls for social responsibility or citizen activism outside of the family. It is not an accident that America has given the world the game plan for modern democracy and the example of a culture which continually works to improve itself.[86]

This statement is a no-frills version of the racist American exceptionalism that runs through much of the rhetoric undergirding U.S. nativism. Dick Lamm seconded Christian's statement when he declared, "Our best course is to model sustainability for the rest of the world."[87] Considering how much pollution and hazardous waste the U.S. government, military, and businesses produce, and the enormous volume of ecological wealth these institutions consume, this idea is internally contradictory.

The second major claim Jonette Christian made is that immigrants are, in conjunction with rich corporations, making life hard for working people in the United States:

[W]e are seeing increasing disparity between rich and poor, and massive immigration is largely responsible. . . . In other words, our current immigration policy is making it increasingly difficult for our most vulnerable populations—blacks, minorities, recent immigrants, and the poor to earn a living wage. . . . Do we have an obligation to protect the living standard of unskilled workers in this country, or are we going to require them to compete with third world wages?[88]

In the past decade, the Valley Alliance has continued to gather support for its cause; they found it in the form of nationally recognized and respected authors, activists, and foundations. Lester Brown, chair of the board of the World Watch Institute, attended a conference on sustainability in Aspen in 2004, and he has frequently appeared at many events sponsored by nativist and population-control organizations. Population has always been one of the key indicators of the global ecological crisis according to World Watch over the years. Brown spoke directly to many of the main concerns the Alliance shares with regard to the impact of population growth on ecosystems.[89] We would not describe Brown as a nativist environmentalist but his emphasis on Malthusian theories of population growth lends credibility to that perspective.[90]

Members of our research team had a chance to sit down with the Alliance founders Terry Paulson and Mike McGarry. They spoke candidly and forthrightly. McGarry described the region's social problems in this way:

[O]ur problem is that we got this monster looming just outside the city limits. A population monster. Because this thing's going to bury us all. . . . You know if you just conceptualize no growth in the sense that you don't need growth if you're a person, you have an infrastructure called your anatomy, your physiology. You're not built to be 6'5", 500 pounds, you know? Herman Daly, our ecological economist, he would make the distinction between qualitative and quantitative development. You could continue to improve your body. But you don't necessarily have to grow the body.[91]

McGarry's analogy, like those used by many nativist environmentalists, draws on biological or "natural" models for much of its logic. On the sensitive subject of immigration, it becomes clear that, for many nativists, there are desirable and undesirable immigrants. We asked about the numerous Australians and Europeans we have noticed in Aspen, working on the ski slopes and in upscale restaurants. Referring to the town's iconic resort, Paulson stated, "The Ski company has been lobbying pretty heavily in the Southern Hemisphere to get people to come up here when their off-season is, so we get people from Queenstown, New Zealand, Australia, Argentina, Chile." McGarry added, "It's their summer experience, it's great, it's great for everybody." These immigrants are viewed ethnically as white. Unfortunately, for McGarry and Paulson, these immigrants are in short supply in comparison to people from Mexico and Central America.

McGarry and Paulson located the origins of the current immigration "crisis" in the Roaring Fork Valley in part to earlier European immigrants who liked to call in sick on days when the skiing was good. So, according to Paulson, employers soon switched to recruiting non-European immigrants who had little interest in skiing, and who would also work for less money. Terry Paulson recalled:

> I came here in '82. That time here, I thought I was in Sweden because there were a bunch of Swedes here [laughs]. They were washing dishes, skiing, you know, whatever. I think there was a business concern here about finding workers that were reliable and wouldn't call in sick on powder days. I really think that's what started the whole move to look for a work force that wasn't interested in the sports that we enjoy.

McGarry picked up the story from there:

> [T]the people washing dishes in the restaurants were more native people, people who have lived here, they were part of the Alpine culture too, they were skiers and backpackers and so forth. So we had a schedule that said whoever was there the longest, if they could find someone to replace them, they could go on out and go skiing on good days. So everyone adapted to the culture, so then we had people hired from out of the country because they were cheaper, they were not going to participate in the culture. They will work day and night no matter what. . . . So we get more and more dependent on these guys who will work for low wages. The employers rigged how all these things developed.

Here again we see the populist anti-corporate rhetoric combined with a soft racism of permanent cultural difference between people from European versus non-European nations and ethnic groups. Terry Paulson jumped in to say, "Also in terms of the cultural, I think Europeans in general have a sense of population and where they want their countries to be. Other parts of the world, I don't think have that same concept of over population as Europeans."

These two founders of the Valley Alliance spoke about the strength of ecological ethics and policies in the Aspen area. They both embraced a recent anniversary celebration of the Aspen Wilderness Workshop—a local environmental group—because, as Paulson claimed,

> They're one of the few environmental organizations that I admire that really goes out and does something. . . . They've taken the Aspen ski company on for various issues, making them be responsible. As a result, the ski company has been getting a lot of these green awards for recycling, they even started using a kind of diesel fuel that's more ecological. As a corporation I think that they're ahead of most. You know the sundeck at the top of Aspen Mountain: it's made of all recycled and biodegradable materials. It's made out of plastic, basically. They didn't have to do that, you know, but they decided that this is what they want to do and it's costing them a lot more to do it.

McGarry proudly chimed in, "I have a lot of respect for them, as far as corporations go. I think that if we look at the big picture, Aspen is as environmentally-conscious and as conservation oriented and as aware as any town." Like other towns, Aspen requires positive "mitigations" to offset development that might be ecologically harmful. In other words, projects that are intended to improve local ecosystems when other efforts cause harm. However, in Aspen, these development practices have a distinctive flair. Terry Paulson explained, "For instance if someone wants to put in a heated driveway . . . so you don't have to shovel snow . . . he has to mitigate that somehow, he has to make small changes in his other plans." We queried, "Did you just say a heated driveway?" McGarry stepped in, "They're all over the place up here."

Both men reported disgust with the federal government's response to undocumented immigration from Mexico. When asked about the recent fight over the INS's attempt to locate a detention facility in nearby Glenwood Springs, McGarry retorted:

> They don't come here. They don't do on-sight raids, the INS. That location down there was strictly to deal with the I-70 traffic, you know the vanloads. There's no INS in Aspen. They go on the record all the time and they couldn't be more apologetic, going on profusely about [in a whiny voice] "we're not here to mess with the local businesses, we're only here to stop the trafficking on I-70." It's an addiction. It's turned into just an addiction like heroine. Cheap foreign labor. That's all they see and it's all they invest in. That's the revenue. We need to cold turkey these guys.[92]

Near the end of the interview, two Latinas passed by us on the sidewalk, and Paulson and McGarry stopped talking and glared at them as they walked by.

Backlash against Immigrant Rights Groups

Not only did the Valley Alliance work to build up nativist-environmentalist sentiment against immigrants in the Roaring Fork Valley, they have also set out to target organizations that have provided support services and advocacy for these populations. This effort has had an impact on the public perception of these organizations as undeserving and as an additional indicator of the alleged drain on resources caused by immigration.

Roaring Fork Legal Services (RFLS) opened its offices in Aspen in 2001 with a $3,000 grant from the city of Aspen. Created at the request of the local bar association, RFLS is a nonprofit organization that offers legal advice to immigrants—regardless of citizenship—on civil matters including divorce, landlord-tenant disputes, welfare law, and immigration law. This is a public service given to those who otherwise are unable to afford an attorney. The news of this group's founding created an uproar among local nativists. During one city council meeting, Mike McGarry and a colleague of his—a woman who refused to give her name—lambasted the council for supporting the organization. They demanded that RFLS require proof of citizenship or residency for any Latin American clients they serve. When councilman Tony Hershey pointed out that asking someone from one ethnic group for identification would be racist and probably illegal, McGarry snapped, "Don't even bring up that race crap with me."[93]

When word spread about RFLS, many locals linked that organization to the mission of other groups in the valley that advocate on behalf of immigrants. One particularly virulent letter to the *Aspen Times* called into question these organizations' tax-exempt status:

> [T]heir defenders and heavily financed front organizations—Roaring Fork Legal Services, the Stepstone Center, and Latinos Unidos, race-based organizations with racist, race-based ends—are beneficiaries of tax exempt status as "educational" nonprofits, a status granted them by a U.S. government agency. Go figure. And yes, "criminals." People who invade our borders, against our law, forge and use forged documents to further their dishonest ends while they make up, hide behind, and perpetuate the preposterous (and humorous) charge of racism, a stylistic tactic right out of Joseph McCarthy's playbook, are criminals, and their apologists are subversive, multicultural hypocrites. People, unless you want to be forced to eat the worm at the bottom of the bottle, wake up and smell the tequila.[94]

Again, the language some nativists use is overtly racist, yet they deny that racism. Instead, they claim reverse discrimination by stating that to acknowledge race at all is racist. This is a logical quagmire that has the effect (if not intent) of stopping all conversation and consideration of racial inequality while perpetuating it.

It is true that many organizations have sprung up across the valley to meet some of the needs of the area's growing Latino immigrant population. And yes, they do receive grants for their work. They include the Mountain Family Health Center, which offers subsidized health care to uninsured immigrant families. Catholic Charities of the Western Slope offers resources and advice to undocumented persons seeking citizenship. The activist-oriented Stepstone Center organizes around issues facing Latinos and the broader community to empower people at the grassroots level to confront corporate power, environmental injustices, and nativism. Additionally, the Aspen Valley Community Foundation developed a program for grants around issues facing working Latino families.[95] The fact that none of these groups distinguishes between documented and undocumented persons raised more than a few eyebrows among local immigration critics.

These groups' success at keeping a planned INS facility out of the valley incensed many local Anglos, who let their feelings flow onto the written page. One Aspen resident wrote:

> OK, Latinos, you've scored a coup and stopped a legal action by the U.S. government. The INS can't camp in your back yard. Congrats. Now why don't you address the real reason the community and our government likes you as individuals, but refuses to accept you as a group. Last week there were two stories in the paper—two more Latinos were arrested for peddling cocaine, and a fourteen-year-old girl was taken to the hospital for cocaine overdose. You and your people have proven you have time to protest against our government. How about taking time to form Good Latinos against Drugs, and protest against an activity we all know is evil? You got what you want, how about showing you care for someone other than yourselves?[96]

The association between immigrants, people of color, and drug dealing runs deep in the American psyche, nurtured by news media and film and music industries, which push these images daily.[97]

The evidence presented here leads us to two conclusions. First, the mainstream environmental movement in the United States is most definitely *not* a movement concerned with racial justice. Nor has it shown much willingness to fight for even the broader—and less controversial—goal of social justice. This is not only because it has often traditionally been reserved for middle – and upper-class populations but also because it has always been haunted—indeed fueled—by a strong thread of white supremacy and nativism.

The environmental movement's blind spots are unfortunate and tragic. Environmentalism could become a transformative force that embraces justice for all, considering that the one thing we all share is the global ecosystem. Instead, we have constructed political, economic, and social borders to protect only certain people's ecosystems and human communities: these borders are not only artificial, they are also the source of environmental devastation impacting everyone. The exclusive "protection" of the

backyard of the privileged is absolutely dependent upon the impoverish-
ment of everyone else's common space. The volume of resources—both
human and non-human—required to maintain the heavenly experience of
the very few in Aspen is astounding. If environmentalists are truly committed to ecological sustainability, they must find ways of reducing ecological
damage through an acknowledgement and alleviation of social inequality
rather than fixating on immigrants and population control.

The second conclusion we draw is that nativist movements are also
generally supported by a strong current of ideology, one that is not just
about protecting one's economy, language, culture, or borders but also
about protecting the land, air, and water: in other words, the environment.
These issues are closely held together in nativist ideology. Nativist movements tend to be environmentalist in their outlook, which is why we see
nativism and environmentalism as part of the same, broad continuum of
movements. In fact, environmentalism functions to convey a level of legiti-
macy for some nativists who may seek to smooth over their sharp racist
inclinations. Our view is that nativist movements are not just anti-immigrant in their approach to the world; they are racist and generally white
supremacist.[98] Thus, nativism does nothing but function as a disservice to
environmentalism. Rather than bolstering their membership with restric-
tionist fearmongers, environmental organizations might act as the mass
movement that it could become and separate from and condemn nativist
ideology as fundamentally anti-environmental.

One sign of hope is the transformation of the radical environmental
movement network EarthFirst![99] Begun in 1979 as a response to both the
increased threats to ecosystems and the elite corporatization of the U.S.
environmental movement, EF!'s actions "are tied to Deep Ecology, the
spiritual and visceral recognition of the intrinsic, sacred value of every living thing."[100] EF!'s slogan is "No Compromise in Defense of Mother Earth,"
something sorely needed in the mainstream environmentalist community,
considering the cozy relationship between many of these groups and some
of the world's major corporate polluters like Clorox, Shell, and BP.[101] For example, the National Wildlife Federation and the Nature Conservancy have
accepted money from large oil corporations and rewarded them with positive press coverage and awards for ecological stewardship. When it was
revealed that IKEA was selling dining room sets made from wood taken
from endangered forests, the World Wildlife Fund leapt to IKEA's defense,

claiming that the company could guarantee forest protection in the future. It was soon revealed that WWF was a recipient of money from IKEA at the time. In 2008 the Sierra Club agreed to a deal with Clorox Corporation, endorsing a new line of green products in exchange for a percentage of the sales.[102] In response, the entire board of directors of the club's northern Michigan chapter resigned. Finally, there are countless examples of how large environmental organizations have partnered with extractive industries and governments to create "conservation" projects that expel indigenous peoples from their lands.[103] Grassroots and radical environmentalists associated with groups like EarthFirst! believed there had to be a better way forward.

Dave Foreman, the co-founder of EF!, was known for his radical approach to wilderness defense. But early on, Foreman and Edward Abbey (author of *The Monkey Wrench Gang*) became public advocates of nativist politics, pushing EarthFirst! in that direction. Abbey told a gathering of EF! activists in 1987 that U.S. cultural values were superior to those of Latin America. That same year, Foreman wrote an article in the EarthFirst! journal claiming that AIDS would ultimately be a good thing for the earth's ecological ills, since it would reduce the global population. Many EF!ers challenged this racism by abandoning the *EarthFirst! Journal* and creating a new 'zine called *Live Wild or Die*. At the same time, members of the Biotic Baking Brigade first appeared in an issue of the *EF! Journal* with a letter condemning Abbey and stating that he deserved a "frijoles" pie to the face to silence his racism. Not long afterward, Foreman left EF!, sensing that his bridges had been burned.[104] Another EF!er wrote, in response to this unsavory history:

> Real bridging, which involves listening instead of recruiting, needs to be done due to ingrained racist sentiments of some of the environmental movement's spokespeople. EF! can't let industrialism, capitalism, racism, patriarchy, or privilege go unchecked. That is, not if we really mean it when we say, "No Compromise in Defense of Mother Earth." EF!'s "deep" ecology has not been deep enough.[105]

Since EF! ousted Abbey and Foreman, many of its leading voices have since declared their solidarity with immigrants in the United States. As one EarthFirster explained:

Over-emphasizing the role of population growth in environmental problems ignores who has control of production and consumption decisions. . . . Immigrants are essential allies and leaders of the movement for environmental protection and restoration. Immigrant communities suffer disproportionately from environmental degradation and poisoning, whether from exposure to pesticides in fields, toxic dumps in neighborhoods or solvents in factories. But immigrants have begun to fight back and are among the leaders of the environmental justice movement.[106]

Another EarthFirster wrote that "racist ecology poses a danger to the movement as a whole and, ultimately, to life itself. We must confront white supremacy within the ecology movements as militantly as we would confront ExxonMobil or the U.S. Forest Service; the threat is just as great."[107] Recently, many EF!ers have moved to deepen their deep ecological commitment into something that looks more like a radical approach to environmental justice. This is a great illustration of how a movement with strong nativist tendencies can begin transforming itself and rejecting problematic ideologies while becoming an even stronger force for justice.

Even so, many EF!ers remain firmly committed to stopping population growth and are dismissive of the politics of immigrant solidarity. And, like many grassroots movements, EarthFirst! continues to struggle with its finances to remain solvent. Without the deep pockets of mainstream organizations lined with nativist-tainted funds, EF!'s future may be tenuous.

Most of the major environmental organizations in the United States have (or have had) programs or campaigns focused on population analysis. This includes the Sierra Club, the National Wildlife Federation, the Audubon Society, and many others. This interest in population control extends beyond environmental and nativist groups to federal government agencies, international development organizations, and global philanthropies. Many federal agencies and large foundations in the United States determined, decades ago, that population control is one of the pillars of national and corporate security. Since the early 1950s, the Ford Foundation, John Rockefeller III's Population Council, and other institutions began funding research at U.S. universities on the links between population and political stability. Funding from the federal government for population studies increased soon thereafter. By the mid 1960s, international food aid programs became some of the key players in supporting family planning in the global South. By the 1990s, the U.S. Agency for International Development (USAID) became the world's largest funder of population control initiatives in the global South.[108] This was troubling for women's rights advocates around the world who recalled USAID's troubling history of sterilization policies.[109] Population control efforts have often used the notion of conserving the earth's resources as a vehicle of exerting influence over the world's low-income and global South populations. Therefore, population control is actually very much in tune with nativist ideology.

However, history shows us that early on there was a glimmer of hope that the U.S. environmental movement might have taken a different path. In the early twentieth century, social reformers who advocated on behalf of immigrants working in sweatshops and living in America's slums could also be viewed as environmental justice leaders. They were, after all, critical of the power relations that relegated economically and politically marginal peoples to hazardous living and working environments. These far-sighted individuals included Jane Addams, Florence Kelley, and Alice Hamilton, among others. Together they challenged the social forces that threatened the public health status of European immigrant communities in Chicago and elsewhere, places where men, women, and children were forced to work long hours for low wages, where lead poisoning was a way of life, and where garbage dumps came with the neighborhood.[110] The mainstream environmental movement made a choice *not* to cast its lot with this brand of activists, and the movement suffered greatly in its lack of capacity for melding social justice with ecological protection. We believe that there are those in the movement who might one day challenge their colleagues to remember Addams, Kelley, and Hamilton and embrace a different path.

5

Advocacy and Social Justice Workers

Today, the Roaring Fork Valley is a bustling, thriving series of towns. Despite the nostalgic picture painted by the area's few long-term residents, and contrary to the nativist ideal of Aspen as a stable community with deep local roots, the population here is constantly on the move. In fact, virtually everyone in the valley is a newcomer or a transplant.

Despite the dominant Anglo presence, this is an area marked by rich ethnic and racial diversity, with immigrants from Argentina, El Salvador, Guatemala, Mexico, Paraguay, Peru, and Uruguay. There are many native-born Latinos and a smaller population of Asian Americans and African Americans as well. As one local leader related to us when we asked about the African American population in the valley:

> Actually, it's surprising, I think the census said there are 40–60 in Carbondale, but that doesn't count Latinos who are of African descent. You go to the grocery store and you'll see a lot of afros, but they don't speak English and don't identify as black, they identify as Latino. They are not really counted because they're undocumented.[1]

Thus it seems that a lot of the social diversity of the valley is undocumented, because of the presence of undocumented workers. Moreover, much of the valley's diversity is often *unrecognized*, because many Anglos lump together all people of a darker hue as Mexicans. Beginning in the

1980s employers and towns in the Roaring Fork Valley began recruiting workers from Latin America to fill jobs in the area's growing tourist industry. The expectation was that these were temporary workers, but as they began raising families and setting down roots in the valley, these workers became permanent residents.[2] The influx of a mélange of cultural and ethnic groups to the valley since the 1980s has posed significant challenges for local institutions to serve newcomer populations and to address the sense of anxiety that preexisting populations feel about immigrants. Fortunately, there are many organizations and individuals committed to this kind of work. In this chapter we hear from advocates working from within and on behalf of Latino immigrant communities in the Roaring Fork Valley. These leaders offer critical challenges to nativist environmentalism and environmental privilege in their analytical and grassroots political work. They offer assistance and solidarity to immigrant communities and confront the political forces seeking to expel or restrict the rights of immigrants. Most importantly, they articulate a vision of social, economic, environmental, and global justice and embrace policies in pursuit of these goals.

Immigrant Advocacy

Philanthropy

George Stranahan is what you might call a character. We sat down with this enigmatic and irreverent man one day, and he gave us an earful. For years he has reigned as the Roaring Fork Valley's most visible and flamboyant left-leaning philanthropist. An heir to the Ohio-based Champion Spark Plug Company, with a PhD in physics and formerly a tenured professor at Michigan State University, he left MSU to teach high school and pursue a vision of social and economic justice. A rabble-rouser with plenty of clout, Stranahan counted the late Hunter S. Thompson as a personal friend in addition to the recording artist Don Henley and the actor Don Johnson, who are his neighbors in Woody Creek, a small town just outside Aspen. There, Stranahan owned the Woody Creek Tavern until recently. The pub and restaurant were closed for a time after a dispute with the Colorado liquor license officials who objected to his printing the phrase "Good Beer, No Shit" on his Flying Dog Brewery product labels. In 2007 Stranahan told a reporter, "I've ended up doing a lot of businesses. But it was sort of incidental to some sort of social or political purpose." In fact his business motto is "Do good. If you make money, God bless! That's more fun even."[3]

Stranahan founded the Aspen Center for Social Justice, which, as one journalist quipped, "sounds like a contradiction."[4] That organization gave birth to the Stepstone Center for Social Justice—the left-leaning, Carbondale-based activist group that has led some of the most visible social struggles in the valley during the last decade. Stranahan revealed, "It's modeled on the Highlander Education and Resource Center in Tennessee, [founded by] Myles Horton, which is about popular education. So rather than doing organizing for you, we teach popular education so you can organize yourselves. I used to go down there [to Highlander] a lot."[5] The Stepstone Center, in turn, gave birth to Latinos Unidos (Latinos United)— a group focused on improving Latino-Anglo relations in the valley.

Despite being so jaded about the Crystal City of Aspen, Stranahan has put many resources into some of the most important socially and environmentally progressive activities in the valley, making possible the existence of a strong, organized activist community. Without his assistance, the movement for environmental and social justice in the valley would not be what it is today.

And while Stranahan has been quite influential, there is no shortage of nonprofit groups in the valley, all of them vying for a limited pool of dollars from local government and foundations. One local activist stated, "There's about three hundred right in this valley. All nonprofits. I think the worst part is just competing for funds . . . funding is really difficult and it's getting harder all the time."[6]

Education

There are a number of nonprofit organizations in the valley that work to meet some of the critical needs of the area's immigrant communities. One such organization is Colorado Mountain College (CMC), an important educational support anchor for Latinos pursuing college degrees, various credentials, and pathways to economic stability. We spoke with Leticia Barraza, a representative of CMC's Office of Student Access. Her office began with a basic approach to addressing local needs, starting with the establishment of a "Latino Help Desk," which answers students' questions in Spanish. CMC also initiated the Alpine Bank Scholarship, which is earmarked for Latino students. The Help Desk staff also coordinates an annual Latino Youth Summit to provide mentoring and guidance for the valley's young people who are themselves immigrants or the children of immigrants. Barraza is the main staff person at the Help Desk and is sympathetic to the experiences of young Latinos in the area today because she has lived through some of the challenges they face:

> I was born in Mexico and came here not much different than a lot of these students. I came here illegally but have been able to obtain my citizenship. It would be impossible for me to move back to Mexico with my kids. A lot of these kids here know nothing but the valley.[7]

Barraza contends that one of the barriers to the success of Latino youth here is the official hostility toward bilingual education. She explains that the local school district is "pushing for English only" and has convinced many local families that bilingual education is a bad idea. She objects to the general move away from dual-language classes in the state's schools. The problem and solution are in the politics of education, she says:

> Bilingual education definitely works, but if you don't have the backing of school districts there's not much you can do about it. It's about being able to retain your language. When I grew up, I started school speaking Spanish only. But back then, you couldn't even speak Spanish at school, even on the playground [it was forbidden by school officials]. My mother was a migrant and she pushed for more English at home. Consequently my Spanish is very limited—I can understand it but not speak it very well. That's what happens when you try to force someone who has dual languages to only speak one language. Instead of finding ways to teach in a way that allows them to learn a new language and retain the old one . . . the bottom line is that they are saying "forget everything you've learned, the 5,000 word vocabulary you obtained in your first four years of life. You're starting from scratch." That's why we have a lot of Latino kids placed in "special needs" classes when they don't belong there, but they're being labeled "special needs" kids.[8]

Not surprisingly, many Latino youths never finish high school. In 1997 the Latino dropout rate in the valley school district was 62 percent.[9]

Ultimately, Barraza asserts, local Latino youth tend to remain confined to occupational and residential ghettoes, and without significant institutional support, this is not likely to change anytime soon:

> For the most part I think they end up, most of them, obtaining fake papers and working. Hoping that they can find a job and stay here. As far as education, most of them express interest in wanting to continue. It makes it very difficult because we want to give that to them . . . but most of them end up quitting school unfortunately. [They say] "If I can't keep going, I'll just look for a job." It's very frustrating because they could be a valedictorian, but if they're undocumented—which most of them are—then how can they get a decent job? So many of them work in the service industry. We have many students who take one class at a time [since they have little money or time to commit to more than that]. Many of them hope that this state passes the Dream Act so they can go to college. But for now, we don't see a lot of hope because Colorado is such a conservative state.[10]

The Roaring Fork Valley's public schools and colleges have a monumental challenge ahead of them. Fortunately, there are other organizations in the area working toward the same general goals.

Social Services

Jessica Dove is the coordinator of an Adult Literacy Program in the valley. An Anglo transplant from the East Coast who has strong connections with many Latinos in the valley as a service provider, Dove moved to the area with her husband in the late 1990s. She recalls her initial impressions upon arriving in Colorado: "I noticed that the population here was very bicultural—Anglos and Latinos. They lived in the same area but don't mix together much." She was able to secure her position as coordinator of the literacy program "because I had strong language skills and I wanted to bring people together, by building relationships. My official job is to bring people together in the community. I have fifty volunteers in the literacy program who help tutor students."

Dove is a strong advocate for her students and for the immigrant population in general. When we asked her whether businesses suffer from federal immigration control policies, she responded:

No. Immigrant workers have no rights, no control over their work schedule or working conditions. They often work seven days a week, sixteen-hour days, with no overtime. Businesses are not suffering. I've only heard of perhaps one fine that's been imposed on a business for hiring undocumented folks. The onus is really on the immigrants themselves. Businesses just have to show that they've had paperwork on their employees, and that's easy.[11]

But Dove is hopeful for the future. Like the Latinos Unidos organization, she emphasizes that empowering Latinos will only happen if alliances are built with Anglos:

[N]ot all Anglos have tension with Latinos. We had a graduation ceremony the other day for the . . . Adult Literacy Program and the families of the tutors (Anglo folks), mostly husbands, were coming up to me saying things like "this is so great that you're bringing these two communities together!" They really were so happy to be able to participate in a multiracial, multicultural gathering, and I think it speaks to the desire among many Anglos to work together and cooperate across the two cultures. So that's what I do, my job is not just about having people learn English, it's also about building relationships.[12]

Even so, there are significant stress points, even among immigration advocates. Dove informed us that most of her literacy tutors are Anglo, but not all fully support her mission: "Most volunteers don't ask questions, but some of them insist on tutoring documented persons only. That can be a problem."[13]

Asistencia Para Latinos (Assistance for Latinos/APL) was yet another organization founded and funded by George Stranahan. Since 1992, this Glenwood Springs–based agency provided information regarding housing, citizenship, immigration services, work visas, and much more to members of the Latino community in the valley: APL's mission was "To empower the Latino Community towards self-sufficiency through services, education, advocacy and inter-agency collaboration."[14] Asistencia confronted many of the challenges facing immigrant communities, including the tensions that occur between immigrant parents and their newly Americanized children. To address that particular issue, APL launched an initiative called Strengthening Latino Families. They also went farther than a typical social service approach and offered small loans to Latinos for microenterprise development.[15] One beneficiary of this program is Ernesto Leon, the proud owner of a Mexican restaurant and bakery in the valley. He met with APL's director, who helped him develop a business plan and awarded him a small loan. He is now a successful Latino business owner and credits APL with getting him started.[16]

According to APL's documents, in 1998, their client profile looked like this:

61% male, 39% female;
76% from Mexico, 14% from El Salvador, 2% Guatemala;
37% report little to no English proficiency
70% have no more than a 12th grade education
51% report a monthly income of $1,000–2,000
54% report health insurance, 24% report none
73% are employed[17]

This profile suggests that the client base is working poor, with little formal education, and with minimal healthcare coverage. That same year (1998), APL served 3,500 clients and helped 165 of them become U.S. citizens and 153 more to become legal residents of the United States.[18]

This group was honored with a national excellence award from the U.S. Department of Housing and Urban Development Secretary in 1996. A number of prominent valley immigrant advocates served on the APL board and staff, including Marie Munday, Felicia Trevor, and Jessica Dove. With this level of human capital, it seemed that this organization had a bright future ahead of it. Instead, APL was frequently overwhelmed with daily demands from the community and eventually shut down due to a lack of funding and a high rate of staff and board turnover. One community activist speculated that local governments were given a huge fiscal break because APL provided many of the services that state agencies would normally offer. She stated, "It was one agency that had to do so much. It's not surprising that they were overwhelmed."[19]

The closing of APL's office is an example of the difficulty of immigrant life in the valley. Not only do immigrants themselves face economic and cultural hardships there, but finding adequate, professional help to deal with these issues is also difficult. And even those organizations providing such help have a hard time staying above water, since they operate in such a neglected part of the valley's consciousness.

We asked the Stepstone Center director Scott Chaplin—a leading immigrant rights and environmental justice advocate in the valley—whether burnout was a factor, given the heavy workload at APL:

> Yes, that happened with some people with Asistencia. They were underfunded and trying so much. Even for Latinos who come here looking for help, you could spend two to three solid days with just one person, helping with their problems. Their problems are huge. I have a friend in the trailer park where I live, came in the other day. Her husband passed away in March, he was helping her with her paper work, so now she doesn't know what to do and may be deported, so this is quite common.[20]

Catholic Charities, a social services organization in Glenwood Springs, stepped in to pick up where APL left off when they closed. Peter Jessup, a staff member at Catholic Charities, recalled that when APL

> went under . . . a lot of people started coming to us. . . . Before that, CC didn't even have any emergency assistance, to say nothing of immigrant advocacy, so Asistencia did all that. We didn't do that kind of work before, so then we shifted our focus. So we've been doing cultural orientation days and discussion sessions with people involved in a range of services.[21]

Like other advocate groups in the valley, one of CC's principal pursuits is multiracial unity. Jessup asserted, "We need to educate the broader public so that we're not just preaching to the choir or to only Latinos." And while Catholic Charities generously offered a wide range of immigration services, the loss of APL—a key organization founded to empower Latino immigrants—is still felt today.

Peter Jessup sees himself as a person on the front lines of the fight for immigrant rights, and his efforts as a community leader speak to the difficulty of making progressive change in the interest of marginalized groups. The Glenwood Springs native has a special interest in seeing his hometown evolve into a place marked by social justice:

I went to Colorado Mountain College and transferred to Creighton University in Omaha, Nebraska. The reason why I went there was that they have a lot of classes on social justice. We did a lot of work unionizing and organizing Latinos there. My biggest change was when I did a semester abroad in the Dominican Republic. There was a group of fifteen of us and we did a lot of service work. We studied the structure of oppression in classes—those were the best classes I've ever taken—and we were able to see it for yourself. I came back after that and it was earth shattering for me, and still is. One of the persons I met there told me that "if you really want to do service work that will challenge structures of oppression here, then go back to the United States and do social justice work there where you are, and change the cycles of oppression that are oppressing us." That really struck me and stuck with me because it's true.

Jessup joined the staff at Catholic Charities after returning to the United States and has been working on human rights issues ever since. He stands out in this valley as an Anglo resident who is more than willing to engage in anti-racist politics. He decries the ongoing and very present racism in the area:

It's shocking how much racism actually still exists. There are a lot of businesses and they hear the word "Latinos" and they kind of say "oh." For example, hospitals—I try to call them up and negotiate to see if they could use part of their charitable funds with us, but when they hear "Latinos," they kind of shut down and it's just such an easy way for them to discount wanting to do a human service. So they'll say "we can't help you out because they are undocumented." They say "what are you doing, helping the wetbacks?" Others in churches I've visited have asked "why is the church helping out with these people? They're illegal."

This type of quiet refusal on the part of businesses and other organizations to support immigrant communities suggests that institutional racism and nativism operate on multiple levels in the valley. However, others were not so quiet about their racism. Jessup told the story of an employer who repeatedly hired undocumented Latinos yet boldly refused to pay them:

This story is so amazing . . . an employer went out of her way *not* to pay her workers. . . . She lives in Rifle and she just hires people and contracts them out to Aspen. When I came on board here, I served as an interrogatory on the case. We're just about ready to get her to pay. She has more than twenty people who have filed a suit against her, so to think about how many people she has screwed over in the valley is amazing. So we're trying to get her to pay and to go to jail. We're trying to stage a protest outside her house with a lot of people in the area. We asked a Rifle judge if it was legal to [protest] and he said "Yes, and I'll go down and join you guys!" So we're getting people not to hire her.[22]

This kind of blatant labor exploitation of persons without official status is, unfortunately, all too common across the United States.[23] Catholic Charities also collaborates with other advocacy organizations in the valley, although this process was affected by the nativist environmentalist backlash. Jessup states:

I see it as amazing, how we're able to organize throughout the valley. We do referrals to them [other immigrant social services groups] and they do the same to us, but we always say to each other that we need more of us because there is such a demand. We get funding from the Salvation Army and from Tom's Door—a Carbondale organization that helps us a lot. We also work with Alpine Legal Services, which is a nonprofit legal assistance organization. We used the Aspen Valley Community Foundation (AVCF) in the past, but not any more because they kind of had a problem with that.[24]

The "problem" with the AVCF was a result of public political pressure from Mike McGarry, Terry Paulson, and others who pushed publicly to stop the agency from serving undocumented immigrants.

We asked Jessup, "Where do you get the drive to do this work, which must be so stressful and draining?" Without hesitation he responded, "I get an anger inside me, and anger is good, and that really brings me through. I try to be reasonable with people, demanding justice, but I get really worked up at the inequalities and the injustice that goes on. That's where I get my drive."[25]

Another key social service organization working on immigrant rights in the valley is Roaring Fork Legal Services (RFLS). We spoke with James Knowlton, an attorney who worked for this organization. He said, "Roaring Fork Legal Services was started in about 1996 by a group of lawyers headed by the city attorney who decided it would be important to make access to the legal system easier for people who are on the lower end of the income spectrum." Knowlton pointed out that like most other nonprofits, RFLS "always had to fight for its money, [but] we did get a grant from George Stranahan." They opened an office in Carbondale and immediately saw an overwhelming community response from both immigrants and those who oppose immigration:

> [T]here was a flood of over five hundred calls—basically they took us by storm. We helped a lot of people, [including those] seeking asylum. . . . I do know that when we were doing immigration there was a lot of attorneys who would *not* give us financial support, because we were doing immigration, we were helping "illegals." What happened is just our office wasn't able to keep up with the demands.[26]

Eventually, RFLS merged with Garfield County's legal services unit to form Alpine Legal Services, which offers assistance to Catholic Charities and other core organizations in the valley.

From Social Services to Social Justice

In the late 1990s, a new kind of social movement began sweeping the United States and other nations—the anti-globalization movement. Also known as the global justice movement, its primary targets were large transnational corporations and the governments and international financial institutions (like the International Monetary Fund and the World Bank) that supported them. Among other things, this movement represented an important moment when activists on the Left articulated a more or less common global framework that encompassed and celebrated local differences. The framework fairly coherently linked concerns among workers and labor rights advocates, environmentalists, indigenous peoples, and others who had experienced the violence of cultural and economic globalization processes that were otherwise uncritically celebrated by the mainstream media, elected officials, and economists at the world's leading universities, think tanks, and corporations. This was a time when the now famous "Battle in Seattle" took place, where tens of thousands of activists successfully shut down the Millennium Round of talks among delegates to the World Trade Organization in 1999. That massive uprising was essentially repeated many times over in other cities around the world whenever significant gatherings of global political economic elites took place. The global justice movement lives on and has become more sophisticated. Unfortunately, since the attacks of 9/11, the United States and many other governments have hampered many left-leaning direct action movements, creating serious barriers for future activism.[27]

While the global justice movement captured headlines in Seattle, Miami, Washington, DC, Porto Alegre, Davos, Prague, Mumbai, Caracas, Nairobi, and other places, its real strength came from the countless local actions and mobilizations that constituted the movement and posed a threat to various power brokers. The Stepstone Center for Social Justice and its partner group Mountain Folks for Global Justice play a vital role in the Roaring Fork Valley.[28] George Stranahan founded these groups with a vision drawn from his time at the Highlander Folk School, which is located near New Market, Tennessee. One of the cornerstones of the Highlander philosophy of social change is that the collective possesses the greatest power, not individuals or experts, no matter how brilliant or charismatic they may be. Stranahan stated, "One of us alone ain't gonna make any change, but when everybody gets together, watch out."[29]

The Stepstone Center is a project of COMPASS, formerly the Aspen Educational Research Foundation, another Stranahan-funded organization dedicated to educational reform and, more recently, social justice. The center's first significant victory was the fight to keep the INS out of the valley. They built on that local success by organizing a series of events around the global justice cause in the summer of 2000.

One of their projects offered an excellent exposé of Aspen's extremes and the vast differences that can be seen throughout America between the interests of the elite and the countervailing efforts by grassroots community interests. "The People's Summit on Globalization" was intended to provide a progressive alternative to a decidedly exclusive conference held simultaneously at the Aspen Institute, "Globalization and the Human Condition." The Aspen event—organized to herald the Institute's fiftieth anniversary—featured such luminaries as Henry Kissinger, Gerald Levin (former TimeWarner CEO), and James Wolfensohn (former head of the World Bank). Also featured was a presentation by Norm Augustine, the chairman of the executive committee of the Lockheed Martin Corporation, the global security firm and weapons contractor. While there were some progressive personalities and voices present at this event (including President Jimmy Carter), the dominant theme was a celebration of globalization and twenty-first-century imperialism. This was actually quite fitting considering what Aspen stands for—environmental privileges and excessive financial and political power for the few.[30]

Mountain Folks for Global Justice was not invited to the Aspen Institute event, which perhaps was not surprising since members of this group were known to have recently been involved in the Battle in Seattle protests. Mountain Folks and the Stepstone Center responded by organizing the People's Summit and invited many well-regarded national figures of the Left, including Kevin Danaher of Global Exchange, Njoki Njehu of 50 Years is Enough, Jello Biafra of the Dead Kennedys, and Hunter Lovins of the Rocky Mountain Institute. Labor, environmental, alternative media, and Green Party leaders were also in the lineup of speakers. And while the Aspen Institute's conference charged $750 for admission, the People's Summit charged $7.50, one one-hundredth of the institute's price.[31]

The People's Summit featured a teach-in on the social and ecological devastation associated with economic globalization. This event also showcased a nonviolence training session by John Bach, a Quaker activist who served three years in prison as a conscientious objector to the U.S.–led war in Viet Nam.[32] Activists also led a march near the Aspen Institute, a public rally at Paepcke Park, and an event at which U.S. foreign policy was put on (mock) trial.[33] Hundreds of people participated. The *Aspen Daily News* editorial page later named the People's Summit one of the top news stories of 2000.[34]

This case is important for the larger story surrounding immigration and environmental politics for three reasons: (1) Stepstone became one of the most effective voices for both immigrant rights and environmental justice, (2) Stepstone would later place much of the blame behind undocumented immigration to the United States on economic globalization and

U.S. foreign policy, and (3) the creation of Stepstone signaled a maturity in progressive grassroots politics in the valley, which tied together a vision of environmental justice, social and economic justice, and immigrant rights.

Many activists work as staff members and volunteers for social justice organizations in the area and make the grassroots movement gains in the valley possible. Felicia "Flash" Trevor hails from Chicago and moved to the valley in 1977. She studied renewable energy, solar power, and sustainable housing at a local college and planned to apply that knowledge, along with her Spanish skills, in Latin America. Instead, she fell in love with the valley and never left. She worked as the Stepstone Center director for five years. As someone who still works closely with the center, she stated, "We provide a place for people to organize."[35] Luis Polar is a Puerto Rico–born transplant to the valley and was the editor and publisher of one of the area's only Spanish language newspapers, *La Unión* (formerly *La Misión*). He recalled that when he first arrived in Glenwood Springs he "fell in love with the place, especially the small town atmosphere." He began getting involved with local NGOs and soon realized the distinct need for media that would serve the Latino community:

> I volunteered at KDNK, the public [radio] station, doing a Latino show in Spanish. And ultimately, in early 2000 is when a group of people got together in the Basalt-Carbondale area and they were looking at what was the immigrant community missing in this area. And an informational source was critical. There was no radio show at that moment with news. No newspaper, no TV in Spanish, except for cable that came from all sorts of places. And I connected with these folks.

Some of the major concerns Polar and other leaders shared included the lack of affordable housing for immigrants, poor educational services for Latinos, and the associated high drop-out rate among Latino students. Media as an educational and political tool was understood as critical to addressing these concerns:

> What we needed also was a newspaper, some sort of a way to print what was going on in the valley, put it in Spanish. We decided that we needed to do this. And they gave me a computer, an old Macintosh computer and a scanner, and working out of my home, which I still do,

we started publishing this newspaper, *La Misión*. My job is publishing this newspaper and doing the articles and selling ads. We started in September 2001. . . . At the beginning it was very small, eight pages. And now we're up to thirty-two pages. It still prints once a month, I still work out of my home office, and I've been having a little bit of a struggle finding the resources. In terms of staff it's just myself. We are the only source of news in Spanish in the valley and we are actually also bilingual, bilingual format. That way we can bridge that gap of language between Anglo and Hispanic, and the Anglo community can realize some of the issues that we're facing and the Latino community can learn English.

At that same time, Scott Chaplin was the director of the Stepstone Center and a town trustee in Carbondale. His biography is revealing: he is the son of a Latin American Studies scholar and lived for a while in Spain, where he began learning Spanish. He came to the Roaring Fork Valley after college, and after travels in Nicaragua and Guatemala, found himself living in a mobile home park in Carbondale where the majority of residents were Latino:

> I moved there in '94, and by '97 the owners were thinking of just tearing it down and evicting everybody . . . and we basically engaged in this three-year battle, organizing all the neighbors and trying to get some compensation for the loss of the homes. It was like 80 percent Latino, 10 percent Native American, 10 percent Anglo in the trailer park. We ended up getting ninety thousand dollars between twenty families—not very much. I think around that time . . . I started working at the Stepstone Center. So Stepstone was actually involved in helping with . . . part of that campaign to get some compensation. Also I, on the side I had this little dump truck and I would hire people to help me all the time with different landscaping jobs, just a weekend thing that I would do to make a little extra money. So I got to know a lot of Latinos that way too. I don't see Stepstone's mission as being exclusively Latino . . . we're trying to fight all kinds of discrimination.

We asked Chaplin what it is like being an Anglo man working in this community. He answered:

It's kind of neat because I've got trust in a community that other people don't have access to. We did this collaborative struggle [over the trailer park evictions], so that helped. When you struggle alongside people like that, a different bond develops. My old neighbors, I still sustain contact with them [despite the dissolution of the community when the mobile home park was sold].

As Latinos, Luis and Felicia are frequently overburdened with requests to do volunteer community-based work throughout the valley. Felicia says they are called on to do "anything and everything." She attributes this demand on their schedules to the fact that there are so few Latinos doing community work since most of them are busy working multiple jobs and barely have time for family. "So when Luis started here I said, 'oh you'd better be careful because everybody and their brother's going to ask you,' and sure enough, he was the new Latino poster child in the valley."

And while there may be too few Latino leaders and organizations in the valley, there are other colleagues and friends supporting and collaborating with Trevor, Chaplin, and Polar. Alejandro Manjarrez is a Costa Rican immigrant who serves on the boards of directors of Latinos Unidos, the Stepstone Center, and, before it closed, *La Misión*:

I have lived here in the valley for almost two and a half years and I've been doing different kinds of jobs, like right now I'm gardening [laughs]. But I also work with some nonprofits like Computers for Kids Foundation, I have a couple hours, and basically that's my job.

Alejandro also speaks Russian because the Costa Rican government paid for him to travel to Russia for graduate studies in Forestry. Luis chimes in, "These are the kind of Latinos we were talking about. He doesn't fit the profile of the uneducated. We need more Alejandros in the valley."

Miguel Ortiz and Aurelia Cerda also participated in our discussion at the center that day. Aurelia is deeply involved in community work, although not in such confrontational and public ways as other activists. She said, "Right now I'm a ranch caretaker, I've been in the valley since 1991. And been involved here and there, you know, as part of Latinos Unidos. Right now I'm really involved at the church, I'm a general treasurer and the person that does the Women's Association."

Miguel told us:

This is where I live. I like to help a lot of people that have problems translating, you know. I'm a notary public also, and I get a lot of people that come to get help from me doing letters for them or just translating some papers, things like that. So I know a lot of people in this valley. And I like to get involved with the community. . . . I also was the president of the Head Start Program. And I was the president of the parents association at school. I would go once a month to Grand Junction for meetings and just get information for what was going on in our valley, what we could do for all Latino parents. Then I would come to Carbondale and make a meeting for the parents in the Head Start program and just translate to them everything that I learned up there.

The kind of work that Aurelia and Miguel do is crucial for the day-to-day functioning and survival of the Latino community here. Their efforts challenge the notion of immigrants as temporary sojourners who provide little or nothing to the community in which they reside. Rather, they are just two of many members of the immigrant community who share a strong commitment to improving the schools, social service organizations, churches, and other institutions that support families in the area.

Environmental Privilege and Nativist Environmentalism

Activists in the valley also directly engaged and challenged the problem of environmental privilege. Felicia Trevor noted, "[we reject] the whole idea of only the wealthy can have beautiful [mountain] views and things like that, so that's part of what we deal with."[36] Trevor also spoke to the class dynamics associated with the kind of market chaos that produces environmental privilege found in the valley; a class inequality that cuts across racial groups: "There's a whole group of young people that lived here in Carbondale that have all moved out because they couldn't afford to live here and think about buying a house unless they wanted to work eighty hours a week. They were all white people that were here."

Jessica Dove, the Basalt activist, echoes Felicia Trevor's analysis of class and race inequalities:

The issue of the difference between yesterday's wages, prices, and rents versus today's has really come out in the wake of immigration. But what we really need to be asking is "who benefits from all this?" Years ago working-[class] whites could live here and work here, but no longer. Businesses get labor for lower costs, so they make out very well. The people being hurt are working-class whites and Latinos who are not experiencing upward mobility at all.[37]

While nativist environmentalists blame immigrant populations in the valley for a host of social problems, they seem to ignore the fact that both working-class whites and Latinos face economic and political marginalization. Dove also questions the level of environmental privilege among valley Anglos and speaks to what she sees as the root of the problem—white anxiety over threats to that privilege and power:

I'd also love to get a sense for what kind of ecological footprint these different groups produce and then compare that to immigrants. When my literacy students visit my house they always remark that they can't believe only two people live there because it's so big compared to what they are used to. They can't process it . . . it's kind of curious to me that you're focused on Latinos when it's really Anglos who are the problem—they're the ones who have created this discourse of blame and should be studied. You should focus on white folks because it's about *them*, because they are generating the discourse.[38]

Dove's comment is incisive and powerful. It is also in line with some of the most exciting academic research on the study of whiteness and white privilege, issues that tend to go unexamined by scholars studying race and the experiences of communities of color.[39] One of the goals of the growing field of Critical White Studies or Whiteness Studies is to bring to light the largely invisible and understudied phenomenon of whiteness and the ways in which this category has been created, protected, inhabited, transformed, and undone. For example, well into the twentieth century, only people from northern and western Europe who were Christians were viewed as culturally white in this country, while people of Slavic, Irish, Italian, German, Catholic, and Jewish ethnic and religious heritage—who are understood to be "white" today—were not. The legal standards that define whiteness have constantly changed over time as well, creating confusion for Americans of Asian, European, Middle Eastern, Latin American, and African descent who, depending on a court ruling or legislation, could instantly be defined as white or nonwhite. Research on whiteness also makes clear that white supremacy and white racism have historically been detrimental to the goals of democracy and have done untold harm to white working-class communities.[40] Environmental privilege is often reflective of white racism and the preservation of whiteness.

Catholic Charities' representative Peter Jessup weighed in on the question of race, immigration, and environmental privilege as well:

> There are two really hot issues here. One is immigration and the other is development. I think you can have both. With me, where I take my environmentalism is that I'm really against commercial development, seasonal homes, and golf courses. That's preposterous, it's awful. But at the same time we have to ask what is right for Latinos. Because if we do bring in more commercialism, we provide more jobs for Latinos, so I understand that. But I don't think it's a cycle that can continue, bringing in more commercialism. If we provide more fair housing it'll solve a lot of problems. So I think we can build low-income housing and be environmental at the same time.[41]

Alice Hubbard Laird, a former Rocky Mountain Institute staffer, pointed to the global market forces that make Aspen ecologically and economically unsustainable:

> I'm one of these people that feel like Anglos—North Americans—cause far more environmental damage than people from other countries. The problem is that Aspen has an international market for its real estate. When you have an international market for places to live, it does weird things to the economy. It pushes the millionaires out; people cannot afford to live there. The professional class of Aspen lives in Basalt. When you have people who will pay anything to say they own a piece of property in Aspen, it creates this weird dynamic. The transportation problem

is more that this whole region is a desirable place to live, and it's not at all a result of immigration or greater numbers of people coming here. It's more market forces.[42]

Jonathan Fox-Rubin, of the Basalt City Council, argues that, ironically, the very people who come to the valley to "get away from it all" and enjoy their own tract of unspoiled nature contribute the most to ecological strains in the area:

I think the number of people here is not necessarily a problem, but the impact that the number of people who are here have on the environment and on each other is a problem. The kind of growth that we approve is what Colorado land law allows and that small communities are trying to get a handle on all over the map. You have a person who wants to live on the biggest piece of land they can buy with the biggest possible house with as many possible amenities. So kind of where the capitalist culture meshes with the rural West.[43]

The most common argument by immigration control advocates for building up national borders is the claim that immigrants pose an economic threat to U.S. citizens: they take away "our" jobs or immigrants depress "our" wages. Jessica Dove provided her own analysis:

Wages are deflated here because of the greed of businesses and home owners, not because of immigration. I used to think that we all would benefit from the low prices, but it hasn't happened because it's actually resulted in businesses taking a greater share of profits. There has not been an increase in wages in the valley here in twenty years. My husband is from here and is not making any more today than he was then. There are a lot of white working-class people here who are disgruntled because they used to be able to make $20 an hour cleaning second and third homes, but cannot now. Do people make those connections about low wages and immigration?[44]

Dove's words coincide with leading studies that find that the real wages of Americans have declined or remained stagnant over the past four decades, while the earnings of the wealthiest Americans and the profits of large corporations have skyrocketed.[45] According to data from the Internal Revenue Service, the share of the national income that the richest Americans take home is the highest it has been since World War II, and some scholars believe it has not been surpassed since the 1920s. The richest 1 percent of U.S. residents held 21 percent of all income in 2005, while the bottom 50 percent of income earners received just 12.8 percent. The trends associated with wealth inequality (i.e., property, stocks, and bonds) are even more dramatic. For example, the top 1 percent of income earners in the United States owns 35 percent of the wealth and the bottom 40 percent of income earners owns less than 1 percent. As of 2007, the top 20 percent of income earners in our society controls 85 percent of the wealth. In other words, just 20 percent of the people own a remarkable 85 percent of the nation's wealth, leaving only 15 percent of the wealth for the bottom 80 percent.[46] What is interesting is how tensions over these class inequalities gain expression through racist and nativist language and politics directed at immigrant workers, who actually receive even lower wages than the average Anglo or other citizens. Moreover, wage levels fell and income inequality grew as a result of de-industrialization, capital flight, economic restructuring, and the dismantling of labor unions in the 1970s and —all of which occurred *before* the current influx of immigrants into Colorado.[47] Immigrants, however, remain easy targets during these unsettling times, and the argument that they represent an economic threat seems intractable despite these historical dynamics.

The claim that immigrants are an environmental hazard is equally problematic and disturbing in its implications. We asked Felicia Trevor what she thought was driving elected officials and environmentalists in Aspen to link immigration and ecological harm. She spoke frankly:

> Racism plain and simple. I mean, we went to the conference that they did on the myths of sustainable growth, and finally somebody actually said it, they put this chart up and they said "if we don't curb immigration by 2050, our population is going to be one-quarter white. We'll be the minority." So they actually said it and I was going to ask "so then next will you have laws about interracial marriage to make sure that you keep the population white or what?" As far as I'm concerned, that's totally where it's based.[48]

The environmental and racial privileges on display in Aspen are also rooted in environmental injustices that occur *elsewhere*. That is, the market forces that give rise to the wealth controlled by Aspenites produce social and ecological violence in communities of color and working-class neighborhoods in other locations. Noting that coal-fired plants are disproportionately located in communities of color and poor communities, Felicia Trevor expresses the irony of Aspen's environmental privilege:

> [H]ow much energy and BTUs are we burning to keep their driveways from frosting over? And then they talk about immigrants degrading the environment. How many hours does a coal plant have to run so that their driveway keeps the snow melted?[49]

Despite all of the critiques of nativist environmentalism, Jessica Dove points out, however, that undocumented immigration does have impacts. It is not as if the population of a town, state, or nation can increase by millions of persons without effect. Dove is particularly concerned about the social impacts:

> [S]trains on the educational, medical, and law enforcement systems are the ones most apparent to me. And I think these impacts need to be addressed thoughtfully. What do you do with a classroom of kids where half don't speak English, and the teacher is undersupported and underpaid? What do you do when families are not eligible for medical insurance and people aren't receiving the medical care they need? What do you do when people are afraid to report crimes because they don't want to interface with the "authorities"? And what do you do when lots of drivers are unregistered and driving without insurance? All of these situations impact not just the undocumented immigrants but the greater community as a whole. I think that the scapegoating of "illegal" immigrants for these impacts only distracts and confuses us, making it harder to really think about and find solutions.[50]

Dove maintains that there are responsibilities and obligations that citizens and governments must meet to address the needs of newcomers. Her analysis suggests that we might shift resources toward greater emphasis

on social welfare on the domestic stage. This would require a major transformation of the current policy orientation in the United States, given that
more than 50 percent of its federal discretionary budget goes to military
operations.[51]

The Ambivalent Role of Employers

Roaring Fork Valley employers, temporary services, resort owners, and
business groups frequently advocate immigration reform (increases, not
restrictions) so that they can meet the growth and labor demands of
Colorado's tourist economy. While this hardly constitutes advocacy in the
progressive sense, they do share common ground with social justice advocates on this point. They are *immigration* advocates, not necessarily immigrant *rights* advocates.

Amy McTernan, the manager of a temporary employment service in Aspen, spoke vehemently and openly about her views on immigrant workers:

> [T]his is a temporary labor company and we put people in temporary
> jobs. We're not an immigrant service. I have very high respect for the
> men who work for me. They take care of wives and children, and you
> know what? They pay taxes. I take taxes out of their checks, you know?
> So I don't understand what the big whoop is. And everybody deserves
> the same chance if they're willing to work for it. You know? I don't care
> what color they are, what language they speak.[52]

Actions by business leaders in support of immigration often carry great
weight. Scott Chaplin remarked, "Luckily, for the wrong reasons, a lot of
the business community—the landscaping community, golf course community, and hotel community, the people who really depend on these
workers, right or wrong, because they need the cheap labor. So they're
combating it [immigration restrictions] more than we could ever."[53] The
Stepstone Center and resort business leaders are an unlikely alliance, but
they have this one thing in common.

The Rural Resort Region, a multicounty business association, held
a conference in September 2001 titled, "The Immigrant Workforce . . .

Opportunity, Pain and Profit in Paradise: An Exploration of Issues Surrounding Foreign Workers in Colorado's Premier Resort Areas." The RRR, made up of commissioners from Eagle, Garfield, Lake, Pitkin, and Summit counties, had planned to lobby the U.S. Congress to relax laws on immigration so that they could meet the needs of their resorts, which were projected to be 63,000 workers short in a few years. The RRR sought to push Congress to go beyond the H1-B visa and other related foreign worker categories and allow for more workers to gain documentation without being tied to particular employers. The RRR contended that "documented foreign workers with full rights and responsibilities under U.S. labor laws will not only pay taxes to support the community services they use, but will be less susceptible to employer abuse and more likely to participate in the affairs of the communities in which they live."[54] The RRR representatives visited the White House to lobby for a new class of visas that would allow foreign nationals to live and work in the United States for up to three years. Members of the Bush administration reportedly were inclined to consider these proposals. That was before September 11, 2001.

The RRR conference was scheduled to take place less than two weeks after the attacks of September 11, 2001. The attacks that day in Washington, DC, New York, and Pennsylvania quickly set off a spike in nativist sentiment throughout the country. Reactionary response in Colorado was predictable, given the state's long history of nativism. Always reliable, Mike McGarry stepped into the fray, denouncing the RRR for undermining Colorado's culture and economy. But this time, he took the brash and creative step of addressing the Mexican government because a representative of the Mexican Consul General in Denver was planning on attending the RRR conference. McGarry wrote a letter to the Consul that stated:

> Dear Madam Consul . . . It has come to my attention you will be appearing in Snowmass, Colorado, on September 20–21 at the invitation of the Rural Resort Region. I ask you to reconsider doing that. The U.S. is in a national emergency because of the murderous destruction illegal aliens from the Middle East perpetrated on the thousands of innocent people. Your coming to Snowmass at this time to a forum designed to encourage the "normalization" of illegal aliens and by implication, the encouragement of further illegal immigration could be seen by many here as indelicate at best, but more likely as grossly inappropriate. The choice is yours,

of course, but if you do decide to attend the meeting—a meeting which I and others believe in violation of Colorado law—you should know you will be asked some very challenging questions, questions you will not be able to dismiss with rhetorical slights[*sic*]-of-hand, platitudes or clichés.[55]

McGarry's letter created a minor international incident when the Mexican General Consul Leticia Gomez had authorities check into his past to assure the Consul that he was no security threat.[56] McGarry and Aspen councilman Terry Paulsen tried to secure a legal injunction against the RRR to prevent them from holding the meeting, but they were denied. Ultimately, however, the "War on Terror" drowned out any possibility of discussion of immigration and the economy, and the RRR tabled its campaign for immigration reform.[57] Even so, it is important to acknowledge the complexities of immigration and environmental politics, which are evident in the efforts of area employers to recruit immigrant labor to a town whose city council has rejected the idea.

Law Enforcement and Advocacy

Depending on whom you ask, Marie Munday is either a saint or a handmaiden to all that is evil and contemptuous in Aspen. She is that city's Anglo-Latino liaison at the police department. Munday is a veteran of the police force, and her current job is to facilitate a more cooperative relationship between the sheriff's office and the immigrant communities in the areas surrounding the city. "110 percent of my time is spent with the Latino community. And a lot of that is outreach. I go to their English classes at night once a quarter and talk to them about legal rights and responsibilities."[58] She is bilingual, having studied Spanish in Sevilla and Mexico City while she was enrolled at the State University of New York. Like many transplants to the Roaring Fork Valley, Munday came to the area for recreation and soon decided she loved the place and stayed: "In 1979 I moved here to play, to learn how to ski after grad school, and was general manager of a radio station here." She remembers when "there were about five Latinos in the valley" and estimates that there are upwards of twenty thouisand today. She is outspoken about the nativism and racism that emerged in response to that population shift:

It's sad because . . . Aspen was known as being open to the whole world and so liberal and lenient. It's amazing to hear educated—what we always thought were decent people—speaking out like this. And of course they always use excuses. Like ex-Governor Dick Lamm. And it's always a green thing that they're hiding behind. They're saying "it's just the environment, it's overpopulation, it's not just because they have dark skin or they speak funny. It's because we can't have more people coming into the state or into our valley." And I don't buy that, because when you really get 'em hot, the statements will come out about "those people" and it's pretty obvious that it has nothing to do with polluting our rivers or overpopulating the area. So why don't they go after the wealthy homeowners that have these huge estates with servants and they're not even here half the year? What depletes our resources more, you know? It doesn't fit, what they're saying.[59]

Mike McGarry, Terry Paulsen, and other nativists have attacked Munday in public fora and in the newspapers. Munday told us "Mike McGarry slams me in the papers every chance he gets, and he's written letters to the editor saying that I should be fired for working with 'illegals', and a few people have done that over the years." But when she's not waging a war of words on the editorial page on a day-to-day basis,[60] Munday works as an advocate for immigrant communities:

A lot of times it's civil stuff. A lot of times it's about an employer that didn't pay. "I quit" and now he says "you can't get your last paycheck. I know you're here illegally so there's nothing you can do about it." So I often make a phone call and say "do you know that you can be fined for hiring someone you know was undocumented? And did you know that state labor law says if you hired them you have to pay them?" A lot of times it just takes that phone call and they'll say "it was just a misunderstanding or a language barrier. Tell him his paycheck's ready."[61]

Munday has a rock-solid reputation in the valley's Latino community. Every immigrant resident we met who knew her offered praises and had stories about selfless deeds she had performed. Munday explains how she earned this respect:

I love the immigrant community. They are—for the most part—the hardest-working people I've ever seen. When I go to classes I tell them "if you screw up and break the law, I'll probably be the one arresting you, but I'll treat you with dignity and respect.". . . If I hear that somebody didn't show up to traffic court, I'll call them directly and figure out a way to keep them out of jail and to avoid the $300 fine and get them right on the docket. Gringos don't do that. They'll embarrass a guy right in front of his family, which is the worst thing for Latinos, to lose face. So they trust me. I like to break the ice and say, "It's not like you killed somebody! It's just a traffic violation!"[62]

But she is more than just an officer of the law. Munday works directly with all the immigrant rights groups in the valley. "I'm going to be on a panel with Peter Jessup of Catholic Charities. I've worked with Stepstone for years, I've been on committees with them. We all work together."

Munday also puts in a great deal of time training other police officers to achieve a deeper understanding of issues facing the valley's immigrant communities. She recounted an experience during which she was giving a presentation at the police academy. She remembered, "I was in the middle of the presentation and talking about the minimum wage and argued 'who wouldn't move to a foreign country to feed their families?' You see a lot of lights go on and people getting won over little by little." However, some officers at the class session expressed concerns that undocumented immigrants were prone to lethal violence:

> One female officer said "well, do you know that the people who live on the border now have to arm themselves because the immigrants coming over are armed and they're [Anglos] fearing for their lives?" And I said, "No, actually it started the opposite way, the immigrants started arming themselves because of the vigilantes that were out there for sport, pickin' them off." And three slides later I have a picture of a guy who was lynched, it shows the body with the mark around his neck and it says "lynching victim," and she said "OK," so it was perfect timing! But that's the propaganda that's out there and it's hard to fight.[63]

Munday's story is remarkable because she is the exception to the rule. Immigrants feel routinely harassed and profiled by law enforcement in the valley, and she works to bring both communities to a place of mutual respect. Aside from local law enforcement units like Munday's, there has been a strong presence of federal immigration agencies in the area. Recently, that presence—and local perceptions of the actions—of federal agencies created significant social impacts in the valley.

The INS Showdown

In the fall of 1999, the Immigration and Naturalization Service (INS, now ICE) announced that it would locate what it called a "Quick Response Team" center in Glenwood Springs, right in the middle of the Roaring Fork Valley.[64] The center would be a site where "criminal aliens" would be held for twenty-four hours before being transferred to a detention center in Denver, where they would await official actions that would result either in their release or deportation. This move came in response to (1) continuous reports of undocumented persons living, working, and traveling through the I-70 corridor that links the Roaring Fork Valley with much of the Rocky Mountain region; (2) a congressional assessment that the INS had not been achieving its goals with regard to stemming the flow of undocumented immigration; and (3) a new law that provided the INS with additional operational resources.

Local law enforcement officials had complained that the understaffing of INS offices created a burden for police who regularly encounter vanloads of undocumented persons traveling on Colorado highways but have little capacity to apprehend and detain them. Congress then passed legislation that funded forty-five new facilities around the nation, five of which would be located in Colorado (at a cost of $21 million for Colorado's expansion alone). Colorado congressman Scott McInnis (R-Grand Junction) and Senator Ben Nighthorse Campbell (R-CO) both supported the legislation. In addition to adding five new offices in Colorado, the INS doubled its staff to meet the goals outlined by Congress, and the Glenwood Springs facility was an important part of that plan.[65] Many local law enforcement authorities greeted these developments with open arms. Terry Wilson, a Roaring Fork Valley area police chief, pledged to work with the INS and praised their greater capacity for surveillance and monitoring "criminal aliens" with the agency's state of the art computer systems. He stated admiringly, "Big Brother has a lot of computer databases out there."[66]

Historically, concerns regarding "criminal aliens" have ever been present in the United States. One of the earliest laws passed in this country was the Naturalization Act of 1790. This law—passed by the U.S. Congress the year after the Bill of Rights was signed—limited citizenship to "free white persons." Later amended to include African Americans (in 1870), after Emancipation, the law was used repeatedly to exclude Asians, who were barred from citizenship under later legislation based on this precedent. From the beginning, citizenship was defined and marked by race, not just national origin. In 1798 Congress passed the Alien and Sedition Acts, which gave the president new powers to censor the activities and speech of foreign nationals and to deport them if they were deemed a threat to national security (at the time, it was feared that radical sympathizers with the French Revolution would stir up dissent within the United States).

Finally, at the turn of the twentieth century, the U.S. Border Patrol was in formation, in large part to control Chinese immigration across the U.S.–Mexico border. The 1882 Chinese Exclusion Act was the first law to regulate who could enter the country based on race and became the cornerstone of the unfolding national body of law on immigration. The forces that gave birth to this immense agency, which we now associate mainly with the control of the flow of Mexicans and other Latin Americans to the States, were first set into motion to control Chinese immigration. The fear of an Asian ethnic invasion became the foundation of our current immigration legal framework and drove racial anxieties over threats to the cultural fabric of a white Anglo-Saxon dominant nation.[67] For more than two hundred years, the United States has formalized presidential and federal powers to monitor, control, repel, and expel foreigners for certain political activities or for being members of particular racial, ethnic, religious, gender, sexual, political, or national populations. Again, this was all before September 11, 2001.

Then, in the wake of the attacks of 9/11, on March 1, 2003, the functions of several border and security agencies, including the U.S. Customs Service, the Federal Protective Service (FPS), and former Immigration and Naturalization Service (INS) were transferred into the Directorate of Border and Transportation Security within the Department of Homeland Security. As part of this transition, these agency functions were reorganized into the Bureau of Immigration and Customs Enforcement (ICE), whose mission became to link the enforcement and investigation branches of the Customs Service, of the former INS, and the FPS.

This integration of powers was intended to enhance information sharing among federal agencies and facilitate more cohesive enforcement of immigration laws.

From this legacy, the "criminal alien" is derived. The U.S. federal government defines a "criminal alien" as a person who is a noncitizen convicted of crimes while in this country legally or illegally.[68] Documented foreign nationals and legal residents of this nation can be defined as a "criminal alien" if convicted of a crime. Clearly the terms "criminal alien" and "illegal alien" are pregnant with explosive symbolism. They blatantly combine and draw on every negative stereotype and hot-button image associated with immigration; they dehumanize immigrants while avoiding crucial questions about why they might be in a new country, who is benefiting from their labor, what kinds of conditions they live and work under, what rights they are entitled to, and what their contributions to society may be. The terms eviscerate all of that in just two words. The political linguists George Lakoff and Sam Ferguson write:

> "Illegal," used as an adjective in "illegal immigrants" and "illegal aliens," or simply as a noun in "illegals" defines the immigrants as criminals, as if they were inherently bad people. In conservative doctrine, those who break laws must be punished—or all law and order will break down. Failure to punish is immoral. "Illegal alien" not only stresses criminality, but stresses otherness. As we are a nation of immigrants, we can at least empathize with immigrants, illegal or not. "Aliens," in popular culture suggests nonhuman beings invading from outer space—completely foreign, not one of us, intent on taking over our land and our way of life by gradually insinuating themselves among us.[69]

Consequently, this is not simply rhetoric. These words have enormous cultural, ideological, and political power. They are also solidified by federal governmental policies and practices. For example, ICE has a Criminal Alien Program (CAP) whose mission is to focus on "identifying criminal aliens who are incarcerated within federal, state and local facilities thereby ensuring that they are not released into the community by securing a final order of removal prior to the termination of their sentence."[70]

Mike Davis and Alessandra Moctezuma write about the "second border" as the mobile dragnet of state surveillance and detention practices directed at immigrants within the U.S. domestic interior.[71] Indeed, ICE's own language and practices support their thesis. Consider this statement from the federal government to the city of Glenwood Springs, concerning the application for a permit to build and locate the new ICE facility there: "Quick Response Team facilities are an integral component of the ICE *interior enforcement strategy*. They support this strategy nationwide by minimizing the impact of *criminal alien* and smuggling activity on local law enforcement and the communities they serve."[72]

The initial plan for locating the INS office in Glenwood Springs changed when it was decided that there was not enough space for a sally port for the intake of "a bus full of 'criminal aliens.'"[73] The INS estimated that between thirty-five thousand and forty-five thousand undocumented persons lived in the state, lending strong emotive support from many quarters for this project.[74] This may account for their surprise at the reception they received from local activists and community leaders when they tried to move the proposed facility to Carbondale.

The Community Responds

Throughout the Roaring Fork Valley and beyond, residents, activists, and others protested against the proposed INS facility. The editorial board of the *Denver Post* fired one of the first salvos. A mainstream-to-conservative paper, the *Post* voiced support for the cheap labor-hungry employers of the state's resort regions. They wrote:

> [T]his mandate, indeed all federal law governing immigration, conflicts sharply with our economic necessity. Ski resorts, agricultural areas, commercial kitchens and other businesses desperately need hard-working employees, and not enough US citizens are willing to take on these low-paying jobs. When federal agents and local cops swooped through Jackson, Wyo., in late 1996, they ousted 153 immigrants—marking numbers on their arms with felt-tip pens as if they were cattle and herding some into a horse trailer to haul them to jail. . . . Yet the INS in Colorado will crack down hard on these very workers, quite possibly smashing the viability of ski resorts, a key factor in our vibrant economy.[75]

This quote recalls our earlier discussion of the simultaneous economic dependence upon and social contempt for poor immigrant labor. We often defend immigration because it is economically profitable, not because immigrants are fellow human beings. Of course, not all immigrants experience social contempt. One news story on the Stepstone Center's response stated, "Felicia Trevor sees the INS move as a blatant act of racism. 'There are (Anglo) undocumenteds all over the valley. They won't get harassed.'"[76] Trevor gave voice to the frustration over the double standard that allows white Australians and European immigrants into the valley to live and work unmolested, even though many may overstay their visas.

The Stepstone Center and Latinos Unidos soon organized a petition drive and a public campaign around the proposed INS facility, and they held a town hall meeting on the issue. At that forum, one Latino resident stated her fears of deportation and the need for organizing: "If one member of my family has to leave, the whole family will have to leave, and we've been here a long time. . . . If we don't get involved, we might as well start packing up now."[77]

Since Carbondale was the site of the facility proposal, activists decided to stage a major public protest march in town in early November 1999. Hundreds of people descended on Carbondale for several hours of marching and speeches at a rally. One of the protesters was Sister Maria José, of St. Vincent's Catholic Church in Basalt and St. Mary of the Crown Catholic Church in Carbondale. She carried a framed likeness of Our Lady of Guadalupe, one of the most potent symbols of Catholicism in Mexico. She declared, "I am here to support the Hispanic community and Our Lady of Guadalupe . . . is always there to walk with the needy, those people who are suffering. . . . She is the patron of Mexico, and I believe she will help us not have immigration offices here in Carbondale."[78] Other participants carried colorful signs emblazoned with messages organized around the same theme. The following is a sampling of those placards: "*Permite vivir en paz* (Let us live in peace)"; "*Respeto a los derechos humanos* (Respect human rights)"; "There goes the neighborhood"; "We want the Latinos to stay, the INS should go";[79] "Deport the INS"; and "Aliens=people."[80] A significant percentage of marchers were Anglos demonstrating their solidarity with Latino immigrant communities in the valley. But not all Carbondale residents shared these sentiments. Vicky Johnson, a local resident, told a reporter, "I don't know much about what's going on, but I wouldn't mind if all of them would go back home."[81]

In addition to public actions like this, Latinos Unidos and the Stepstone Center eventually adopted a triple-pronged approach to fighting the INS facility proposed for Carbondale. One component was to frame the concern as one of a jail being located in a quiet neighborhood and how that would be hazardous because of the risk to public safety associated with criminals being held there. Of course, that framing explicitly accepted the INS's own labeling of immigrants as criminals. Another frame was that the danger the public building posed to the community constituted a "taking" of property owners' rights under the U.S. Constitution—a classic conservative populist argument. And still a third frame, built on a more critical social justice perspective, argued against the broader ripple effects of such a facility's presence—that it would instill fear, terror, and lend itself to racial profiling of Latinos, whether documented or not. Felicia Trevor, as a resident of Carbondale, filed an appeal of the building permit issued for the facility. Her letter read: "One of the primary uses of this facility would be as a detention point for dangerous criminals, and the building would become a staging point for detaining and transporting these criminals. . . . This will present a danger to many Carbondale residents, both in the kinds of persons that will be processed, as well as the danger of this office becoming a target from those outside." The letter also stated,

> There is a highly populated residential neighborhood surrounding the site, and property owners in this area have not been provided adequate notice that this "public building" would include a secure facility designed to harbor federal criminals. Permitting occupation of the site by the QRT [Quick Response Team] is an unjustified taking of these property owners' rights to quiet enjoyment of their homes in safety, and a violation of the residents' constitutional rights.[82]

Trevor and the Roaring Fork Legal Services director Kathy Goudy appeared before the town board to express their concern that the presence of the INS facility would lead to more harassment of Latinos, causing many to leave the area. Activists deliberately combined these three seemingly contradictory frames to gain the widest possible support for opposition efforts directed at the facility.

While the controversy continued in the Roaring Fork Valley, the other four proposed locations for new INS/ICE facilities in Colorado raised eyebrows as well. One of these facilities was slated to be built in Durango, Colorado, where a newly formed advocacy group emerged to challenge the INS's plans there. Olivia Lopez, an organizer with Compañero Latino in Durango, stated that she had collected more than four hundred names on a petition asking the INS to stay away.[83]

Back in Carbondale, Latinos Unidos, Asistencia Para Latinos, and the Stepstone Center got a boost when the Public Counsel of the Rockies joined them in their challenge to the INS facility. The PCR is a well-funded legal group, which up to that point focused on battling threats to ecological sustainability, but it deepened its analysis of the environmental problems facing the valley to support affordable housing and public transportation.[84] Eventually, in January 2000, the Carbondale Zoning Board of Adjustment voted to deny the INS its building permit.[85] Not simply savoring this victory, Latinos Unidos and Stepstone took proactive steps to propose new directions for the agency. In a letter to an area newspaper, they stated "We also believe the INS should restructure their present immigration procedures to include greater emphasis and resources on processing of immigration documents and the creation of temporary work visas, and to lessen the focus on the detention of undocumented workers."[86]

As a Basalt City Council member, Jonathan Fox-Rubin recalled this battle as a great moment when different racial and ethnic groups built solidarity and unity locally: "I think it was a major success of a couple of organizers who brought in some of the Anglos as allies on that. As you probably know, a lot of the undocumented Latinos are not in a position to fight."[87] Because of the past and continuing harms visited upon undocumented communities by the ICE, Scott Chaplin still becomes emotional when he talks about this case:

> Interstate 70 is a major corridor for people being shipped around the country, that's why the INS wanted a presence here. For them to put a detention center in Carbondale, we thought that would be very detrimental. A lot of us didn't like the INS tactics. They've done such horrific things in Colorado. Arresting people, taking off all their clothes down to their underwear and putting them into a hotel room, and that's a detention center. Taking their shoes so they can't run away. And they'd leave.

This was down in Durango. Somehow they [the detainees] wedged a window open and there were like fourteen Latinos running around in their underwear. This was about a year and a half ago. So that kind of cowboy treatment is pretty bad. A lot of times people call the police for help, the police show up and ask for an ID, and they don't have proper documentation and they get deported. This has happened with a domestic violence case or when a guy got his car stolen. I think we ought to be able to call the police without getting deported. Once Mexicans get arrested, they just kind of disappear. You don't hear about it.[88]

Unfortunately for immigrant residents and advocates, ICE eventually succeeded in building its detention facility in the valley, and, according to Marie Munday, that development has been accompanied by a rise in arrests and deportations. We asked Munday if her approach to advising valley immigrants has also been altered. She stated,

I used to say "Oh don't worry about Immigration, you only have a traffic ticket." But that's changed. If they're in Glenwood and have to go to court for some reason and Immigration's just around the corner, they could get scooped up down there. I used to say, "They're not lurking around every corner. You can live a semi-normal life here in Aspen if you're not committing crimes," but that's no longer true. If you happen to be in the wrong place at the wrong time. . . . If people go to visit someone in jail down in Glenwood Springs, if Immigration happens to be there, I've heard of people getting arrested. And that was very rare years ago but now it's better for them to just not go visit someone in jail if they don't have documents.[89]

Munday says she has a working relationship with ICE personnel in the valley. But she is also blunt about their intentions and approach: "They've made it clear to me that they really don't care if people are scared, they want people to be scared."

On the other hand, immigrant rights and social justice groups in the region have stepped up their efforts as well. Luis Polar told us about the formation of new organizations like the Colorado Immigrant Rights Coalition (CIRC) and Congregations and Schools Empowered (CASE), which have organized rallies around immigration reform and community building across divides of race and nationality in the valley:

So in the last few years we've been getting more groups that are *pro* immigrant, that are supporting immigrants. We know we're getting more immigrants coming to this valley, and so we are organizing people. You'd be really impressed to see what people have been doing with not much resources.[90]

Politics beyond Borders and Citizenship

It is not just the ardent, vicious, right-wing political forces that support nativist environmentalism; it is often the liberal, left-of-center folks who share these ideas as well. Consider the following words from two Aspen area environmentalists who consider themselves liberal on a range of issues:

[Liberal 1]: I think there are different cultural . . . sort of responses to the environment. I mean I know I've just witnessed certain times where I see Latino people throwing trash out the window or on the trails and things like that. And I talk to my friends who are from Mexico and they say "yeah that's just the way we do it." I mean, that is sort of more of a litter issue, but I think more people [coming] and again the development pressure, pressure on water and other resources and things like that. Ripple effects . . . and development to house people and then limited water. All throughout the west, rivers are down and we've just had drought for the last couple years.[91]

[Liberal 2]: There has been a huge amount of growth here. We're seeing probably not the best type of growth that we would like to see and that's a problem that all communities face. . . . So and of course, with the population expansion, we're getting more people here who don't have that type of appreciation for the environment. They're coming here for different reasons now. A lot of which are simply opportunities for jobs. They're not choosing this particular place because of the environment. I think there are—there's a segment of the population that's growing pretty rapidly that isn't here for that reason. And . . . whenever you have a shift in values, that's going to have an impact.[92]

Again, these two quotes come from liberal to progressive voices in the valley. The battle among liberals and progressives who maintain views consistent with nativism requires greater critique. There appear to be two paths in this immigration-environment debate in the Roaring Fork Valley and the United States in general. One path is to continue to pursue a nativist environmentalist agenda, which ultimately facilitates violence and exclusion not only in the name of selective entitlement but also in the service of racial and environmental privileges. Jessica Dove, the Anglo social services provider in Basalt, critiqued that path:

> In a way, the discourse surrounding undocumented immigrants and the environment has little to do with the immigrants themselves, and more to do with the perceptions and misperceptions of the white people engaged in the discourse. It's kind of like the excuses for racism in general. These excuses function to help white people "accept" the mistreatment of (and denial of access to resources to) the majority of the world's population. The excuses do not have a whole lot to do with people of color themselves, who are not, of course, the cause of racism, but merely its target.[93]

The other path is to challenge the social violence embodied in the way we use national borders. George Stranahan spoke to this possible direction:

> Well, I'm very much a "one world" person. It's a small enough world for us that we should feel like we're all in the same lifeboat. And it doesn't do any good to not give biscuits to half of the members and throw the other half into shark water. I say open the doors.[94]

It will be up to the Roaring Fork Valley community as a whole to make the choice as to which path it will chart. And, since virtually everyone in the valley is a newcomer ("transplant" is the term generally used for Anglo immigrants), a helpful way to move forward might be to develop a "framing of belonging" that does away entirely with the division between "immigrant" and "citizen." As Amy McTernan of the Aspen Temporary Labor Service told us, "the thing about Aspen is that nobody's really from here."

Conclusion

Dreams of Privilege/
Visions of Justice

'Nativist environmentalism' is clearly not a passing fad or a recent development in U.S. politics. It has much of its roots in the Western European concept of the "virgin land" or "empty land," born centuries ago. European explorers and colonizers judged themselves to be the rightful and dominant inhabitants of these lands; thus indigenous peoples would no longer enjoy that entitlement. This myth of the virgin land undergirds nativist environmentalism and facilitates the maintenance of environmental privilege in many settler-colonial societies like the United States, Canada, Australia, and New Zealand. That myth remains strong today and supports the broader ideological power of the Aspen Logic—the driving force behind mainstream environmental movements in the United States.

Within the Aspen Logic, environmentalism and capitalism work in concert, claiming that we can achieve ecological and social sustainability by supporting capitalism, not transforming or transcending it.[1] What this also means is that existing social hierarchies are, at root, not problematic; they only need be tapped, along with other resources such as innovative thinking and the kind of "breakthrough" entrepreneurial creativity that is popularly associated with free markets.[2]

'The Aspen Logic is dependent upon the continued practices of racism' and other forms of social domination but is resolutely blind to these realities. It is shrouded in the innocence of whiteness. This idea parallels, in many ways, the phenomenon of post-racialism. Unlike the United States of the pre–civil rights era, today public pronouncements, laws, and general mores in this nation disavow, deny, and condemn racism, offering a kindler, gentler social order of official racial equality. Never mind that this is contradicted by continued racist violence on the part of states, institutions, and individuals domestically and abroad (through the prison industrial complex, education, health care, labor markets, and U.S. foreign policy, for example). But it is precisely the words and promises of equality that make this country's post-racial paradigm parallel—and a core part of—the Aspen Logic.

Consider many of the nativist environmentalists in the Roaring Fork Valley who go to great pains to declare themselves "not racist," all the while writing open letters calling for public policies that are indeed thoroughly racist. The idea is to change the veneer, the message, or the façade of the machine, while further fueling its functions. The Aspen Logic is simultaneously a project of racial domination and one that refuses to see the world it produces and does great harm to. Post-racialism is an idea that entices many of us, as Lani Guinier and Gerald Torres write:

> [C]olorblindness disables the individual from understanding or fully appreciating the structural nature of inequality . . . it disables groups from forming to challenge that inequality through a political process . . . [it] is a deterrent to collective political action . . . such an ideological approach guards oligarchies from moral reproach and promotes a popular disengagement from politics . . . .the colorblindness attack has destabilized the movement for transformative social change within communities of color as well.[3]

The Aspen Logic is also implicated in persistent gender inequalities across societies. The Native American Studies scholar Andrea Smith makes profound connections among the domination of ecosystems, Native peoples, and gender politics as part of current-day colonialism. Smith explores the ways in which indigenous peoples and people of color experience sexual violence at the hands of states and corporations that harm their communities while enriching other communities (through environmental racism and land theft, for example). In other words, Smith uses the concept of sexual violence in both a literal and metaphorical sense, to underscore that many communities have experienced a process in which resources were taken without permission and in which land and bodies were violated without consent.[4] This is a fundamental part of the Aspen Logic and environmental privilege because they thrive on social and ecological domination. Not only is the Aspen Logic blind to its race and gender effects, it does not allow for the acknowledgement of the capitalist engine it fuels and the path of devastation it leaves in its wake (thus it is purposely blind to class dynamics as well). James Gustave Speth's book *The Bridge at the Edge of the World* speaks directly to the Aspen Logic.[5] Speth, an environmental studies scholar, argues that capitalism as we know it is incompatible with ecological sustainability, social justice, and democracy. The Aspen Logic seems to be oblivious to this reasoning. Speth also finds that U.S. environmental movements possess a number of shortcomings, most of which revolve around their ultimate acceptance of the inequalities capitalism produces as a matter of course. Ultimately, Speth concludes that markets *can* be made to work, if the system itself is transformed in ways that value both human beings and ecosystems. Whether that would constitute a new kind of capitalism or something different altogether remains to be seen.

On the contrary, in *The Enemy of Nature*, the philosopher Joel Kovel unabashedly contends that capitalism must die so that humankind and the planet we inhabit may live. He asks, "where is the serious, systematic reflection of the brutal truth—that humanity is in the hands of a suicidal regime?"[6] Kovel likens capitalism to "a trusted and admired guardian . . . who . . . is in actuality a cold-blooded killer who has to be put down if one is to survive."[7] He writes, "Capital's combined ecodestructivity and incorrigibility forces open the prospect of a total revolution."[8] Like other progressive scholars of ecological and social crises, Kovel also argues that a societal transformation beyond capital must embrace a feminist orientation (specifically ecofeminism) that recognizes how capitalism thrives off of hegemonies of humans over ecosystems, Europeans over people of color, the rich over the poor, men over women, citizens over noncitizens, and heterosexuals over gays/lesbians/bisexuals/transgendered/queer communities. Without integrating these systems of inequality into our analyses of the problem, we will fall short.

The Aspen Logic is fundamentally a neoliberal idea with a message of hope and redemption, but without a change in policy direction. The following quote from the World Resources Institute's *Guide to the Global Environment* captures the Aspen Logic that dominates U.S. environmentalism:

Energy conservation was once unfairly linked to the need for drastic cutbacks in living standards. Although some changes in human behavior are clearly appropriate, conservation efforts are now strongly focused on introducing new technologies for producing and using energy more efficiently and on improving energy management. By increasing energy efficiency, demand can be reduced without adversely affecting personal lifestyles or a country's economic growth. In fact, increasing energy efficiency can even enhance them.[9]

According to the sociologist Michael Goldman, for "Global Resource Managers [like the World Resources Institute] 'sustainable development' is just another way of saying that world economic growth rates can be sustained without destroying the earth."[10] This is nothing new. In fact, the early twentieth-century precursor to the "sustainable development" discourse and policy framework (dominant since the late 1980s) was termed "sustained yield." The idea was that the U.S. federal government might serve as a steward to the nation's ecological wealth in a way that does not exhaust it, while at the same time wholeheartedly supporting capitalism.[11] The term "sustained yield" remains in wide use today among foresters. Sustainable development and sustained yield are concepts that speak to the Aspen Logic's ability to incorporate and co-opt genuine concerns about *un*sustainability into a language of sustainability. Allan Schnaiberg's "Treadmill of Production" sociology thesis captured this dynamic years ago when he argued that national and global political-economic power structures will attempt to solve social and ecological crises by simply speeding up or reinforcing the system itself.[12]

James Speth writes, "today's environmentalism believes that problems can be solved at acceptable economic costs—and often with net 'economic benefit—without significant lifestyle changes or threats to economic growth."[13] In other words, the cure for the ills of capitalism is more capitalism. We must also note that many socialist societies have produced their fair share of social inequalities and ecological devastation, so this is not a feature that is exclusive to capitalist economies. Any system of governance that produces violence against people and ecosystems is a part of the problem.

Many leaders in environmental organizations believed that the 1992 Earth Summit in Rio de Janeiro would catapult the world community toward a consensus and action plan around global sustainability. Unfortunately, among other things, the summit's "effect has not been to stop destructive practices but to normalize and further institutionalize them."[14] What has become clear is that Garrett Hardin's 1968 "Tragedy of the Commons" thesis—despite being challenged thoroughly by numerous scholars over the years—has served as a guide for global ecological management within the United Nations, global corporations, and nation-states. Hardin's thesis that individuals will overconsume resources within common spaces has taken hold at the highest levels. Generally speaking, as global capitalism has gained in strength and force since World War II, the privatization of the commons has occurred at a parallel rate. People fighting for open space in urban parks, for rights to grazing lands, for the right to live on ancestral forest lands, and for public airwaves and the digital spectrum are facing an uphill battle because capitalism views these spaces as potential profit sources, indeed, as sites of future enclosures.

But they also face a difficult road because of the strength of nativist environmentalism. So in Aspen and other places around the world, people who construct themselves as the rightful inhabitants or owners of ecological systems and resources exclude others from gaining access to those spaces. What this practice also does is to naturalize the idea of nation. That is, some people "naturally" belong, are naturally a part of this nation, while others naturally do *not* belong. The idea of "carrying capacity" makes this plain and simple in the most basic biological terms. This is a new twist on the "old" racism associated with biological differences; it just comes wrapped in a green package. And while racism always hurts those who suffer its indignities, it also works in the service of privilege.

White Privilege and Environmental Privilege

In his powerful book *The Possessive Investment in Whiteness*, George Lipsitz denotes how whites value and invest in whiteness "to remain true to an identity that provides them with resources, power, and opportunity."[15] We see this in housing, education, banking, environmental protection, voting, health care, and virtually any other space of social interaction. There is a payoff for being white. The transportation infrastructure of the United States is a classic example of white privilege in action. The interstate highway system provides suburban white communities access to resources while locking inner-city communities into local dead-end labor markets, crumbling school systems, and contaminated industrial spaces. The construction of interstate highways is also reflective of this process by repeatedly being directed *through* neighborhoods of color, destroying and displacing African American communities like Rondo in St. Paul, the Chicano communities of Sal Si Puedes in San Jose and Barrio Logan in San Diego, and the Coldwater Springs area of Minneapolis, a site viewed as sacred to the Lakota and Dakota nations. The result is the preservation and maintenance of white communities and the identity of whiteness.

Environmental racism and environmental privilege are often part of the problem of white privilege. The possessive investment in whiteness drives white communities to maintain the social, economic, political, and environmental privileges they have secured through histories of dominance over other groups. But since there are many nonwhite communities around the globe that enjoy environmental privilege, white privilege is not always at the root, but some combination of racial, class, political, and cultural privilege is always at work in this process.

The ultimate difficulty with social privilege of any variety is that it is often unrecognized and unmarked. Privilege is the experience of being a part of a social group that benefits from inequality—and rarely having to account for it—because privilege is socially invisible.[16] That invisibility is what makes privilege so difficult to challenge, and this is especially so with regard to environmental politics. When a tourist stands at the head of a ski run in Aspen, they rarely consider the labor of all of the people from around the world who make their leisure possible. Nor do they consider the ecological costs involved in maintaining their "get away" in the mountains. And as they stare at the sunset or dip their toes into the Roaring Fork River, they can easily fool themselves into thinking that such simple pleasures are a universal part of life, available to everyone.

The Price of Privilege

Contrary to what one might believe upon first consideration, people with social privilege have paid a heavy price for their position and participation in the systems of power that maintain their dominance. Much of the scholarship on the costs of racial privilege focuses on the harm that white supremacy visits upon the white working class. The sociologist Joe Feagin and his colleagues argue that since the nineteenth century, the white working class in the United States has failed to prioritize the struggle against their own exploitation by capitalists and, instead, focused much of its energy on securing and maintaining privileges for white communities. This has resulted in enormous lost opportunities for collaboration and unity with working-class communities of color, therefore reducing the economic and political power of all working-class people in the United States.[17] No less disturbing is W. E. B. DuBois's conclusion in *Black Reconstruction in America* that both black and white workers' inability to stand together against the white propertied class during the Reconstruction era revealed the persistent power of white capitalist supremacy and ushered in the failure of democracy in the United States at a time when there was a real opportunity to secure a democratic system for all.[18] Thus the thirst for white privilege has undermined the very basis of democracy.

If the future of democracy is at stake, then clearly the problem of white privilege impacts whites at the bottom and at the top of the social structure. But those at the top seem increasingly impervious to the realities of racial and environmental injustice, precisely because their privileges have distanced them from these experiences and, because to seriously address these injustices they would necessarily have to give up those privileges. The environmental journalist Hervé Kempf believes that this creates an indifference to injustice that will eventually harm all of humanity. He writes that elites are "[b]lind to the explosive power of manifest injustice. And blind to the poisoning of the biosphere that the increase in material wealth produces, poisoning that means deterioration in the conditions for human life and the squandering of the chances of generations to come."[19] After all, ultimately everyone will pay the price of climate change; it may just take a little longer for the rich to feel to pain. But the blindness of power is a disease that is difficult to cure.

The anti-racist activist and author Tim Wise inveighs against social privileges associated with white racism. He contends that privilege is dysfunctional because it feeds a collective narcissism, abuses of power, a sense of self-righteousness, and mythologies of invincibility, which are unfounded and unsustainable. He writes "if we are going to truthfully analyze what is wrong with our culture . . . we should begin with the folks at the top, not the bottom, for as the old saying goes, the fish tends to rot from the head down."[20] We argue the same with regard to environmental privilege. Environmental racism and injustice are facts of life in many communities. The social distance between environmentally privileged communities and those communities suffering from environmental injustice reinforces the problem and feeds into the blindness to the ultimate outcome for all of us.

Many elites believe that they can shield themselves against the effects of the ecological and social violence they produce and profit from. No one is exempt from ecological harm, even those who live in the cocoon of environmentally privileged spaces. This is what Guinier and Torres call the problem and opportunity of the "miner's canary": that the conditions people of color suffer under racism are a warning sign that the general social atmosphere that we all must breathe is increasingly toxic and dangerous to all of us.[21] The blindness to the social and ecological violence that environmental privilege produces and rewards in the short term will be shattered by the scourges of climate disruption and the pollution of air, watersheds, and the soil we all depend upon.

Environmental privilege is made possible by and works in concert with white supremacy, racism, class domination, heteropatriarchy, capitalism, and the world's most unsustainable ecological practices. The illogic of environmental privilege is that it supports the very ideas and practices that produce ecological and social devastation, so it undermines itself in the long run. There is yet one more reason to harbor concern about this issue. On a philosophical level, Tim Wise urges us to consider that "ignoring the essential humanity of another living soul . . . does something to a person, and what it does is never a good thing."[22] When we enjoy privileges and benefits at someone else's expense—which is generally how social inequality works—we lose a bit of our humanity.

In their groundbreaking book *From the Ground Up*, Luke Cole and Sheila Foster, both environmental justice scholars, write about the need for "transformative politics" and how this phenomenon is already occurring within some social movement circles. Transformative politics occurs when individuals, communities, institutions, and national policies change dramatically in ways that produce new spaces for the imagination and creation of environmentally just realities. When a person evolves from being a bystander to a movement participant, or when an institution reprioritizes its energies to support the goals of social justice, or when a social movement experiences "fusion" with another movement to create a much more inclusive and powerful whole than the two parts, *this* is what is meant by transformative politics.[23] We could use a little transformative politics right now.

The pioneering journalist Bill Moyers writes that "America needs a different story" because so many people have been written out of the dominant national narrative that has been so full of half truths, omissions, and distortions.[24] Our new story must be one in which major differences in life chances (meaning the opportunities, living conditions, and life experiences that people have in common by virtue of belonging to a particular class), vast gulfs between the wealthy and the poor, and Gilded Ages must be confronted and disallowed. That new story can be written about environmental justice—where ecological sustainability and social justice meet.

Ending Nativist Environmentalism

Immigrants and social justice advocates in the Roaring Fork Valley have confronted nativist environmentalism locally. But they are just one node in a larger network of communities challenging this phenomenon. Since the mid-1990s, the San Francisco–based Political Ecology Group (PEG) has spearheaded what it calls the Immigration and Environment Campaign. The group started around the time the nativist Proposition 187 passed in California, and tackles several nativist environmentalist claims in its campaigns and writings. In one article they write:

> Overemphasizing the role of population growth in environmental problems ignores who has control of production and consumption decisions. Many of the causes of environmental decline in the U.S. have nothing to do with population growth or individual consumer choices. The military, the nation's largest single polluter, and corporations produce much more toxic wastes than households. Corporate advertising drives overconsumption and creates demand for new products that are often more environmentally destructive than old products. Sprawling suburbs, planned and built by developers, gobble up prime agricultural land and wildlife habitat. The public has little control over these decisions. Corporate lobbying

against regulations often undermines attempts to make companies clean up after themselves or make new developments more compact and efficient. Corporate actions also limit individual decisions for more sustainable lifestyles, such as taking mass transit instead of driving.[25]

PEG's Immigration and Environment Campaign position statement identifies seven strategies for movements to challenge nativist environmentalism. They include:

1. Creating alliances between environmental and immigrant rights movements to embrace an environmentally sustainable economy that works for all people
2. Working for immigrant rights, civil rights, and human rights
3. Combating environmental deregulation efforts by corporations and the federal government
4. Confronting nativist environmentalism and making more visible the contributions immigrants have made to this nation
5. Supporting policies that significantly lower U.S. consumption of global resources while encouraging the invention and application of ecologically sound technologies and practices
6. Ensuring that the state and corporations are accountable to public demands for environmental justice
7. Supporting universal and equal access to education, health care, and living wages.[26]

We observed and documented each of these objectives in the work and dreams articulated by activists and immigrant residents in the Roaring Fork Valley. They constitute a vision of a society where social and environmental justice, inclusivity, and democracy thrive.

Another organization doing work similar to PEG is the Committee on Women, Population and the Environment, a multiracial alliance of feminist community organizers, scholars, and health professionals working to realize a vision of global peace, environmental justice, economic sustainability, and women's empowerment. This group challenges ideologies of population control and nativism in the United States and in international politics. Both the PEG and the CWPE take credit for forcing the Sierra Club to take immigrant rights seriously in that organization's recent elections.

Penn Loh, the former executive director of the Boston-based environmental justice organization Alternatives for Community and Environment
(ACE), has been active in opposing nativist environmentalism as well. He
writes:

> Reducing immigration will not solve environmental problems, but will
> militarize borders, criminalize migrants, and increase the divide be-
> tween haves and have-nots. A true ecological approach, one that sees
> everything as connected to everything else, broadens environmental
> concerns to include human rights, health, and livelihood issues.[27]

Finally, one contributor to the main publication of the radical environmental movement EarthFirst! declares unconditional solidarity with immigrants and contends that national borders only serve to divide people
who should otherwise be working for environmental sustainability and
against capitalism:

> The U.S. Empire isn't falling because of any "invasion along the border."
> It's crumbling from being faced with its own greed, indifference and pre-
> cariously unsustainable industrial foundation. This machine is coming
> down, and it's our work to ensure that its fall is as ecological, liberat-
> ing and permanent as possible. Cross-border solidarity and anti-border
> struggle are a crucial part of that effort.[28]

When such radical environmentalists like this EarthFirster—who comes
from a movement that has traditionally been charged with not seeing the
people but seeing only the forests and the trees, a movement with deep
nativist roots—casts their lot with immigrants and the cause of anti-im-
perialism, this is significant. Unfortunately, precisely because EarthFirst! is
such a radical organization, it is viewed as a part of the political fringe and
therefore irrelevant or perhaps a threat to many of us who are pragmatists.

But perhaps it is high time for some outrageous and creative thinking
about our future. As James Speth bravely states on this subject, "if some
of these answers seem radical or far-fetched today, then I say wait until
tomorrow. Soon it will be abundantly clear that it is business as usual that
is utopian, whereas creating something very new and different is a practi-
cal necessity."[29] We look forward to a future in which people work to create

something as outrageous as social justice and ecological sustainability. A good place to start might be to name the social forces that obstruct this vision. Let us name these forces out loud. Let us look at ourselves honestly, question our own assumptions, and acknowledge the various forms of privilege so many of us take part in and benefit from. Let us listen to the voices that come from all corners of our communities, especially those that come from the innumerable "down valleys" all over America. Let us create a different story to live by.

NOTES ON OUR RESEARCH METHODS

This book is the result of research we conducted in Colorado's Roaring Fork Valley, primarily between 2000 and 2004, and in periodic subsequent visits through 2009. We began by conducting an archival search of the area's history to understand the roots of the contemporary conflicts over immigration and ecological sustainability. We focused on issues related to immigrant labor, environmental politics, race, and economic development. We examined a wide range of sources—government documents, scholarly books, personal letters, newspapers, and nongovernmental organizational reports—at the Aspen Historical Society, the Pitkin County Public Library, the Colorado Historical Society (Denver), the Denver Public Library, and the library at the University of Colorado–Boulder.

We conducted a series of research trips to Aspen and the Roaring Fork Valley region to interview key players in the local debate concerning immigration, labor, and environmental policy. We interviewed city council members, county commissioners, service industry employers, social service providers, housing advocates, local immigration attorneys, local and federal law enforcement and immigration control officials, school teachers, nonprofit immigrant advocacy organizations, ethnic media personnel, and most importantly Latino immigrant residents, workers, and their families. In face-to-face meetings and focus groups, we interviewed seventy people. In our references to these interviews, we used pseudonyms for those who requested anonymity.

In addition, we analyzed the contents of several local newspapers, including the *Aspen Times*, *Aspen Daily News*, *Glenwood Springs Post Independent*, *Valley Journal*, *Mountain Gazette*, *Carbondale Echo*, and the recently established Spanish-language paper, *La Misión* (now *La Unión*). We also scoured the pages of historical periodicals, including the *Rocky Mountain*

Sun and the *Aspen Democratic-Times* and the more contemporary *Aspen Magazine*. This range of research methods allowed us to approach this study from multiple vantage points, exploring differing points of view on the key themes examined herein.

NOTES

NOTES TO THE INTRODUCTION

1. Heiman 1999.

2. Aspen Chamber Resort Association, City and County Information. http://www.aspenchamber.org/htdocs/city.cfm, accessed March 18, 2002.

3. For an insightful study of social conflicts in wealthy tourist destinations, see Dolgon 2005.

4. Agyeman 2005; Bullard 2000; Cole and Foster 2001; Pellow 2002; Pellow and Park 2002; Sze 2007; and Williams 2005.

5. For research on extractive industries see Gedicks 2001 and Khagram 2004. For research on "natural disasters" see Boyce, Wright, Bullard, Pastor, Fothergill, and Morello-Frosch 2006; Bullard and Wright 2009; and Mileti 1999.

6. Bullard 2005; Clapp 2001; Hoerner and Robinson 2008; Pellow 2007.

7. Pellow and Park 2002.

8. Pellow 2002.

9. Bullard, Mohai, Saha, and Wright 2007; Faber and Krieg 2001; United Church of Christ 1987; Mohai and Saha 2007.

10. Agyeman, Cole, Haluza-DeLay, and O'Riley. 2009; Moore, Kosek, and Pandian 2003; Stein 2004; and Weaver 1996.

11. See Freudenburg 2005; Gould 2006; Lipsitz 2006; and Pulido 2000. See also Pellow 2009.

12. Millennium Ecosystem Assessment 2005, 19–20.

13. Kempf 2007, 25.

14. It is certainly not the case that one either is or is not environmentally privileged; there are gradations of privilege and disadvantage, and some people may experience privilege on one issue or axis and disadvantage on another (such as being a citizen of the United States but also being a person of color or working class). So this is a dynamic concept that can be applied across populations and life experiences.

15. Heiman 1999.

16. Hooper 1999.

17. Mutrie 2001. NumbersUSA is based in Washington, DC.

18. The resolution adds, "Fifty percent of our original wetlands have been drained to accommodate growth. Ninety-five percent of all U.S. old-growth forests have been destroyed. It is estimated that we have consumed approximately

three-fourths of all our recoverable petroleum, and we now import more than half of the oil we consume in the United States. America's underground aquifers are being drawn down 23 percent more than their natural rates of recharge."

19. Ibid.

20. Ibid.

21. Terry Paulson's opening statement, December 13, 1999, Aspen. Emphasis added.

22. For excellent historical data on nativist perceptions of immigrants as pollutants in the United States, see Washington 2005, 79. She also makes a similar argument for the way that many African American populations have been treated. See also Briggs and Mantini-Briggs 2004; Molina 2006; and Shah 2001. These important works also present evidence that various groups of marginalized "others" are viewed as public health and environmental threats, depending on the place and historical moment.

23. SPLC 2001.

24. Aztlán is the Aztec name that many Chicana/o activists have used to describe what is now the U.S. Southwest, which used to be northern Mexico before it was annexed by the United States. Aztlán became a powerful symbol of the historical presence that Chicanos have had in pre-Columbian North America.

25. Stiny 1999c.

26. A resolution of the Board of County Commissioners of Pitkin County, Colorado, Supporting Population Stabilization in the United States, March 22, 2000.

27. Ibid.

28. Ibid.

29. Smith 2005.

30. Chung 2000.

31. See the letter from the SouthWest Organizing Project (SWOP) to the "Group of Ten" national environmental organizations, written by environmental justice activists Pat Bryant and Richard Moore, February 21, 1990; see also Bullard 2000, and Nordhaus and Shellenberger 2007, for critiques of mainstream environmentalism's elitism.

32. For data on the ecological impacts of the California Gold Rush, see Pellow and Park 2002. For similar information on the rush in the Rockies, see chap. 2, this volume.

33. Davis 1999.

34. For example, White River, Yosemite, Yellowstone, Great Smoky Mountains, and Glacier National Parks. See Spence 1999.

35. Hartmann 2003.

36. See De Genova 2005; Higham 2002; and Jacobson 2008.

37. Lowe 1996.

34. Gutierrez 1995; Ngai 2004; and Roediger 2005.

39. See Pellow 2009.

40. Massey 2003.

41. Cornelius 2002; Kotlowitz 2009; and Harris 2009.

42. Ong 2006; and Sassen 1998.

43. Davis 2007.

44. Ibid.

45. Among the numerous anti-immigrant policies and laws in U.S. history are the Chinese Exclusion Acts, the Cable Act, the Page Act, the Alien Land Laws, the Asiatic Barred Zone, the Gentleman's Agreement, the Tydings-McDuffie Independence Act, and the Johnson-Reed/National Origins Act. In addition, there are numerous anti-immigrant Supreme Court, federal court, and district court rulings, the FBI, local police forces, the Texas Rangers, and countless nongovernmental organizations and social movements that have organized into militias, terrorist organizations, and political pressure groups to control, expel, or repel immigrants over the centuries. See Lowe 1996.

46. Sassen 1998.

47. California voters approved Proposition 187 in November 1994, during the same election when Republicans retook the U.S. Congress and launched the "Contract with America"—a massive series of policies designed to roll back progressive gains from the 1960s and 1970s. Proposition 187 would have banned access to public education, public social services, and nonemergency public health care for undocumented immigrants in California. Later ruled unconstitutional, the legislation was never implemented. Under the Immigration Reform and Control Act of 1986 and the 1996 Welfare and Immigration reforms, noncitizens became vulnerable to indefinite detention by federal authorities: they were denied access to judicial review of deportation orders and thus were no longer eligible for basic federal public benefit programs. In fact, the 1996 laws barred hundreds of thousands of *legal* immigrants (foreign nationals with authorization to be in the United States) from receiving food stamps and federal disability assistance.

48. The films *Falling Down* and *Menace II Society* are particularly troubling depictions of anti-immigrant sentiment. Challenges to these nativist images such as Morgan Spurlock's television show *Thirty Days* and the film *A Day Without a Mexican* have far less impact, judging by the small audiences they have reached. The "Right Wing Revolution" in the United States helped launch and sustained the prominence of nativist AM talk radio hosts and authors such as Rush Limbaugh, Don Imus, and Ann Coulter. One of the most popular shows on the Cable News Network (CNN) during the 2000s was *Lou Dobbs Tonight*, a major voice in the nativist movement (Dobbs moved from CNN to host a national radio show in 2009). Coupled with Glenn Beck's and Bill O'Reilly's shows on Fox TV, the nativist message enjoys prime time most nights each week.

49. SPLC 2007.

50. The term "War on Terror" was the hallmark of the George W. Bush regime. While the Obama administration has decided against using the phrase (and substituted the "War on al Qaeda" and other variations on this theme), many of the same features of the previous polices remained in place (Solomon 2009).

51. NAPALC 2001.

52. Takaki 1998.

53. Aoyagi-Stom 2008.

54. Wayne Cornelius, a political scientist at the University of California–San Diego, indicated that the recent spike in anti-immigrant sentiment is the eighth major wave of nativism in U.S. history (Cornelius 2006).

55. For a best-selling nativist tract that blames immigrant populations for ecological harms, see Brimelow 1995.

56. See Gottlieb 1993; Hunter 2000; Hurley 1995; Kong and Chiang 2001; and Ortiz-Garcia 2004. Ortiz-Garcia's report reveals that "35 percent of Hispanics live in areas that violate the federal air pollution standard for particulate matter, known commonly as soot, which causes premature death and other serious health effects. More than 19 million, or 50 percent of Hispanics, live in areas that violate the federal air pollution standard for ozone, one of the major triggers for asthma attacks. Thirty-nine percent of the Latino population lives within thirty miles of a power plant—the distance within which the maximum effects of fine particle soot from the smokestack plume are expected to occur." (3) The report also maintains that "Hispanics are regularly excluded from federal research activities and data collection efforts. The exclusion of Hispanics from these critical national data systems means that environmental health issues affecting Hispanics are going undocumented. Although many Latino communities are in close proximity to power plants, they have the least amount of representation with the health researchers who inform our nation's policymakers." (4). See also Pellow and Park 2002; and Perfecto and Velasquez 1992.

57. Sierra Club 2004. This report underscores the Sierra Club's dual pressures vis-à-vis Latino populations and immigration: there are many progressives within the organization who seek to build common cause with immigrants and Latinos while there remain members who view these populations as a threat to the ecological and cultural sustainability of the United States.

58. Heiman 1999.

59. Ibid.

60. Jacoby 2001.

61. See Balibar 1991; and Cornelius 2002.

62. Winant 2001, 35.

63. While many scholars use the terms "colorblind" and "post-racial" interchangeably, there are important differences. We often need reminding that throughout our history, race has rarely been exclusively defined by skin color

alone. Race in U.S. history has variously been defined by one or more of the following factors (among others): skin color, nationality, language, religion, politics,
culture, phenotype, blood quantum, class, gender, sexuality, space, place, surname,
fashion, cuisine, hair, and sound. There seems to be no end to and no consistency
in the ways in which race can be defined. So "*color*blindness" is not the only way
to conceive of a "post-racial" condition or practices.

64. Maldonado 2004.

65. It is not surprising that biological notions of population control continue
to arise in environmental and immigration debates. The language that environmental scientists use to describe the behavior of nonhuman species is powerful
and spills over into popular discourses. For example, "Invading alien species are
responsible for a worldwide biodiversity crisis, driving large numbers of native
plant and animal species to extinction on every continent. The damage is documented by IUCN—the World Conservation Union in a new survey of the 100 worst
alien species issued in time for Biodiversity Day, May 22." The Indian mynah bird,
the Asian long-horned beetle, the Asian tiger mosquito, and the yellow Himalayan
raspberry are all species that are "like unwanted house guests [because] they can
take over ecosystems to which they are alien species" (Environment News Service
2001). The similarities between the way that these animal and insect species and
human immigrants to the United States are described is striking.

66. Sibley 1997.

67. We are indebted to Juliana Smith for reminding us of the importance of
Reagan's campaign.

68. Sibley 1997, ix.

69. Ibid., xv.

70. Limerick 1987, 181.

71. Veblen 1994.

72. Chaplin 2000.

73. For book-length treatments of this topic, see Blum 2003; Johnson 2004ab;
and Kinzer 2007.

74. Taylor 2009, 117–21.

75. Dolgon 2005, 3.

76. AOL Travel website. http://travel.aol.com/travel-ideas/galleries/resort-
towns, accessed January 2010.

NOTES TO CHAPTER 1

1. Jesse Jackson once gave a speech in Aspen on the movement to empower
women, gays, and poor people, and raised thousands of dollars from a single event
(Conover 1991, 64). On the growing number of politicians raising funds in Aspen,

see Shaw 2004, 52. A recent feature story in *In Style Weddings Magazine* showcased Kevin Costner and his fiancée, Christine Baumgartner, planning a three-day wedding feast and party for five hundred guests on his 165-acre Aspen ranch (Schneller 2004).

2. Conover 1991, 9. This is not only pretentious but true to Aspen's bad case of Europhilia. Davos, Switzerland, is particularly appropriate as a sister city since it is the location of the annual World Economic Forum, the meeting of the heads of state and ministers of finance of the world's wealthiest nations, who come together to chart policymaking for the rest of the planet. Davos has, not surprisingly, been the location of some of the most spectacular global justice movement protests.

3. The average sale price of a single family home in Aspen in 2000 was $3.8 million. Aspen Chamber Resort Association. City and County Information. http://www.aspenchamber.org/htdocs/city.cfm, accessed March 18, 2002.

4. Paid advertisement in the *Aspen Times*, July 17–18, 2004. "Pay no Estate Tax." "I choose to leave all my assets to my family and favorite charities; not the IRS." "Many wealthy people have not done the necessary planning to keep the IRS from being a primary beneficiary of their estate." "Using a case study, this seminar will show you how to . . . pay no estate tax to the IRS." "Free Lecture. The Aspen Institute."

5. Aspen Music Festival and School. 2002. June 20–August 18 Season Calendar. Emphasis added. See www.aspenmusicfestival.com.

6. *Aspen Times*, January 6, 1977, "Aspen is a Fashion Show."

7. Clifford 1999, 33.

8. George Stranahan, interview by authors, Spring 2004.

9. Like many immigrant laborers, she follows the tourists. She works in Aspen during the summers and in Florida during the winters.

10. Bartender, interview by authors, Aspen, July 23, 2004.

11. *Aspen Times*, July 24–25, 2004, C19.

12. Ibid.

13. *Aspen Times*, August 4–5, 2001, C31.

14. *In Snowmass*, Summer 2004, 3B. Snowmass, CO.

15. McGovern 2006.

16. Hooper 2004b.

17. Ibid.

18. Rebecca Doane, city of Aspen's director of Human Resources, Aspen, interview by authors, Spring 2004.

19. Brady 2002.

20. Doane, interview.

21. Tony Hershey, city councilmember, interview by authors, Spring 2004.

22. Clifford 1999.

23. Stranahan interview.

24. U.S. Census Bureau. 2000. Aspen City. In 2000, 95 percent of the population of Aspen was white, followed by Mexicans at 4 percent. Carbondale's white population was 84 percent that year, with a 15 percent Mexican population (U.S. Census Bureau. 2000. Carbondale City). Glenwood Springs' white population in 2000 was 90 percent with a 10 percent Mexican population. (U.S. Census Bureau. 2000. Glenwood Springs City). Mexicans are the single largest Latino population by far, and all others plus African American and Asian Americans are statistically quite small.

25. Conover 1991, 239–40.

26. Johnson 2007.

27. Ibid.

28. Conover 1991, 245.

29. Harvey 2002.

30. Doane, interview.

31. The city of Aspen received an environmental award from the USEPA "that will make it the only municipality in the nation to be designated as one of the Best Workplaces for Commuters District." To qualify for the award, the city's employers must offer benefits to employees who commute, like showers, lockers, monthly transit passes, etc. (Hooper 2004a).

32. Author's interview with Ellen Friedman, executive director of the Aspen Valley Community Foundation, spring 2002. The AVCF was started by the Aspen Ski Company in 1980. According to Friedman, its mission is to support and strengthen nonprofits from Aspen to Parachute, to increase private giving, to promote philanthropy and volunteerism, and to identify and address human needs. Friedman recalled, "Last year we gave out about a million-and-a-half [dollars] in grants."

33. Conniff 2004.

34. McGovern 2004.

35. "In the Ski Area Citizen's Coalition annual report . . . Aspen Mountain and Buttermilk claimed top honors, scoring a grade of A, recording 93.9 points out of 100" in a report on environmentally progressive ski areas in the West. The SACC is a trade association that represents more than three hundred ski area owners and operations in the United States, so this report is likely to have a pro-industry bias. "Resorts . . . are evaluated on snowmaking and its drain on resources, water quality protection and energy and water conservation" (Staff and Wire reports. 2003).

36. O'Grady 2004.

37. Coleman 1996. Coleman argues that the whiteness of ski resorts "has clear historical roots" based on the fact that so many Americans who learned to ski in the 1930s and 1940s were wealthy persons who did so while vacationing in Europe; many of the first ski instructors in the United States were from Europe; and many

ski resorts were purposely modeled after European ski resorts and as "Alpine" villages. Even the state of Colorado launched a campaign, which advertised the Rockies as "the 'other' Alps," featuring alpine bowls, gondolas, and even ski villages to go with the state's high quality snow and "genuine western camaraderie" (593). This created a "whitewashing" of ski culture that remains with us today.

38. O'Grady 2004, 80.

39. A similar bumper sticker by the radical environmental group EarthFirst! has a graphic of the earth and the word "NATIVE" in capital letters. This is a big improvement over the Colorado "Native" bumper stickers that visually suggest Colorado as the exclusive domain of Anglos.

40. Ibid.

41. Ward 1996. See also Ward 1997. The negative impacts of outdoor recreational activities on ecosystems have been well documented for years.

42. Stranahan interview.

43. Hershey interview, spring 2004.

44. Doane, interview.

45. Jon Fox-Rubin, interview by authors, Spring 2004.

46. Scott Chaplin, Carbondale, interview by authors, July 24, 2004.

47. Carol O'Brian, program coordinator, Advocate Safehouse Project, Roaring Fork Valley, interview by authors, Spring 2004.

48. Browne and Colson 2004, 23.

49. Colson 2004. For more information on this campaign see www.pantsonfire.net.

50. Fowler 2009.

51. Aspen Times Staff Report 2004.

52. Brokaw 2006.

53. Vader 1999.

54. Passel and Cohn 2009.

55. U.S. Census 2000. "Population by Race and Hispanic Origin: Colorado Counties." http://www.garfield-county.com/docs/population_race_2000.pdf.

56. Marie Munday, interview by authors, July 24, 2004.

57. Jessica Dove, interview by authors, July 15, 2004.

58. Associated Press 1994.

59. Fox-Rubin, interview.

60. See McCully 2001; Pellow 2007.

61. Scott Chaplin interview, July 24, 2004.

62. Alice Hubbard Laird, interview by authors, July 26, 2004.

63. Gretchen Wroblewski, Red Rooster Inn owner, Glenwood Springs, conversation with authors, July 22, 2004.

64. Condon 2000b.

65. Condon 2001.

66. Condon 2004.

67. Fox-Rubin interview.

68. McGregor 2001.

69. Davis and Moctezuma 1999.

70. We acknowledge that the Mexico–U.S. border—like many international boundaries—is often contested. For example, many Mexican American students protesting anti-immigrant bills in the House of Representatives in 2005 chanted "We didn't cross the border, it crossed us!"

71. In 2000, the INS launched its Interior Enforcement Strategy, which was "designed to strategically and systematically reduce the overall population of illegal residents in the United States. . . . Building on the success of the INS border enforcement strategy, the agency is now focusing its capabilities on the nation's interior, in areas that had previously not been affected by illegal immigration" (Mutrie 2000). This issue was at the heart of congressional questions almost from the beginning of the Border Patrol's founding in the early twentieth century. The concern was that "The Border Patrol's capacious definition of its jurisdiction illustrates the nation's borders (the point of exclusion) collapsing into and becoming indistinguishable from the interior (the space of inclusion)" (Ngai 2004, 63).

72. Border crossings by undocumented persons are hazardous, claiming one life every day, according to an Associated Press report published in 2004 (Pritchard 2004). As we noted earlier, thousands of people are known to have died crossing the desert into the United States, but once inside the country proper, transportation routes can also be fraught with danger. In February 2000, two vans transporting undocumented persons slid off an icy highway and into a snow bank in Wolf Creek Pass, Colorado. No one was hurt in that accident, but in January 2000, fifteen people were injured and three killed in a similar accident near Walsenburg, Colorado. An INS supervisor in Alamosa told reporters that these "smuggle vans . . . remind me of slave ships. . . . They jam people into them just like the holds of slave ships. They are being exploited" (Hunter 2000). Once migrants reach their destinations, they are often working the most unrewarding, lowest-paid, and high-risk jobs available, even if they arrive here legally through the federal H2-A visa program (Yeoman 2001). The job-related death rate in Colorado for a Mexican worker is four times greater than the average U.S.–born worker. Susan Feldman works for the federal Centers for Disease Control and Prevention and takes calls from Spanish-speaking workers concerned about occupational safety issues. She told a reporter, "They're considered disposable" (Pritchard 2004).

73. Staff report 2000.

74. Ibid.

75. Frey 2003a.

76. Webb 2000.

77. Virginia Kice, ICE Agent in Los Angeles, interview by authors, July 22, 2004.

78. Ibid.

79. Park 2009.

80. Democracy Now! 2007.

81. *Denver Post* Wire Report 2009.

82. Davis and Moctezuma 1999.

83. These laws might also be interpreted and supported as public safety measures aimed at reducing fire hazards and the like.

84. Chung 1999.

85. Massey and Denton 1998.

86. Belson and Capuzzo 2007.

87. Associated Press 2001.

88. Parker 2001.

89. For the text of Colorado's Ethnic Intimidation statute, see http://www.cuah.org/co199718.htm.

90. Associated Press 2002.

91. Chaplin interview, July 24, 2004.

92. Slotkin 1998.

93. Peter Jessup, interview by authors, July 2004, Glenwood Springs.

94. Amy McTernan, Aspen Temporary Labor Service manager, interview by authors, July 2004.

95. Leticia Barraza, interview by authors, Colorado Mountain College, Glenwood Springs, July 26, 2004.

96. Munday interview, July 24, 2004.

97. Chaplin interview.

98. See Havlen 2004; and Carroll 2004.

99. Munday interview.

100. Ibid.

101. Aspen Temporary Labor Service, interview by authors, July 2004, Aspen.

102. Munday interview.

103. Jessup interview. There was a concern that our ability to do field research in July 2004 would be jeopardized by this incident. Jessica Dove coordinated one of the focus groups we held during that time, but in the days before that session she was apprehensive about whether it would even take place: "I am worried about whether . . . I can actually put together the focus group we had agreed to do. The main reason is because of the recent rumors that ICE raids are going on. My focus group has dropped from four people to two people because of the fear surrounding all this. So ultimately it may not materialize." Fortunately, Dove was able to bring nearly a dozen people to the focus group, a testament to the trust she has earned among Latino immigrants in the valley.

104. Quino, from focus group at the Roaring Fork Area Adult Literacy Program (RFAALP), interview by authors, July 26, 2004. We note that stopping traffic to bring attention to police racism is what students at the University of California–San Diego did after the Rodney King verdict. Students marched from campus to Interstate 5 and held up traffic during rush hour for three hours. This is a tactic also used by activists during the Civil Rights Movement (Lipsitz 1988).

105. Colson 2000b.

106. See Smith, Sonnenfeld, and Pellow 2006.

107. Basalt city council member, interview by authors, Spring 2004.

108. See Jacoby 2001. Even today, most of the mainstream environmental organizations in the United States reflect the interests and values of middle – and upper-class, white, American males. The class and racial orientation of these groups is an extension of the broader societal exclusion of people of color, women, and the working class from participation in the formal U.S. political system. Up until the 1980s, most environmental movement groups in the United States were based and located in white communities. Directly or indirectly, people of color were excluded. For example, the 1915 bylaws of the Fraternal Order of American Sportsmen limited membership to "white male citizens of the U.S." (Fraternal Order of American Sportsmen 1915).

109. Some classic studies in this area of scholarship include: Anderson 1992; Jencks 1991; and Wilson 1990. For excellent critiques of this tradition, see Briggs 2002; and Goldberg 1993.

110. C. Wright Mills, G. William Domhoff, and Rosanna Hertz have all pursued outstanding research agendas on the ruling classes, for example. See Domhoff 2009; Hertz and Imber 1995; and Mills 2000.

111. Stranahan interview.

112. See Brimelow 1996.

113. Johnson 2003, 183.

114. We are indebted to Juliana Smith for inspiring this point as a result of several conversations. See Chang and Zinn 2002; Gilmore 2007; and Parenti 2000.

115. Krugman 2002, 62.

116. Ibid..

117. Davis and Moctezuma 1999.

118. Millennium Ecosystem Assessment 2005.

119. For an excellent analysis of the increasing irrelevance of the mainstream U.S. environmental movement—particularly with respect to its lack of a social justice orientation—see St. Clair 2007.

NOTES TO CHAPTER 2

1. 1941. "Another Kind of Boom for Aspen, Historic Mine Camp." *Aspen Times*, March 6.

2. Glick 2001, 256.

3. Limerick 2000, 226.

4. Two important earlier laws were the Graduation Act of 1854, which reduced the price of public land to twenty-five cents per acre, and the Homestead Act, which allowed white settlers to own the land they farmed (Clifford 2003, 67).

5. Andrews 2007.

6. DeVoto 2000, 9.

7. Ibid., 53.

8. Turner's paper was presented at a special meeting of the American Historical Association in Chicago, July 12, 1893. The overseas imperialism around that period would include U.S. invasions of Hawai'i, Guam, Cuba, Puerto Rico, and the Philippines.

9. Limerick 2000, 19, emphasis added.

10. For an excellent critique of the post-materialist position, see Faber 2005.

11. Gedicks 2001; Khagram 2004; and McCully 2001.

12. See Limerick 1987; Lorah 1996; and Worster 1992.

13. Worster 1992, 13.

14. Davis 1999.

15. See Gottlieb 1998.

16. Spence 1999.

17. Limerick 1987, p. 89.

18. Slotkin 1998.

19. Ibid., 3

20. Kaplan 2006.

21. "The history of the West is the history of boom and bust. More than any other region of the United States, the West has found it difficult to find a happy average." Richard Lamm, former democratic governor of Colorado (cited from the foreword in Gulliford 1989).

22. West 1998, 153.

23. Monnett and McCarthy 1996, 21.

24. West 1998, 308.

25. Cornwell n.d.

26. *Aspen Daily Times*, September 7, 1887.

27. Emmitt 1954, 21–22.

28. *Daily Chronicle*, October 11, 1879, Colorado, cf. Buys 2001, 6.

29. See Athearn 1976; and "A Walk Through Time: Historic Glenwood Springs." *Glenwood Springs Colorado: 2001 Official Guide to Glenwood Springs*, 27.

30. Churchill 2003.

31. "Homeward Bound." *Aspen Daily Times*, September 6, 1887. If this seems reminiscent of the pass laws for blacks in apartheid-era South Africa, it may be because that system was deliberately modeled after the U.S. reservations system.

32. J. W. Atkisson, a resident of Aspen in 1886, stated "Colorado people were not to blame in a single instance for trouble with the Indians. Helped bury twenty men in one year that had been killed by Indians" (Dictation of J. W. Atkisson, Aspen, December 16, 1886; archives, University of Colorado at Boulder Libraries, Bancroft Box 1); See also "The Ute War." *Aspen Daily Times,* September 3, 1887. This article reported that many Utes had been killed in the latest skirmish between them and the settlers and the military; see also "WAR! WAR! The Utes Must Go!" *Aspen Daily Times*, September 7, 1887. This headline says it all.

33. Burns 1993.

34. Ibid.

35. *Glenwood Springs Colorado: 2001 Official Guide to Glenwood Springs,* 53.

36. Abbott, Leonard, and McComb 1982.

37. Ibid., 196.

38. Bridges 1883, 408.

39. Rohrbough 2000, 76.

40. Athearn 1976, 179.

41. Monnett and McCarthy 1996.

42. Cities that saw major riots or incidents of anti-Chinese violence or expulsions during this time included Los Angeles, Rock Springs (Wyoming), San Francisco, San Jose, Seattle, Tacoma, and Tonopah (Nevada).

43. Taylor 1929.

44. Rohrbough 2000.

45. Jung 1999.

46. Rohrbough 2000, 161.

47. Ibid., 40.

48. Gulliford and the Grand River Museum Alliance 1983. Garfield County includes the Roaring Fork Valley towns of Silt, Parachute, Rifle, Glenwood Springs, and Carbondale.

49. Ibid. Apparently, many people still view the lives of wild animals in the county as available for the taking. The following advertisement appeared in a recent guide to the city of Glenwood Springs: "Hunting in the Glenwood Springs area: Where the wildlife roams free . . . big game hunters choose Glenwood Springs for many reasons. Of course, the biggest reason is bringing home meat for the freezer. Other reasons include enjoying the outdoors, the sport of stalking prey and spending time with friends and family." *Glenwood Springs Colorado: 2001 Official Guide to Glenwood Springs,* 30.

50. Voynick 1984. By 1948 every state had workers' compensation laws. In 1970, the Occupational Safety and Health Administration (OSHA) became the first federal agency charged with monitoring and regulating workplace safety. And in 1977, the Mine Safety and Health Administration was launched to address the particular needs of miners and regulate that industry. Some observers might view this as progress while others argue that it took far too long to bring these efforts to fruition and that, in the end, these agencies have minimal regulatory authority over industry.

51. Kimmell 1975; See also *Rocky Mountain Sun*, May 26, 1892; *Rocky Mountain Sun*, September 24, 1892.

52. Gilbert 1991.

53. Rohrbough 2000. 206.

54. *Aspen Times*, April 23, 1881.

55. *Aspen Times*, May 28, 1881 (cf. Gilbert 1991, 22).

56. Urquhart 1970, 100.

57. *Aspen Times*, April 30, 1881.

58. Gilbert 1991.

59. State of Colorado Census Returns, 1885, "Pitkin County."

60. "Mass Meeting Held," *Aspen Daily Times.* July 7, 1893.

61. *Aspen Daily Times*, August 26, 1893.

62. Athearn 1976, 91.

63. Gage 1900.

64. Athearn 1976, 96.

65. "Harvey Young. Colorado Spring, October 13, 1886. Dictation." Archives, University of Colorado–Boulder Libraries. Bancroft box #2.

66. Colorado Territorial and State Board of Immigration Collection, 1916. "Pitkin County." 105–6.

67. Severy 1978.

68. Athearn 1976, 336.

69. Ibid., 337.

70. Anoe 1955, 14–15.

71. Morris 1950.

72. Haddock 1948.

73. "Outsider Says Aspen is Peopled with Mossbacks." *Aspen Democrat-Times*, August 26, 1913.

74. A term used to characterize a "countercultural" white person likely (or who soon will be) living off of a trust fund, courtesy of their parents or grandparents.

75. Clifford and Smith 1970a, 101.

76. Ibid., 100.

77. Colestock n.d.

78. Editorial, n.d. "Reign of Injustice," *Aspen Times*.

79. Clifford and Smith 1970a, 19–20.

80. Ibid. 1970b. The Pitkin County Park Association was founded to promote "the activities of all citizens of Pitkin County, Colorado, interested in preserving and enhancing the natural beauty around them, to further the growth and development of outdoor recreation and scenic beauty, and to make the general public aware of the value of such natural resources and of the need for upgrading and improving existing areas" (see Open Space Advisory Board and Aspen/Pitkin County Planning Office, 1980, *Aspen/Pitkin County Open Space Master Plan*, Pitkin County Planning Office, 4).

81. Gilmore and Duff 1974.

82. *Aspen Times*, October 9, 1969, 5A.

83. City of Aspen 1966.

84. Hammond 1995, 23. See City of Aspen, City Council Minutes, October 4, 1971. Only San Francisco and Denver had similar ordinances at the time, and this legal approach had yet to be challenged in a court of law.

85. Aspen City Council and Pitkin County Commission. 1977, *Aspen/Pitkin County Growth Management Policy Plan*, Aspen, Colorado. See also *Aspen Times*, February 24, 1977.

86. Rollins 1982.

87. "Anti-Discrimination Law Given 1st OK," *Aspen Times*, November 17, 1977.

88. One of the rare exceptions was James Knowlton, an attorney with Roaring Fork Legal Services, who stated that the growth control seemed to exempt affordable housing, thus contradicting its very purpose: "they have excluded—much to my chagrin—affordable housing, basically saying 'affordable housing at all cost.'" James Knowlton, interview by authors, Spring 2004). Of course, the price of "affordable housing" in the Roaring Fork Valley is often far out of reach for working-class people.

89. Alice Hubbard Laird, July 26, 2004.

90. Garnsey 1965.

91. Clifford 2003, 77.

92. Ibid., 184–85.

93. Birch 2006.

94. Mattern 2001.

95. Ibid. For example, the Telluride Ski and Golf company illegally destroyed nearly seventy acres of wetlands in order to construct a new golf course (Clifford 2003, 179).

96. Glick 2001, 137.

97. Ibid.

98. The voters of Colorado passed Amendment 8 in 1972, a measure that prohibited the expenditure of public dollars on the Olympic Games. The Games were moved to Innsbruck, Austria.

99. Ellis and Smith 1991, 214.

100. George Stranahan, interview by authors, Summer 2004.

101. Rebecca Doane, interview by authors, Summer 2004.

102. Lamm 2004.

103. Athearn 1976, 363.

104. *U.S. News and World Report* 1975.

105. Hartman 2001.

106. Ibid.

107. Clifford 2003, 192.

108. Ibid., 238.

NOTES TO CHAPTER 3

1. Aguilera 2004.

2. Luisa, from focus group at the RFAALP, interview by authors, July 2004.

3. Luis Polar, Scott Chaplin, and Felicia Trevor, interview by authors, Stepstone Center, Carbondale, July 2004.

4. Jorge, from focus group with undocumented workers, interview by authors, Stepstone Center, Summer 2004.

5. Veronica, from focus group at Catholic Charities, interview by authors, Summer 2004.

6. Renaldo Menjívar, interview by authors, Stepstone Center, Carbondale, July 24, 2004.

7. Jessica Dove, interview by authors, Basalt, CO, Spring 2004.

8. Polar, Chaplin, and Trevor interview.

9. Marie Munday, interview by authors, Aspen, July 24, 2004. "Tijuanita" means "little Tijuana" in English and "Chihuahuita" translates to "little Chihuahua."

10. Ibid.

11. Polar, Chaplin, and Trevor interview.

12. Aguilera 2004.

13. Dove interview.

14. Many Roma communities in Central and Eastern Europe endure involuntarily living next to rivers and flood plains (Pellow 2007).

15. Romig 2001a.

16. "Home talk," *Glenwood Post Independent,* April 30, 2001.

17. Familias de Bonanza Proyecto para Hogares Seguros, 2001. Petition to the Carbondale Trustees, April 24.

18. Daniels 2001a.

19. Scott Chaplin, letter to Roaring Fork Area lawyers seeking legal assistance for Bonanza Families' Secure Homes Project/Familias de Bonanza Proyecto para Hogares Seguros. Carbondale, Colorado, May 21, 2001.

20. Scott Chaplin, n.d., Bonanza Residents Survey, Carbondale.

21. "Benefit Dance for the Bonanza Families' Secure Home Project." Carbondale Community School flyer, August 4, 2001.

22. Grauer 2001a.

23. Romig 2001b.

24. Grauer 2001b.

25. Scott Chaplin, interview by authors, Carbondale, July 24, 2004.

26. Simon Silva, interview by authors, focus group at the RFAALP, July 26, 2004.

27. All quotations in this section are from authors' focus group with Scott Chaplin, Luis Polar, and Felicia Trevor, Stepstone Center, Carbondale, July 2004.

28. We note that Marie Munday contends that employers must pay an employee for time worked, see chap. 5 this book.

29. Melinda, focus group at Catholic Charities, interview by authors, Glenwood Springs Summer 2004.

30. See Gutiérrez 1995.

31. Ibid.

32. Javier, authors' focus group with employees of the Aspen Temporary Labor Service, interview by authors, translated by Felicia Trevor, July 2004.

33. Celia, authors' focus group at Catholic Charities, interview by authors, Glenwood Springs. July 2004.

34. Leticia Barraza, interview by authors, Colorado Mountain College, July 26, 2004.

35. Laura, interview by authors, July 27, 2004.

36. David, authors' focus group at the Aspen Family Visitor Program, interview by authors, July 2004.

37. Barraza interview.

38. Carlsen 2007. See also Clarke 2006; Environmental Health Coalition 2004; Filner and Takvorian 2004.

39. Amy McTernan, Aspen Temporary Labor Service manager, interview by authors, July 2004. Loveland is another resort destination in Colorado.

40. Gloria, focus group at the RFAALP, interview by authors, July 26, 2004, translated by Jessica Dove.

41. Jorge Carrillo, focus group at the Stepstone Center, interview by authors, July 2004.

42. Rosalinda, focus group at the RFAALP, interview by authors, translated by Jessica Dove.

43. Carla (RFAALP), interview by authors, Summer 2004.

44. Federico (RFAALP), interview by authors, Summer 2004.

45. Lupe, Catholic Charities, Glenwood Springs, interview by authors, July 21, 2004.

46. McTernan interview, July 27, 2004.

47. Juanita, Catholic Charities, Glenwood Springs, interview by authors, July 21, 2004.

48. Magdalena and Corazon, focus group at the Aspen Family Visitors Program, interview by authors, July 2004.

49. Evita Salinas, interview by authors, July 2004.

50. Gustavo, focus group at the Stepstone Center, interview by authors, translated by Felicia Trevor, July 20, 2004.

51. Appleby 2006; Associated Press 2009.

52. Emergency Medicaid, for which undocumented immigrants qualify, covers maternal labor and delivery. Colorado is one of twelve states that provide prenatal care coverage for "qualified" immigrants who have resided in the United States for less than five years (see Kaiser Family Foundation and Center on Budget and Policy Priorities 2004).

53. Josefa and Tomas, focus group at the Stepstone Center, interview by authors, translated by Felicia Trevor, July 20, 2004.

54. Prenatal care for undocumented pregnant immigrants can be serviced through presumptive eligibility programs in many states. Presumptive eligibility allows uninsured pregnant women to obtain immediate prenatal care while their Medicaid eligibility is processed (National Latina Institute for Reproductive Health 2005).

55. Juanita interview. All quotations in this section are from interviews with the authors, Catholic Charities, Glenwood Springs.

56. Marisa, interview by authors, Stepstone Center, Carbondale, July 2004.

57. Polar interview.

58. Gabrielson and Giblin 2008. This is the Pulitzer Prize–winning series about the notorious nativist sheriff Joe Arpaio, who became infamous for diverting law enforcement resources away from traditional activities toward punitive treatment of immigrants, including public humiliation associated with parading undocumented detainees through town in prison blues.

59. Amelia, focus group at the Aspen Family Visitors Program, interview by authors, July 2004.

60. Karina interview.

61. Aguilera 2004.

62. Frey 2004.

63. "Parent Issues at Rifle schools." Flyer announcing a meeting organized by concerned parents after the shooting, 2001.

64. Barraza interview.

65. José Cordova, interview by authors, Stepstone Center, Carbondale, July 24, 2004.

66. Ibid.

67. See Gould, Schnaiberg, and Weinberg 1996; Szasz 1994.

68. Ibid.

69. See Agyeman, Bullard, and Evans 2003; Boggs 2000; Gould, Pellow, and Schnaiberg 2008; Pellow 2007; and Smith, Sonnenfeld, and Pellow 2006.

70. Karina interview.

71. Lorena, focus group at the Stepstone Center, interview by authors, Carbondale, July 2004.

72. Aura interview, Stepstone Center.

73. Karina interview.

74. Marisa interview.

75. Juliana interview, Stepstone Center.

76. Julio interview, Stepstone Center.

77. Cordova interview.

78. Javier, focus group with employees of the Aspen Temporary Labor Service, interview by authors, translated by Felicia Trevor, July 2004.

79. Josefa, focus group at the Stepstone Center, interview by authors, July 20, 2004.

80. Aguilera 2004.

81. Carla and Roberto, RFAALP focus group, interview by authors, translated by Jessica Dove, July 26, 2004.

82. Eva, focus group with employees of the Aspen Temporary Labor Service, interview by authors, translated by Felicia Trevor, July 2004.

83. Elena, interview by authors, Carbondale, July 27, 2004.

84. Cordova interview.

NOTES TO CHAPTER 4

1. Burke 2000. Negative Population Growth is a Washington, DC–based organization whose mission is embodied in its name.

2. Feagin 1997.

3. Gottlieb 1993, 256.

4. See *Johnson v. McIntosh* (1823), *Cherokee Nation v. Georgia* (1831), *Worcester v. Georgia* (1832), and *Lone Wolf v. Hitchcock* (1903).

5. This argument was perhaps best embodied in the Dawes Severalty Act of 1887, which forced Native Americans to move beyond collective and commons property arrangements to individual private property allocations. The act also imposed European American agricultural practices on these populations.

6. Gottlieb 1993.

7. Gottlieb and Dreier 1998.

8. panagioti 2006.

9. Ibid., 8.

10. See Roediger 2005.

11. Schmitt 2001a.

12. Dugger 2003. This article reports on a study by the Carnegie Endowment for International Peace on the failed promises of NAFTA proponents.

13. McClintock 1995.

14. Churchill 2003; and Horsman 1981.

15. Hardin 1968.

16. Sferios 1998a.

17. Hardin 1968. See also Gottlieb 1993, 257.

18. See Sferios 1998b.

19. panagioti 2006, 10.

20. Flynn 2006.

21. Ibid.

22. Tactaquin 1994.

23. ZPG representatives have testified in public hearings against anti-sterilization laws (Roberts 1998, 96).

24. Population Connection's website: www.populationconnection.org, accessed March 2008.

25. Rosenfeld 2004.

26. Tanton 2004.

27. http://www.NumbersUSA.com, accessed March 2008.

28. Roy Beck served in this capacity for the Aspen City Council and the Pitkin County Commission when they developed their "population stabilization" resolutions.

29. Motavalli 2001.

30. panagioti 2006, 11.

31. Pear 2007.

32. Camarota 2001. Emphasis added.

33. http://www.cis.org/aboutcis.html, accessed March 2008.

34. Krikorian 2007.

35. Preston 2007.

36. Pear 2007.

37. Schmitt 2001b.

38. Preston 2007.

39. Duke was invited to speak to nativist whites in Siler City, North Carolina, where anti-Latino passions were running high over the increase in Mexican immigrants working at local poultry plants (Schmitt 2001).

40. Rondeaux and Loder 2000.

41. Crass, n.d. See also Huang 2008.

42. Faber 2008; Guha 1989.

43. Hartmann 2003. This argument has a strong parallel with the claim many social scientists have made that Puerto Rican and African American female-headed households are the cause of poverty in those communities (see Briggs 2002 for a critique).

44. Population Institute. Full-page advertisement in the *New York Times*, June 19, 2002, A9.

45. Federation for American Immigration Reform; Immigration and Urban Sprawl. http://www.fairus.org/html/04177001.htm, accessed March 10, 2002.

46. NumbersUSA.com pamphlet.

47. See Bullard, Johnson, and Torres 2000; Avila 2006; and Hayden 2004.

48. Klein and Olson 1996.

49. Navarro 2001.

50. DinAlt 1997.

51. Sferios 1998a.

52. This was known as the abortion "gag rule"; President Obama overturned it during his first months in office in 2009.

53. Tactaquin n.d.

54. Burke 2000.

55. Ibid.

56. Werbach 2004.

57. Barringer 2004.

58. For more on the 1924 immigration law, see Ngai 2004 and Roediger 2005.

59. Sierrans for U.S. Population Stabilization. www.susps.org. The authors are grateful to Angelic Willis for sharing her research on this group.

60. Weiss 2004.

61. Sierrans for U.S. Population Stabilization 2004.

62. Sierra Club Policy on Population and the Environment, adopted by the board of directors, March 13, 1965; amended July 8, 1995. www.sierraclub.org. Emphasis added.

63. Sierra Club Population Policy, adopted by the board of directors, March 13, 1966.

64. Sierra Club Population Policy: Slowing U.S. Population Growth, adopted by the board of directors, May 3–4, 1969.

65. Sierra Club Policy on Population and Environment, adopted by the board of directors, June 4, 1970; amended July 8, 1995. Emphasis added.

66. Gottlieb and Dreier 1998.

67. Sierra Club Policy on Immigration, adopted by the board of directors, February 24–25, 1996.

68. Carl Pope, n.d. "Ways and Means, Moving On: Lessons from the Immigration Debate." http://www.sierraclub.org/sierra/199807/ways.asp.

69. McGarry 2002.

70. Hill 2000. The letter's author is from Carbondale.

71. See Craddock 2004. See also Molina 2006; and Shah 2001.

72. Lich 2004. The letter's author is from Gypsum, CO.

73. Callison 2004. The letter's author is from Denver, CO.

74. Hubbell 2000.

75. See Gutiérrez 1995.

76. Espinoza 2004. The letter's author is from Nuevo, CA.

77. An advertisement for the Alliance reads "Are you curious, concerned, or disturbed that your city and county resources and ski company efforts are going to further an artificial population growth in the Roaring Fork Valley? Are you curious, concerned, or disturbed that massive, endless legal and illegal immigration are the principal causes of these developments?" (Harvey 1999a).

78. Hooper 2001.

79. Lamm was governor of Colorado from 1975 to 1987.

80. Stiny 1999a.

81. Ibid.

82. This comes from a presentation Lamm gave at the Rural Resort Region conference. The title of his talk was "The Agonizing Dilemma of Immigration." He is now director, Center for Public Policy and Contemporary Issues, University of Denver (Harvey 2001b).

83. Carroll 2002.

84. In 2009 Tancredo lambasted Supreme Court Justice Sonia Sotomayor for her affiliation with the National Council of La Raza, which he called "nothing more than a Latino KKK" (CNN Live, May 28, 2009). At the 2010 Tea Party Convention, he called for a return to literacy tests for voters, in order to prevent the election of candidates like Barack Obama, whose ascendancy he blamed on the "cult of multiculturalism." He earlier argued that if the United States bombed holy Muslim sites in the Middle East, such a practice would deter Islamic extremists from attacking domestic U.S. targets (Associated Press 2005). Tancredo's official website describes him as a "lone voice in the wilderness. Speaking out against the ills of the illegal alien invasion. . . . Doing whatever it takes to protect our borders, the language of our country's founders and to save our shared American culture" (http://www.tancredo.org, accessed March 11, 2010).

85. This group includes the Colorado Alliance for Immigration Reform (CAIR), a state affiliate of FAIR. The CAIR website reads: "Advocating for the rights of future generations of Americans." The website logo is fitting: it is simply a picture of a snow-capped mountain range, with no people and no evidence of human

settlement whatsoever. This is a true preservationist approach to immigration and environmental policy. http://www.cairco.org/, accessed July 2004.

86. Christian 1999. The conference was sponsored by the Sopris Foundation, whose motto is "Creating Awareness of Population and Environmental Issues Worldwide." The similarities between Christian's speech here and EarthFirst! activist Edward Abbey's words at the 1987 Round River Rendezvous are striking in terms of their contemptuous views of Latin American cultures.

87. Lamm 1999.

88. Ibid.

89. Fifth Annual State of the World Conference, Aspen, Colorado, July 2004.

90. Brown spoke at a "Reinventing Malthus for the Twenty-first Century" conference sponsored by Negative Population Growth and the Federation for American Immigration Reform in 1997. In his remarks that day he said "We have this infatuation with technology, which is understandable, whether it's exploring Mars or the Internet and all the things one can do now in the telecommunications field. It's fascinating, it's exciting, but it doesn't solve the food problem. And it doesn't bring about the balance that we need between our continuously expanding numbers and the earth's resources, which have not changed very much since the time of Malthus" (National Press Club. July 14, 1997, Washington, DC).

91. Terry Paulson and Mike McGarry, interview by Traci Voyles (Research Assistant), Aspen, Spring 2002.

92. Paulson and Mike McGarry interview.

93. Harvey 2001a.

94. Barber 2000. This letter to the editor was written in response to the protest against the INS plans to build an immigrant detention facility in Carbondale. The author of the letter is from Aspen. See also Baumli (2000), a letter to the editor from a Carbondale resident. This letter specifically targets the Stepstone Center, since, like the letter's author, it is based in Carbondale. Baumli writes "As for the Stepstone Center it should be investigated for saying they are tax 'exempt.'"

95. Harrell 2004.

96. Taylor 2000. Letter to the editor from an Aspen resident.

97. Hall et al. 1978; Bullock et al. 2001.

98. This includes movements such as the Proposition 187 mobilization, which was supported by many Latinos. People of color can work in the interest of white supremacy, so this "diversity" of support does not negate that fact (see Lipsitz 1998).

99. EF! describes itself not as an organization but as a movement. Or, as the website states, "EarthFirst is a priority not an organization" http://www.earthfirst.org/about.htm, accessed on October 22, 2007.

100. Ibid.

101. For an analysis of how the big green groups like the Nature Conservancy, the Sierra Club, Conservation International, and the World Wildlife Federation are ethically compromised by accepting corporate money and then opposing serious regulation, see Hari 2010. Groups like Friends of the Earth and Greenpeace have officially remained steadfastly independent of direct corporate influence.

102. See Hari 2010 and MacDonald 2008.

103. For excellent sources on the conflicts between environmentalists and indigenous peoples, see Chapin 2004, and Dowie 2009.

104. The Biotic Baking Brigade is an group of activists that challenges elites in positions of authority who enact ecologically destructive policies. The methods used include throwing biotically baked pies in the faces of such persons during public events; these events are almost always caught on television. Their slogan "No Pastry, No Peace!" is heard wherever they appear, and they deliver "just desserts" to economists, politicians, and "sell out" leaders of nongovernmental organizations. See http://bioticbakingbrigade.org/aboutbbb.html, accessed October 22, 2007.

105. Abzug 2001, 21.

106. Ibid., 19. See also panagioti 2006.

107. Animal 2005, 38.

108. Hartmann 1995, 2003.

109. In 1977, R. T. Ravenholt of USAID announced the agency's plan to sterilize one-quarter of the world's women. He stated, "Population control is necessary to maintain the normal operation of U.S. commercial interests around the world." (Wagman 1997; cf. Smith 2005).

110. Gottlieb and Dreier 1998.

NOTES TO CHAPTER 5

1. Scott Chaplin, interview by authors, July 26, 2004.

2. Associated Press 1994.

3. Fillion 2007.

4. Colson 2000b.

5. Ibid.

6. Felicia Trevor, interview by authors, July 2004.

7. Leticia Barraza, interview by authors, Colorado Mountain College, July 26, 2004.

8. Ibid.

9. Mutrie 1999. According to this source, the Latino high school dropout rate fell to 50 percent in 1998, but it is not clear if that was part of a larger trend.

10. Ibid. The DREAM Act (Development Relief and Education for Alien Minors) is a legal initiative that would allow undocumented high school graduates greater financial access to colleges and universities (and the military) in the United States. The effort to make this a federal law failed in 2010 as a result of a Congressional Republican filibuster.

11. Jessica Dove, interview by authors, July 15, 2004.

12. Dove, interview, August 26, 2004.

13. Ibid.

14. Asistencia Para Latinos. 2000. Flyer (translated from Spanish).

15. Frey 2000b. APL received some funding from Garfield, Pitkin, and Eagle counties, the city of Aspen, Snowmass Village, the state of Colorado Department of Health and Environment, and the Aspen Valley Community Foundation.

16. Mutrie 1999.

17. Asistencia Para Latinos 1998.

18. Mutrie 1999.

19. Harvey 2001d. See also Daniels 2001b.

20. Chaplin, interview by authors, July 24, 2004.

21. Peter Jessup of Catholic Charities, interview by authors, July 26, 2004.

22. Ibid. Jessup interview.

23. Chang 2000; Milkman 2006; and Pellow and Park 2002.

24. Jessup interview.

25. Ibid.

26. James Knowlton, Roaring Fork Legal Services, interview by authors, Spring 2004.

27. The passage of the USA PATRIOT Act, for example, continues the practice of allowing the FBI to open and expand investigations into citizens' lives and activism based solely on legally and constitutionally protected First Amendment activities. In other words, if you are reading material or speaking or writing words that the state believes is threatening to national security in any way, you may be placed under surveillance.

28. "Best Local Activist Organization: Mountain Folks for Global Justice," *Aspen Times* editorial, July 1–2, 2000.

29. Frey 2000a.

30. As one local journalist wrote regarding the protest against the Aspen Institute's elite extravaganza, "It will be refreshing to see some countervailing winds of opinion blowing round our town this weekend" (Colson 2000b).

31. Frey 2000a.

32. Colson 2000a.

33. Condon 2000a.

34. "The Top News Stories of 2000," *Aspen Daily News* editorial, January 1, 2001.

35. All quotations in this section are from authors' focus group with Scott Chaplin, Luis Polar, and Felicia Trevor, Stepstone Center, Carbondale, July 2004.

36. Trevor interview, July 2004.

37. Dove interview, July 15, 2004.

38. Ibid.

39. See for example, Allen 1997; Ignatiev 1996; Jacobson 1998; Lipsitz 2006; and Roediger 2007.

40. Excellent sources on critical whiteness and ethnic studies include Brodkin 1998; Gualtieri 2009; Lipsitz 2006; and Roediger 2005 and 2007. For historical antecedents and foundations of Whiteness Studies, see DuBois 1998 and Horsman 1981.

41. Jessup interview.

42. Alice Hubbard Laird, interview by authors, July 26, 2004.

43. Jonathan Fox-Rubin, interview by authors, Spring 2004.

44. Dove interview.

45. Ip 2007; Yen 2009.

46. The first set of figures concerning income inequality comes from Ip 2007 and Yen 2009. The second group of figures concerning wealth inequality comes from Wolff 2010.

47. See Calavita 2008; see also Milkman 2006, 9.

48. Trevor interview, July 2004.

49. Ibid. For data on the exposure of people of color to power plants, see Ortiz-Garcia 2004.

50. Dove, email correspondence with authors, July 5, 2004.

51. Gould 2007.

52. McTernan, Aspen Temporary Labor Service manager, interview, July 2004.

53. Chaplin interview, July 26, 2004.

54. Rural Resort Region. 2001. "The Immigrant Workforce . . . Opportunity, Pain and Profit in Paradise: An Exploration of Issues Surrounding Foreign Workers in Colorado's Premier Resort Areas." Rural Resort Region Conference, Silvertree Hotel, Snowmass Village, September 19–21, 2001.

55. Mike McGarry, letter to Leticia Gomez, Mexican Consul General, Denver, September 2001.

56. Harvey 2001c.

57. Frey 2002.

58. Marie Munday, interview by authors, July 24, 2004.

59. Ibid.

60. See, for example, Munday 1999. In her letter to the editor, Munday points out that while many people ask why Latino immigrants don't just get temporary work visas, "there is no such thing available to unskilled laborers . . . visas are only

issued to people with college degrees who have special expertise which U.S. citizens do not possess, especially in the sciences. . . . Incidentally, [being undocumented or living "out-of-status"] this is a 'civil' offense, not 'criminal.'"

61. Munday interview, July 24, 2004.

62. Ibid.

63. Ibid.

64. Frey 2003b, and Daniels 1999a.

65. Stroud 2000a.

66. Craig 1999a.

67. Lee 2007.

68. U.S. Government Accountability Office (GAO). 2005. "Information on Criminal Aliens Incarcerated in Federal and State Prisons and Local Jails." Letter to the Subcommittee on Immigration, Border Security, and Claims, and to the Committee on the Judiciary, April 7, Washington, DC.

69. Lakoff and Ferguson 2006.

70. U.S. Immigration and Customs Enforcement website. http://www.ice.gov/partners/dro/cap.htm, accessed November 30, 2007.

71. Davis and Moctezuma 1999.

72. Sharon Conger, letter to Andrew McGregor, Community Development director, City of Glenwood Springs. April 25, 2003. Regarding application for special use permit, U.S. Dept of Homeland Security/ICE, Midland Center. Conger was the contracting officer, U.S. General Services Administration, Public Buildings Service. Emphasis added.

73. Craig 1999a.

74. Vader 1999.

75. "INS on wrong track," editorial board, *Denver Post*, December 31, 1999.

76. Daniels 2000a.

77. Stroud 1999. This fearful sentiment is reflected in federal law. We located a copy of the minutes from a meeting of Asistencia Para Latinos concerning the question of deportation. The minutes reflect a discussion among activists, residents, and legal counsel:

Q: What happens to the families of a deportee?

A: If the family is legal, they are welcome to stay. When a criminal alien is deported, the family will not automatically be deported too.

Q: What will happen to families with illegal parents and children who are US citizens?

A: The problem is that their parents' illegal status negatively affects the children's well-being. INS can only apply the laws fairly and humanely." (Minutes of a meeting of Asistencia Para Latinos and the Latino Networking Council, July 22, 1999, re: INS office expansion in the region).

78. Stiny 1999b.

79. Ibid.

80. Craig 1999b. See also *Aspen Times,* Saturday/Sunday, August 4–5., 13A.

81. Harvey 1999b.

82. Daniels 1999a.

83. Associated Press 2000.

84. Gagnon 2000.

85. Daniels 2000b.

86. Stroud 2000b.

87. Fox-Rubin interview, Spring 2004, Basalt, CO.

88. Chaplin interview, July 2004, Carbondale, CO.

89. Munday interview, June 2, 2009 (via telephone).

90. Polar interview, January 10, 2010 (via telephone).

91. Anonymous Aspen community leader, interview by authors, Spring 2004, Aspen. CO.

92. Anonymous Aspen community leader, interview by authors, Spring 2004, Aspen, CO.

93. Dove, email correspondence with authors, July 5, 2004.

94. George Stranahan, interview by authors, Spring 2004, Woody Creek, CO. Here, Stranahan is deliberately engaging the late eugenicist Garrett Hardin, who popularized the "lifeboat" metaphor for a nation and a world with too many people who would be passengers. Instead of using the lifeboat metaphor to argue for closed borders, Stranahan does the opposite.

NOTES TO THE CONCLUSION

1. We want to be clear that by arguing for the end of capitalism, we in no way wish to uncritically embrace socialism or related systems of economic organization. It is well known that socialist states have produced deep inequalities and ecological rifts in many parts of the world. Our position is that any system that devalues human beings and ecosystems should be challenged. Even so, one cannot deny that capitalism is the dominant global economic, cultural, social, and political force at this point in history, so any so-called socialist society is ultimately and intimately linked to this reality. However, Erik Olin Wright argues that community-based socialist practices that seek to avoid many of these pitfalls exist in various forms today (Wright 2010)

2. Nordhaus and Shellenberger 2007.

3. Guinier and Torres 2002, 65. Since race can be defined in so many ways (e.g. nationality, color, religion, voice, sound, space, place, politics, etc.), we prefer not to limit the definition of post-racialism to colorblindness.

4. Smith 2005.

5. Speth 2008, 70.

6. Kovel 2002, 6.

7. Ibid., 8.

8. Ibid., 7.

9. World Resources Institute 1990; cf. Goldman 1999, 37.

10. Goldman 1999, 38.

11. Hays 1959.

12. Schnaiberg 1980, and Schnaiberg and Gould 2000.

13. Speth 2008, 70.

14. Goldman 1999, 23.

15. Lipsitz 2006, vii.

16. Kimmel and Ferber 2009.

17. Feagin, Vera, and Batur 2001, 27–28.

18. DuBois 1998.

19. Kempf 2007, 59.

20. Wise 2008, 324.

21. Guinier and Torres 2003.

22. Wise 2007, 335.

23. Cole and Foster 2001, chap. 7.

24. Moyers 2007.

25. Political Ecology Group 1996.

26. Crass 2004.

27. Penn Loh, n.d. "Linking Immigrants and Environmentalists for Sustainability and Justice." http:www.igc.org/envjustice/rep/loh.html, accessed March 1, 2002.

28. panagioti 2006, 9.

29. Speth 2008, xiii and xiv.

REFERENCES

Abbott, Carl, Stephen J. Leonard, and David McComb. 1982. *Colorado: A History of the Centennial State*. Rev. ed. Colorado Associated University Press.

Abzug, Bonnie. 2001. "Shouldering EarthFirst!'s Baggage: Wilderness, Privilege, and Immigration." *EarthFirst!* May-June.

Aguilera, Elizabeth. 2004. "A Wealth of Diversity in a Valley of Riches," *Denver Post*, July 20.

Agyeman, Julian. 2005. *Sustainable Communities and the Challenge of Environmental Justice*. New York University Press.

Agyeman, Julian, Robert Bullard, and Bob Evans, eds. 2003. *Just Sustainabilities: Development in an Unequal World*. MIT Press.

Agyeman, Julian, Peter Cole, Randolph Haluza-DeLay, and Patricia O'Riley, eds. 2009. *Speaking for Ourselves: Environmental Justice in Canada*. University of British Columbia Press.

Allen, Theodore. 1997. *The Invention of the White Race: The Origin of Racial Oppression in Anglo-America*. Verso.

Anderson, Elijah. 1992. *Streetwise: Race, Class, and Change in an Urban Community*. University of Chicago Press.

Andrews, Edmund. 2007. "Inspector Finds Broad Failures in Oil Program." *New York Times*, September 26.

Animal, Problem. 2005. "The Peace That Must End: White Supremacy and Ecology." *EarthFirst!* March-April, 38–40.

Anoe, Pearl. 1955. "Aspen Was No Ghost Town." *Chrysler Owners' Magazine*, August.

Aoyagi-Stom. 2008. "Anti-Asian Column Becomes Rallying Cry in Boulder." *Pacific Citizen*, March 15.

Appleby, Julie. 2006. "Ranks of Uninsured Americans Grow." *USA Today*, August 29.

Asistencia Para Latinos. 1998. "Client Statistics." Glenwood Springs, CO.

Aspen Times Staff Report. 2004. "Glenwood man gets jail, fines for killing bighorn." *Aspen Times*, July 26.

Associated Press. 1994. "Immigrant Workers Putting Down Roots." *Colorado Springs Gazette-Telegraph*, September 6.

———. 2000. "Group Says New INS Office Will Mean More Exploitation."

———. 2001. "Charges Are Filed in Rifle Slayings." *Boulder Camera*, July 6.

———. 2002. "Residents Upset over Court Verdict Issued in Rifle Slaying Case." *Aspen Daily News*, October 10.

———. 2005. "Tancredo: If They Nuke Us, Bomb Mecca." July 18.

———. 2009. "Census Bureau: Number of Americans without Health Insurance Rises to 46.3 Million." September 10.

Athearn, Robert G. 1976. *The Coloradans*. University of New Mexico Press.

Avila, Eric. 2006. *Popular Culture in the Age of White Flight: Fear and Fantasy in Suburban Los Angeles*. University of California Press.

Balibar, Étienne. 1991. "Is There a Neo-Racism?" In *Race, Nation, Class: Ambiguous Identities*, ed. Étienne Balibar and Immanuel Wallerstein, 16–28. Verso.

Barber, Alan. 2000. Letter to the editor. *Aspen Times*. January 7.

Barringer, Felicity. 2004. "Bitter Division for Sierra Club on Immigration." *New York Times*, March 16.

Baumli, Mildred. 2000. "Bleeding Hearts." Letter to the editor. *Valley Journal*, February 3.

Belson, Ken, and Jill P. Capuzzo. 2007. "Towns Rethink Laws against Illegal Immigrants." *New York Times*, September 26.

Birch, Simon. 2006. "Is it Possible to Ski without Ruining the Environment?" *Independent* (London), February 6.

Blum, William. 2003. *Killing Hope: U.S. Military and CIA Interventions since World War II*. Common Courage Press.

Boggs, Carl. 2000. *The End of Politics: Corporate Power and the Decline of the Public Sphere*. Guilford Press.

Boyce, Jim, Beverly Wright, Robert Bullard, Manuel Pastor, Alice Fothergill, and Rachel Morello-Frosch. 2006. *In the Wake of the Storm: Environment, Disaster and Race After Katrina*. Social Science Research Council.

Brady, Lois Smith. 2002. "A Birthday Party in a Trailer Park is Completely Different in Aspen." *New York Times*, May 26.

Bridges, Mrs. F. D. 1883. *A Journal of a Lady's Travels Round the World*. London.

Briggs, Charles, and Clara Mantini-Briggs. 2004. *Stories in the Time of Cholera: Racial Profiling During a Medical Nightmare*. University of California Press.

Briggs, Laura. 2002. *Reproducing Empire: Race, Sex, Science, and U.S. Imperialism in Puerto Rico*. University of California Press.

Brimelow, Peter. 1995. *Alien Nation: Common Sense about America's Immigration Disaster*. Random House.

Brodkin, Karen. 1998. *How Jews became White Folks and What That Says about Race in America*. Rutgers University Press.

Brokaw, Tom. 2006. "The Twenty-first Century Immigrant Story." NBC News. December 27.

Browne, Vicki, and John Colson. 2004. "Hightower Shows Carbondale a Good Time." *Valley Journal*. July 22-28.

Bullard, Robert. 2000. *Dumping in Dixie: Race, Class and Environmental Quality.* Westview.

———, ed. 2005. *The Quest for Environmental Justice: Human Rights and the Politics of Pollution.* Sierra Club Books.

Bullard, Robert, and Beverly Wright. 2009. *Race, Place, and Environmental Justice After Hurricane Katrina.* Westview Press.

Bullard, Robert, Glenn Johnson, and Angel Torres, eds. 2000. *Sprawl City: Race, Politics, and Planning.* Island Press.

Bullard, Robert, Paul Mohai, Robin Saha, and Beverly Wright. 2007. *Toxic Wastes and Race at Twenty: 1987–2007. Grassroots Struggles to Dismantle Environmental Racism in the United States.* Report prepared for the United Church of Christ Justice and Witness Ministries.

Bullock, Heather, Karen Fraser Wyche, Wendy R. Williams. 2001. "Media Images of the Poor." *Journal of Social Issues* 57, no. 2: 229–46.

Burke, Meredith. 2000. "Immigration's Dire Effect on The Environment." *Seattle Times.* June 15.

Burns, Cameron. 1993. "The Return of the Utes: A Historic Pow-wow of Valley's First Residents." *Aspen Times*, April 24 and 25.

Buys, Christian J. 2001. *Historic Aspen in Rare Photographs.* Western Reflections Publishing Company.

Calavita, Kitty. 2008. "Deflecting the Immigration Debate: Globalization, Immigrant Agency, 'Strange Bedfellows,' and Beyond." *Contemporary Sociology* 37, no. 4: 302–5.

Callison, Anne. 2004. "Council Praised, Governor Dogged." Letter to the Editor. *Aspen Daily News*, January 4.

Camarota, Steven. 2001. "The Impact of Immigration on U.S. Population Growth." Testimony prepared for the U.S. House of Representatives Committee on the Judiciary. Subcommittee on Immigration, Border Security, and Claims. August 2.

Carlsen, Laura. 2007. "NAFTA, Inequality and Immigration." Americas Policy Program. October 31, 1–4. www.americaspolicy.org.

Carroll. Rick. 2002. "Strange Bedfellows Made in Quest for Immigration Reform." *Aspen Daily News,* August 19.

———. 2004. "False Raid Rumor Sparks Hysteria in Latino Community." *Aspen Daily News*, July 13, 5.

Chang, Grace. 2000. *Disposable Domestics: Immigrant Women Workers in the Global Economy.* South End Press.

Chang, Nancy, and Howard Zinn. 2002. *Silencing Dissent: How Post-September 11 Anti-Terrorism Measures Threaten Our Civil Liberties.* Seven Stories Press.

Chapin, Mac. 2004. "A Challenge to Conservationists: Can We Protect Natural Habitats without Abusing the People Who Live in Them?" *World Watch Magazine* 17. no. 6. November/December.

Chaplin, Scott. 2000. "Immigration, Globalization, and U.S. Foreign Policy." Guest editorial. *Valley Journal*, August 17.

Christian, Jonette. 1999. "Population, Immigration, and Global Ethics." Presentation at the Myth of Sustainable Growth Conference. Aspen Institute, Aspen, CO. October 9.

Chung, Sarah S. 1999. "Crowded Conditions in C'dale Raise Concerns." *Aspen Times*, November 12.

———. 2000. "City softens immigration stand." *Aspen Times*. April 25.

Churchill, Ward. 2003. *Perversions of Justice: Indigenous Peoples and Anglo-American Law*. City Lights.

City of Aspen. 1966. *Aspen General Plan*. Aspen, CO.

Clapp, Jennifer. 2001. *Toxic Exports: The Transfer of Hazardous Wastes from Rich to Poor Countries*. Cornell University Press.

Clarke, Chris. 2006. "The Battered Border: Immigration Policy Sacrifices Arizona's Wilderness." *Earth Island Journal* (Autumn): 21–26.

Clifford, Hal. 1999. "Aspen's Extremes." *Ski Magazine*, January, 33–37.

Clifford, Hal. 2003. *Downhill Slide: Why the Corporate Ski Industry is Bad for Skiing, Ski Towns, and the Environment*. Sierra Club Books.

Clifford, Peggy, and John M. Smith. 1970a. *Aspen: Dreams and Dilemmas*. Swallow Press.

———. 1970b. "The Distressing Rebirth." *Empire Magazine*, August 16.

Cole, Luke, and Sheila Foster. 2001. *From the Ground Up: Environmental Racism and the Rise of the Environmental Justice Movement*. New York University Press.

Coleman, Annie Gilbert. 1996. "The Unbearable Whiteness of Skiing." *Pacific Historical Review* 65, no. 4: 583–614.

Colestock, Gil. n.d. "Our Readers Speak: Our Laws?" *Aspen Times*.

Colson, John. 2000a. "'Warm-up' Events Will Start Saturday." *Aspen Times*, August 10.

———. 2000b. "Nothing More Refreshing Than a Good Protest." *Aspen Times*, August 17.

———. 2000c. "Raising the Bar." *Aspen Times*, November 11–12.

———. 2004. "'Pants on Fire' Mobile Visits Downtown C'dale." *Valley Journal*, July 15–21.

Condon, Scott. n.d. "Look Who's Coming to Develop Down Valley." *Aspen Times*, (ca. 2004.)

———. 2000a. "Protest Planned for Institute Summit." *Aspen Times*, August 10.

———. 2000b. "Jockeying for Position: Carbondale Enters Race to become Commercial Powerhouse." *Aspen Times*, October 14–15.

———. 2001. "Basalt: A Community Struggles to Keep Its Small-town Character." *Aspen Times*, June 30–July 1.

Conniff, Michael. 2004. "Natural High." Mountain Marketplace. July 21–August 3. *Aspen Daily News*.

Conover, Ted. 1991. *Whiteout: Lost in Aspen*. Random House.

Cornelius, Wayne. 2002. "Ambivalent Reception: Mass Public Responses to the 'New' Latino Immigration to the U.S." In *Latinos: Remaking America*, ed. Marcelo Suarez-Orozco and Mariela Paez, 165–89. University of California Press.

———. 2006. Presentation on historical trends in nativist politics, at the Department of Ethic Studies Colloquium Series, University of California–San Diego. Fall.

Cornwell, Robert. n.d.. "Ashcroft: Its Natural and Human History." Aspen Historical Society. Aspen, CO.

Craddock, Susan. 2004. *City of Plagues: Disease, Poverty, and Deviance in San Francisco*. University of Minnesota Press.

Craig, Bill. 1999a. "INS Office to Open in C'dale, Not Glenwood." *Glenwood Post*, October 27.

———. 1999b. "Protesters Decry Possible INS Move." *Glenwood Post*, November 6.

Crass, Chris. 2004. "Controlling Gendered Immigrants and Racialized Populations: Overpopulation, Immigration and Environmental Sustainability." http://www.infoshop.org/texts/immigration.html, accessed April 2008.

Daniels, Donna. 1999a. "Appeal Filed against INS Office." *Glenwood Independent*, December 29.

———. 1999b. "Latinos Organize to Protest INS." *Glenwood Independent*, December 30.

———. 2000a. "Two Groups Lead Charge against INS." *Glenwood Post Independent*, January 5.

———. 2000b. "INS Loses in C'dale, Renews Search for Office." *Glenwood Independent*, January 28.

———. 2001a. "Citizens Voice Concern for C'dale's Bonanza Trailer Park." *Glenwood Post Independent*, April 26.

———. 2001b. "Services Curtailed as Asistencia Para Latinos Prepares to Close." *Glenwood Springs Post Independent*, December 7–8, A9.

Davis, Kenneth. 2007. "The Founding Immigrants." *New York Times*, July 3. A21.

Davis, Mike. 1999. "Dead West: Ecocide in Marlboro County." In *Over the Edge: Remapping the American West*, ed. Valerie Matsumoto and Blake Allmendinger, 346–47. University of California Press.

Davis, Mike, and Alessandra Moctezuma. 1999. "Policing the Third Border." *ColorLines* 2, no. 37, October 31.

De Genova, Nicholas. 2005. *Working the Boundaries: Race, Space, and 'Illegality' in Mexican Chicago*. Duke University Press.

Democracy Now! Broadcast. 2007. Pacifica Radio Network. October 5.

Denver Post Wire Report. 2009. "Latinos Make up 40 Percent of Federal Prison Population." February 19. Denverpost.com. http://www.denverpost.com/ci_11735475, accessed April 5, 2009.

DeVoto, Bernard. 2000. "The West: A Plundered Province." In *The Western Paradox: A Conservation Reader,* ed. Douglas Brinkley and Patricia Nelson Limerick, 3–21. Yale University Press.

DinAlt, Jason. 1997. "The Environmental Impact of Immigration into the United States." *Focus.* Carrying Capacity Network. Vol. 4, no. 2.

Dolgon, Corey. 2005. *The End of the Hamptons: Scenes from the Class Struggle in America's Paradise.* New York University Press.

Domhoff, G. William. 2009. *Who Rules America? Challenges to Corporate and Class Dominance.* McGraw-Hill.

Dowie, Mark. 2009. *Conservation Refugees: The Hundred-Year Conflict between Global Conservation and Native Peoples.* MIT Press.

DuBois, W. E. B. 1998. *Black Reconstruction in America, 1860–1880.* Free Press.

Dugger, Celia. 2003. "Study: NAFTA Failed to Create Mexican Jobs." *Aspen Times* (originally a *New York Times* story), November 19.

Ellis, Richard N., and Duane A. Smith. 1991. *Colorado: A History in Photographs.* University Press of Colorado.

Emmitt, Robert. 1954. *The Last War Trail: The Utes and the Settlement of Colorado.* University of Oklahoma Press.

Environmental Health Coalition. 2004. *Globalization at the Crossroads: Ten Years of NAFTA in the San Diego/Tijuana Border Region.* San Diego, CA.

Environment News Service. 2001. "Alien Species: Common, Costly and Destructive." May 14.

Espinoza, Priscilla. 2004. "Illegal Creeps." *Aspen Times,* July 23.

Faber, Daniel. 2005. "Building a Transnational Environmental Justice Movement: Obstacles and Opportunities in the Age of Globalization." In *Coalitions Across Borders: Negotiating Difference and Unity in Transnational Struggles against Neoliberalism,* ed. Joe Bandy and Jackie Smith. Rowman and Littlefield.

———. 2008. *Capitalizing on Environmental Injustice: The Polluter-Industrial Complex in the Age of Globalization.* Rowman and Littlefield.

Faber, Daniel, and Eric Krieg. 2001. *Unequal Exposure to Ecological Hazards: Environmental Injustices in the Commonwealth of Massachusetts.* Northeastern University.

Feagin, Joe. 1997. "Old Poison in New Bottles: The Deep Roots of Modern Nativism." In *Immigrants Out!: The New Nativism and the Anti-Immigrant Impulse in the United States,* ed. Juan F. Perea, 13–40. New York University Press.

Feagin, Joe, Hernan Vera, and Pinar Batur. 2001. *White Racism.* 2nd ed. Routledge.

Fillion, Roger. 2007. "Rebel with a Cause." *Rocky Mountain News,* September 22.

Filner, Bob, and Diane Takvorian. 2004. "Promoting Free Trade Isn't Really Free." *San Diego Union-Tribune*, December 17.

Flynn, Kevin. 2006. "Funding Questioned: Critics Say Some Defend Colorado Money Tainted." *Rocky Mountain News*, July 15.

Fowler, Pete. 2009. "New Bilingual Paper Hits the Streets in Glenwood Springs." *Vail Daily*, April 27.

Fraternal Order of American Sportsmen. 1915. *Bylaws*. 7.

Freudenburg, William. 2005. "Privileged Access, Privileged Accounts: Toward a Socially Stuctured Theory of Resources and Discourses." *Social Forces* 84, no. 1: 89-114.

Frey, David. 2000a. "A Step Away from Trouble." *Roaring Fork Sunday*, July 16–22.

———. 2000b. "Barbera Resigns at Asistencia Para Latinos." *Valley Journal*, July 20, 9A.

———. 2002. "Rural Resort Region Backs Off Immigration Reform." *Aspen Daily News*, March 10.

———. 2003a. "Small Offenses Can Mean Return Home for Illegals." *Aspen Daily News*, July 26.

———. 2003b. "Immigration Detention Facility Planned for Glenwood." *Aspen Daily News*, July 29.

———. 2004. "Latinos Voice Concerns to School Officials." *Aspen Daily News*, January 14.

Gabrielson, Ryan, and Paul Giblin. 2008. "Reasonable Doubt." *East Valley Tribune* (Phoenix, AZ), July.

Gage, Emma Abbott. 1900. *Western Wanderings and Summer Saunterings through Picturesque Colorado*. Lord Baltimore Press.

Gagnon, Ben. 2000. "A New Kind of Cavalry." *Roaring Fork Sunday*, April 23–29.

Garnsey, Morris. 1965. "Aridity and Politics in the West." *Colorado Quarterly* 14 (Autumn): 158.

Gedicks, Al. 2001. *Resource Rebels: Native Challenges to Mining and Oil Corporations*. South End Press.

Gilbert, Anne M. 1991. *The People of Aspen and the Roaring Fork Valley: A History of the Families and Daily Life of Miners and Ranchers, 1879–1960*. Aspen Historical Society. November.

Gilmore, Ruth. 2007. *Golden Gulag: Prisons, Surplus, Crisis, and Opposition in Globalizing California*. University of California Press.

Gilmore, John S., and Mary K. Duff. 1974. *The Evolving Political Economy of Pitkin County: Growth Management by Consensus in a Boom Community*. University of Denver Research Institute.

Glick, Daniel. 2001. *Powder Burn: Arson, Money, and Mystery on Vail Mountain*. Public Affairs.

Goldberg, David Theo. 1993. *Racist Culture: Philosophy and the Politics of Meaning*. Blackwell.

Goldman, Michael, ed. 1999. *Privatizing Nature: Political Struggles for the Global Commons.* Rutgers University Press.

Gottlieb, Robert. 1993. *Forcing the Spring: The Transformation of the American Environmental Movement.* Island Press.

———. 1998. "The Meaning of Place." In *Reopening the American West,* ed. Hal K. Rothman, chap. 10. University of Arizona Press.

Gottlieb, Robert, and Peter Dreier. 1998. "Sierra Club Wrestles with the Nativism in Environmentalism." *Los Angeles Times,* March 1.

Gould, Kenneth. 2006. "Promoting Sustainability." In *Public Sociologies Reader,* ed. Judith Blau and Keri Iyall Smith, 213–29. Rowman and Littlefield.

———. 2007. "The Ecological Costs of Militarization." *Peace Review* 19, no. 3: 331–34.

Gould, Kenneth, David N. Pellow, and Allan Schnaiberg. 2008. *The Treadmill of Production: Injustice and Unsustainability in the Global Economy.* Paradigm Publishers.

Gould, Kenneth, Allan Schnaiberg, and Adam Weinberg. 1996. *Local Environmental Struggles: Citizen Activism in the Treadmill of Production.* Cambridge University Press.

Grauer, Bernie. 2001a. "Carbondale to Aspen: Buy Our Trailer Park." *Aspen Daily News,* August 22.

———. 2001b. "Arts Council Members Resign in Protest of Trailer Park Evictions." *Aspen Daily News,* September 20.

Gualtieri, Sarah. 2009. *Between Arab and White: Race and Ethnicity in the Early Syrian American Diaspora.* University of California Press.

Guha, Ramachandra. 1989. "Radical American Environmentalism and Wilderness Preservation: A Third World Critique." *Environmental Ethics,* 11, no. 1: 71–83.

Guinier, Lani, and Gerald Torres. 2002. *The Miner's Canary: Enlisting Race, Resisting Power, Transforming Democracy.* Harvard University Press.

Gulliford, Andrew. 1989. *Boomtown Blues: Colorado Oil Shale, 1885–1985.* University Press of Colorado.

Gulliford, Andrew, and the Grand River Museum Alliance. 1983. *Garfield County, Colorado: The First Hundred Years, 1883–1983.* Gran Farnum Printing.

Gutiérrez, David. 1995. *Walls and Mirrors: Mexican Americans, Mexican Immigrants, and the Politics of Ethnicity.* University of California Press.

Haddock, Laura. 1948. "Aspen Comes Back on Skis." *Christian Science Monitor,* January 24.

Hall, Stuart, Charles Critcher, Tony Jefferson, John Clarke, and Brian Robert. 1978. *Policing the Crisis.* Palgrave Macmillan.

Hammond, Jennifer. 1995. "Growth Management in Aspen, Colorado, 1960–1977." Aspen Historical Society. Aspen, CO. July.

Hardin, Garrett. 2004. "Carrying Capacity and Quality of Life." 1968. Reprinted in *The Social Contract.* Inaugural Issue 1991. March 5.

Hari, Johann. 2010. "The Wrong Kind of Green." *Nation*, March 22.

Harrell, Eben. 2004. "The Changing Face of the Valley." *Aspen Times Weekly*, June 12–13.

Harris, Pat. 2009. "City of Nashville Rejects English-Only Law." *Reuters*, January 22.

Hartman, Todd. 2001. "Two Sides of Colorado: Second homes become large growth factor." *Rocky Mountain News*, March 25.

Hartmann, Betsy. 1995. *Reproductive Rights and Wrongs*. South End Press.

———. 2003. "Conserving Racism: The Greening of Hate at Home and Abroad." *Znet*. December 10. http://www.zmag.org.

Harvey, Allyn. 1999a. "New Watchdog Group Puts Eye on Immigration." *Aspen Times*, June 24.

———. 1999b. "Protest March Targets INS." *Aspen Times*. November 8.

———. 2001a. "Issue of Racism Sparks a Fierce City Council Debate." *Aspen Times*. April 12.

———. 2001b. "Lamm Speaks on Foreign Labor 'Addiction.'" *Aspen Times*, September 24.

———. 2001c. "Local's Letter Raised Authorities' Alarm." *Aspen Times*, September 24.

———. 2001d. "Future Is Bright for Asistencia." *Aspen Times*, December 10, 3A.

———. 2002. "Deal Likely in Andlinger vs. Pitkin County." *Aspen Times*, March 12.

Havlen, Naomi. 2004. "Immigration Rumor Causes Some Latinos to Miss Work." *Aspen Times*, July 13.

Hayden, Dolores. 2004. *Building Suburbia: Green Fields and Urban Growth, 1820–2000*. Vintage.

Hays, Samuel. 1959. *Conservation and the Gospel of Efficiency*. Harvard University Press.

Heiman, Jeremy. 1999. "City Council Passes Resolution Requesting Immigration Limits." *Aspen Times*, December 20.

Hertz, Rosanna, and Jonathan Imber, eds. 1995. *Studying Elites Using Qualitative Methods*. Sage.

Higham, John. 2002. *Strangers in the Land: Patterns of American Nativism, 1860–1925*. Rutgers University Press.

Hill, Tracy. 2000. Letter to the editor. *Glenwood Post Independent*, January 6.

Hoerner, J. Andrew, and Nia Robinson. 2008. *A Climate of Change: African Americans, Global Warming, and a Just Climate Policy*. Environmental Justice and Climate Change Initiative.

Hooper, Troy. 1999. "City Council May Begin Statewide Immigration Campaign." *Aspen Daily News*, December 21.

———. 2001. "Illegal Immigration Critic Jumps into Council Race." *Aspen Daily News*, April 6.

———. 2004a. "EPA Lauds Aspen for Getting Around." *Aspen Daily News*, April 27.

———. 2004b. "AVH Hopes a Nip Here, a Tuck There Boosts Revenues." *Aspen Daily News*, July 26.

Horsman, Reginald. 1981. *Race and Manifest Destiny: The Origins of American Racial Anglo-Saxonism.* Harvard University Press.

Huang, Priscilla. 2008. "Anchor Babies, Over-Breeders, and the Population Bomb: The Reemergence of Nativism and Population Control in Anti-Immigration Policies." *Harvard Law and Policy Review* 2:385–406.

Hubbell, Gary. 2000. "Why Do We Love All Our Illegal Aliens So?" *Aspen Times*, February 5–6.

Hunter, Lori. 2000. "The Spatial Association between U.S. Immigrant Residential Concentration and Environmental Hazards." *International Migration Review* 34, 2: 460–88.

Hunter, Mark. 2000. "'Slave Ships' Keep INS Busy as Flood of Smugglers Surges." *Denver Post*, February 24.

Hurley, Andrew. 1995. *Environmental Inequalities: Class, Race and Industrial Pollution in Gary, Indiana, 1945–1980.* University of North Carolina Press.

Ignatiev, Noel. 1996. *How the Irish Became White.* Routledge.

Ip, Greg. 2007. "Income-inequality Gap Widens." *Wall Street Journal*, October 12.

Jacobson, Matthew Frye. 1998. *Whiteness of a Different Color: European Immigrants and the Alchemy of Race.* Harvard University Press.

Jacobson, Robin Dale. 2008. *The New Nativism: Proposition 187 and the Debate over Immigration.* University of Minnesota Press.

Jacoby, Karl. 2001. *Crimes Against Nature: Squatters, Poachers, Thieves, and the Hidden History of American Conservation.* University of California Press.

Jencks, Christopher. 1991. *The Urban Underclass.* Brookings Institution.

Johnson, Chalmers. 2004a. *Blowback: The Costs and Consequences of American Empire.* Holt Paperbacks.

———. 2004b. *Sorrows of Empire: Militarism, Secrecy, and the End of the Republic.* Holt Paperbacks.

Johnson, Kevin. 2003. "Immigration, Civil Rights, and Coalitions for Social Justice." *Hastings Race and Poverty Law Journal* 1, no. 1: 181–200.

Johnson, Kirk. 2007. "A $135 Million Home, but If You Have to Ask . . ." *New York Times*, July 2.

Jung, Maureen. 1999. "Capitalism Comes to the Diggings." In *A Golden State: Mining and Economic Development in Gold Rush California,* ed. James Rawls and Richard Orsi, 52–77. University of California Press.

Kaiser Family Foundation and Center on Budget and Policy Priorities. 2004. *Covering New Americans: A Review of Federal and State Policies Related to Immigrants' Eligibility and Access to Publicly Funded Health Insurance.* Menlo Park, California. November.

Kaplan, Robert. 2006. *Imperial Grunts: On the Ground with the American Military, from Mongolia to the Philippines to Iraq and Beyond.* Vintage.

Kempf, Hervé. 2007. *How the Rich are Destroying the Earth.* Chelsea Green Publishers.

Khagram, Sanjeev. 2004. *Dams and Development: Transnational Struggles for Water and Power.* Cornell University Press.

Kimmell, Thomas John. 1975. *A History of a Rocky Mountain Silver Mining Camp: Aspen, Colorado, 1879–1910.* Unpublished BA Honors Thesis. Harvard College, Cambridge, MA.

Kimmel, Michael, and Abby L. Ferber, eds. 2009. *Privilege.* 2nd ed. Westview.

Kinzer, Stephen. 2007. *Overthrow: America's Century of Regime Change from Hawaii to Iraq.* Times Books.

Klein, Jim, and Martha Olson. 1996. *Taken for a Ride.* New Day Films.

Kong, Maria, with Pamela Chiang. 2001. *Fighting Fire with Fire: Lessons from the Laotian Organizing Project's First Campaign.* Laotian Organizing Project and Asian Pacific Environmental Network.

Kotlowitz, Alex. 2007. "All Immigration Politics Is Local (and Complicated, Nasty and Personal)." *New York Times Magazine,* August 5, sec. 6.

Kovel, Joel. 2002. *The Enemy of Nature: The End of Capitalism or the End of the World?* Zed Books.

Krikorian, Mark. 2007. "Fewer Migrants Mean More Benefits: As Immigration Enforcement Takes Hold, Jobs Begin to Open Up to Less-Skilled Americans." Op-ed. *Los Angeles Times,* September 27.

Krugman, Paul. 2002. "For Richer: How the Permissive Capitalism of the Boom Destroyed American Equality." *New York Times Magazine,* October 20.

Lakoff, George, and Sam Ferguson. 2006. "The Framing of Immigration." The Rockridge Institute.

Lamm, Richard. 1999. Presentation at the Myth of Sustainable Growth conference. Aspen Institute, Aspen, CO, October 9.

———. 2004. "I Have a Plan to Destroy America." *Social Contract.* Spring, 180–81.

Lee, Erika. 2007. *At America's Gates: Chinese Immigration During the Exclusion Era, 1882–1943.* University of North Carolina Press.

Lich, Marty. 2004. "Statistics don't lie." Letter to the editor. *Aspen Times,* June 30.

Limerick, Patricia Nelson. 1987. *The Legacy of Conquest: The Unbroken Past of the American West.* W. W. Norton.

———. 2000. *Something in the Soil: Legacies and Reckonings in the New West*. W. W. Norton.

Lipsitz, George. 1988. *A Life in the Struggle: Ivory Perry and the Culture of Opposition*. Rev. ed. Temple University Press.

———. 2006. *The Possessive Investment in Whiteness: How White People Profit from Identity Politics*. Temple University Press.

Lorah, Paul. 1996. *Wilderness, Uneven Development, and Demographic Change in the Rocky Mountain West, 1969–1993*. Unpublished PhD diss. Department of Geography, Indiana University. December.

Lowe, Lisa. 1996. *Immigrant Acts: On Asian American Cultural Politics*. Duke University Press.

McClintock, Anne. 1995. *Imperial Leather: Race, Gender, and Sexuality in the Colonial Contest*. Routledge.

McCully, Patrick. 2001. *Silenced Rivers: The Ecology and Politics of Large Dams*. Zed Books.

McGarry, Mike. 2002. "Ingrates Don't Deserve Citizenship." Letter to the editor. *Aspen Daily News*, October 22.

McGovern, Jeanne. 2004. "Modern-day Movers and Shakers." *Aspen Times Weekly*, vol. 125, no. 29, July 17 and 18, A21.

———. 2006. "Beyond the Glitz and Glamour." *SkyWest Magazine*, July/August. 30–34.

McGregor, Heather. 2001. Latinos Face Many Obstacles in Search of a Better Life." *Glenwood Springs Post Independent*, July 22.

MacDonald, Christine. 2008. *Green Inc.: An Environmental Insider Reveals How a Good Cause Has Gone Bad*. Lyons Press.

Maldonado, Marta Maria. 2004. *Harvesting the Fruits of Colorblindness: Racial Ideology in Employers' Discourse and the Everyday Production of Racial Inequality in Agricultural Work*. PhD diss. Department of Sociology, Washington State University.

Massey, Douglass. 2003. *Beyond Smoke and Mirrors: Mexican Immigration in an Era of Economic Integration*. Russell Sage Foundation.

Massey, Douglas, and Nancy Denton. 1993. *American Apartheid: Segregation and the Making of the Underclass*. Harvard University Press.

Mattern, Elizabeth. 2001. "Ski Areas Issue Sustainable Slopes Report." *Daily Camera* (Boulder, CO), July 6, 2001.

Mileti, Dennis. 1999. *Disasters by Design: A Reassessment of Natural Hazards in the United States*. Joseph Henry Press.

Millennium Ecosystem Assessment. 2005. *Ecosystems and Human Well-Being*. Island Press and the United Nations.

Mills, C. Wright. 2000. *The Power Elite*. Oxford University Press.

Milkman, Ruth. 2006. *L.A. Story: Immigrant Workers and the Future of the U.S. Labor Movement*. Russell Sage Foundation.

Mohai, Paul, and Robin Saha. 2007. "Racial Inequality in the Distribution of Hazardous Waste: A National-Level Reassessment." *Social Problems* 54, no. 3: 343–70.

Molina, Natalia. 2006. *Fit to be Citizens? Public Health and Race in Los Angeles, 1879–1939*. University of California Press.

Monnett, John H., and Michael McCarthy. 1996. *Colorado Profiles: Men and Women Who Shaped the Centennial State*. University Press of Colorado.

Moore, Donald, Jake Kosek, and Anand Pandian, eds. 2003. *Race, Nature, and the Politics of Difference*. Duke University Press.

Morris, Alex. 1950. "The Cities of America: Aspen, Colorado." *Saturday Evening Post*, October 14.

Motavalli, Jim. 2001. "Roy Beck: It's About the Numbers." *E Magazine*, November/December, 33.

Moyers, Bill. 2007. "The Narrative Imperative." TomPaine.com, January 4, 2 and 5.

Munday, Marie. 1999. "Work Visas As Not An Option!" Letter to the editor. *Aspen Daily News*, November 17.

Mutrie, Tim. 1999. "'Asistencia' Means 'Assistance'" *Aspen Times*, May 29 and 30.

———. 2000. "For Some, the Agency Is a Source of Fear—For Others, a Kind of Blessing." *Aspen Times*, January 22–23.

———. 2001. "Pitco to Call for Population Control." *Aspen Times*, April 12.

NAPALC. 2001. *Backlash: Final Report. 2001 Audit of Violence Against Asian Americans*. National Asian Pacific American Legal Consortium. (NAPALC is now the Asian American Justice Center.)

National Latina Institute for Reproductive Health. 2005. *Prenatal Care Access among Immigrant Latinas*. New York. December.

Navarro, Mireya. 2001. "On California's Urban Border: Praise for Immigration Curbs." *New York Times*, August 21.

Ngai, Mae. 2004. *Impossible Subjects: Illegal Aliens and the Making of Modern America*. Princeton University Press.

Nordhaus, Ted, and Michael Shellenberger. 2007. *Break Through: From the Death of Environmentalism to the Politics of Possibility*. Houghton Mifflin.

O'Grady, Janet. 2004. "Editor's Letter." *Aspen Magazine*, Summer, 16.

Ong, Aihwa. 2006. *Neoliberalism as Exception: Mutations in Citizenship and Sovereignty*. Duke University Press.

Ortiz-Garcia, Cecilio. 2004. *Air of Injustice: How Air Pollution Affects the Health of Hispanics and Latinos*. League of United Latin American Citizens. July.

panagioti. 2006. "Down with Borders, Up with Spring!" *EarthFirst!* July–August, 8–11.

Parenti, Christian. 2000. *Lockdown America: Police and Prisons in the Age of Crisis.* Verso.

Park, Lisa Sun-Hee. 2009. "The Politics of Public Charge. Immigrant Women's Health Care Access." Paper presented at the Department of Sociology Workshop Series, University of Minnesota. March 24.

Parker, Jack. 2001. "2,000 in Colorado Protest Racist Killing of Mexican Workers." *Militant* 65, no. 28 (July 23).

Passel, Jeffrey, and D'Vera Cohn. 2009. *A Portrait of Unauthorized Immigrants in the United States.* Pew Research Center. April.

Pear, Robert. 2007. "A Million Faxes Later, a Little-Known Group Claims a Victory on Immigration." *New York Times,* July 15.

Pellow, David. 2002. *Garbage Wars: The Struggle for Environmental Justice in Chicago.* MIT Press.

———. 2007. *Resisting Global Toxics: Transnational Movements for Environmental Justice.* MIT Press.

———. 2009. "'We Didn't Get the First 500 Years Right, So Let's Work on the Next 500 Years': A Call for Transformative Analysis and Action." *Environmental Justice* 2, no. 1: 3–8.

Pellow, David N., and Lisa Sun-Hee Park. 2002. *The Silicon Valley of Dreams: Environmental Injustice, Immigrant Workers, and the High-Tech Global Economy.* New York University Press.

Perfecto, Ivette, and Baldemar Velasquez. 1992. "Farm Workers: Among the Least Protected." *EPA Journal* (March/April):13–14.

Political Ecology Group. 1996. "Immigration and the Environment in the U.S.: Myths and Facts." *Race, Poverty and the Environment* (Summer/Fall):37–38.

Preston, Julia. 2007. "Grass Roots Roared, and an Immigration Plan Fell." *New York Times,* June 10, A1.

Pritchard, Justin. 2004. "U.S. Mexican Worker Deaths Rising Sharply." *Aspen Daily News/Associated Press,* March 14.

Pulido, Laura. 2000. "Rethinking Environmental Racism: White Privilege and Urban Development in Southern California." *Annals of the Association of American Geographers* 90, no. 1: 12–40.

Roberts, Dorothy. 1998. *Killing the Black Body: Race, Reproduction, and the Meaning of Liberty.* Vintage.

Roediger, David. 2005. *Working toward Whiteness: How American's Immigrants Became White.* Basic Books.

———. 2007. *The Wages of Whiteness: Race and the Making of the American Working Class.* Verso.

Rohrbough, Malcolm. 2000. *Aspen: The History of a Silver Mining Town, 1879–1893.* University Press of Colorado.

Rollins, Bill. 1982. "Lawsuit Threatens Courts Policies." *Aspen Times,* August 6.

Romig, Suzie. 2001a. "Developer Plans Phased Fourth Street Projects." *Valley Journal,* n.d.

———. 2001b. "CCAH Offered New Arts Center Location." *Valley Journal,* June 14.

Rondeaux, Candace, and Asjylyn Loder. 2000. "Latino Laborers Targeted." *National Catholic Reporter,* September 7.

Rosenfeld, Steven. 2004. "Population Bombshell." TomPaine.com. February 5.

Sassen, Saskia. 1998. *Globalization and its Discontents.* New Press.

Sferios, Emanuel. 1998a. "Immigration and the Environment: Is Eco-Fascism on the Rise?" *Synthesis/Regeneration* 16 (Summer).

———. 1998b. "Population, Immigration, and the Environment." *Z Magazine,* June: 24–29.

Shaw, Daniel. 2004. "Money, Clout, and Power." *Aspen Magazine,* Midsummer.

Shah, Nayan. 2001. *Contagious Divides: Epidemics and Race in San Francisco's Chinatown.* University of California Press.

Schmitt, Eric. 2001a. "Whites in Minority in Largest Cities, the Census Shows." *New York Times,* April 30.

———. 2001b. "Pockets of Protest Are Rising against Immigration." *New York Times,* August 9.

Schnaiberg, Allan. 1980. *The Environment: From Surplus to Scarcity.* Oxford University Press.

Schnaiberg, Allan, and Kenneth Alan Gould. 2000. *Environment and Society: The Enduring Conflict.* Blackburn

Schneller, Johanna. 2004. "A Fine Romance." *In Style Weddings Magazine,* Spring, 398–403.

Severy, Richard. 1978. "Aspen, Colorado: Unbelievable." December 15. Archives, University of Colorado–Boulder Libraries.

Sibley, David. 1997. *Geographies of Exclusion: Society and Difference in the West.* Routledge.

Sierra Club. 2004. *Latino Communities at Risk: How Bush Administration Polices Harm Our Communities.* San Francisco.

Sierrans for U.S. Population Stabilization. 2004. "For the Love of Money." http://www.susps.org/. Spring.

Slotkin, Richard. 1998. *Gunfighter Nation: The Myth of the Frontier in Twentieth-Century America.* University of Oklahoma Press.

Smith, Andrea. 2005. *Conquest: Sexual Violence and American Indian Genocide.* South End Press.

Smith, Ted, David Sonnenfeld, and David N. Pellow, eds. 2006. *Challenging the Chip: Labor Rights and Environmental Justice in the Global Electronics Industry.* Temple University Press.

Solomon, Jay. 2009. "U.S. Drops 'War on Terror' Phrase, Clinton Says." *Wall Street Journal,* March 31.

Southern Poverty Law Center. 2001. *Intelligence Report.* Spring.

———. 2007. "The Year in Hate." *Intelligence Report* 125 (Spring).

Spence, Mark David. 1999. *Dispossessing the Wilderness: Indian Removal and the Making of the National Parks.* Oxford University Press.

Speth, James Gustave. 2008. *The Bridge at the Edge of the World: Capitalism, the Environment, and Crossing from Crisis to Sustainability.* Yale University Press.

St. Clair, Jeffrey. 2007. "The Withering of the American Environmental Movement." Counterpunch.org. February 3 and 4.

Staff report. 2000. "Two Vans Weaving down Interstate 70 Disgorge 47 Illegal Immigrants." *Glenwood Independent,* May 5.

Staff and Wire reports. 2003. "Report: Aspen Most Environmental." *Aspen Daily News,* June.

Stein, Rachel. 2004. *New Perspectives on Environmental Justice: Gender, Sexuality, and Activism.* Rutgers University Press.

Stiny, Andrew. 1999a. "Former Governor Lamm Heads Growth Conference." *Aspen Daily News,* October 7.

———. 1999b. "Carbondale March Protests INS." *Aspen Daily News,* November 6.

———. 1999c. "Population Resolution Ends Up on Anti-Immigration Web Site." *Aspen Daily News.* December 27.

Stroud, John. 1999. "Latinos Unidos Gears Up to Fight INS Office." *Valley Journal,* December 30.

———. 2000a. "Official: Do Not 'Fear' INS Office." *Western Slope Sunday* (Carbondale, CO), January 9.

———. 2000b. "Zoning Board Denies INS Permit for Carbondale Site." *Glenwood Post,* January 28.

Szasz, Andrew. 1994. *EcoPopulism: Toxic Waste and the Movement for Environmental Justice.* University of Minnesota Press.

Sze, Julie. 2007. *Noxious New York: The Racial Politics of Urban Health and Environmental Justice.* MIT Press.

Tactaquin, Cathi. n.d. "The Greening of the Anti-Immigrant Agenda." *Network News.* National Network for Immigrant and Refugee Rights. Oakland, CA.

———. 1994. "Finding Common Ground." *Environmental Action,* Summer, 24.

Takaki, Ronald. 1998. *Strangers from a Different Shore: A History of Asian Americans.* Back Bay Books.

Tanton, John. 2004. "Description of U.S. and Projects List." *Social Contract Press,* May 30.

Taylor, Alf. 2000. "You Stopped the INS, Now Stop the Cocaine." Letter to editor. *Aspen Times,* January 31.

Taylor, Dorceta. 2009. *The Environment and the People in American Cities, 1600s–1900s*. Duke University Press.

Taylor, Paul S. 1929. "Mexican Labor in the United States: The Valley of the South Platte, Colorado." *University of California Publications in Economics* 6:215–16.

Urquhart, Lena. 1970. *Glenwood Springs: Spa in the Mountains*. Pruett Publishing Company.

U.S. News and World Report. 1975. "Warning from the Rockies: Go Slow in Exploiting Our Fuel." December 22.

United Church of Christ. 1987. *Toxic Wastes and Race in the United States*. UCC Commission for Racial Justice.

Vader, Marija. 1999. "INS to Open New Office in Carbondale Next Year." *Daily Sentinel* (Carbondale, CO), December 23.

Veblen, Thorstein. 1994. *The Theory of the Leisure Class*. Penguin Books.

Voynick, Stephen. 1984. *Leadville: A Miner's Epic*. Mountain Press Publishing Company.

Wagman, Paul. 1977. "U.S. Goal: Sterilizations of Millions of World's Women." *St. Louis Post-Dispatch*, April 22.

Ward, Robert. 1996. "Wilderness Warriors Named 'Local Heroes.'" *Aspen Times*, September 7–8.

———. 1997. "Rush Hour in the Backcountry." *Aspen Times Weekly*, March 1–2.

Washington, Sylvia Hood. 2005. *Packing Them In: An Archeology of Environmental Racism in Chicago, 1865–1954*. Lexington Books.

Weaver, Jace. 1996. *Defending Mother Earth: Native American Perspectives on Environmental Justice*. Orbis.

Webb, Dennis. 2000. "Combating a Crime Where the Criminals Are Often the Victims." *Glenwood Post*, January 19.

Weiss, Kenneth. 2004. "The Man behind the Land." *Los Angeles Times*, October 27.

Werbach, Adam. 2004. "Hostile Takeover: Anti-immigration Coalition Seeks Control of Sierra Club." *In These Times*, March 9.

West, Elliot. 1998. *Contested Plains: Indians, Goldseekers, and the Rush to Colorado*. University Press of Kansas.

Williams, Kara. 2004. "Adoptions from Southeast Asia and Pacific Islands Bring More Color to the Valley." *Mountain Parent* (Carbondale, CO), July–August.

Williams, Orrin. 2005. "Food and Justice: The Critical Link to Healthy Communities." In *Power, Justice and the Environment: A Critical Appraisal of the Environmental Justice Movement*, ed. David N. Pellow and Robert J. Brulle, 117–30. MIT Press.

Wilson, William Julius. 1990. *The Truly Disadvantaged: The Inner City, the Underclass, and Public Policy*. University of Chicago Press.

Winant, Howard. 2001. *The World Is a Ghetto: Race and Democracy since World War II*. Basic Books.

Wise, Tim. 2008. *Speaking Treason Fluently: Anti-Racist Reflections from an Angry White Male*. Soft Skull Press.

Wolff, Edward Nathan. 2010. "Recent Trends in Household Wealth in the United States: Rising Debt and the Middle-class Squeeze—an Update to 2007." *Working Paper No. 589*. Annandale-on-Hudson, NY: The Levy Economics Institute of Bard College.

World Resources Institute. 1990. *World Resources: A Guide to the Global Environment, 1990-1991*. Oxford University Press.

Worster, Donald. 1992. *Under Western Skies: Nature and History in the American West*. Oxford University Press.

Wright, Erik Olin. 2010. *Envisioning Real Utopias*. Verso.

Yen, Hope. 2009. "Income Inequality Widens: Poor Take Big Hit During Recession." *Huffington Post*, September 28.

Yeoman, Barry. 2001. "Silence in the Fields." *Mother Jones*, January/February.

INDEX

ABOUT THE AUTHORS

LISA SUN-HEE PARK is Associate Professor of Sociology and Asian American Studies, University of Minnesota. She is co-author of *The Silicon Valley of Dreams: Immigrant Labor, Environmental Injustice, and the High Tech Global Economy* (with David Pellow, NYU Press 2002); *Consuming Citizenship: Children of Asian Immigrant Entrepreneurs* (Stanford University Press, 2005), and *Entitled to Nothing: The Struggle for Immigrant Health Care in the Age of Welfare Reform (*forthcoming from NYU Press).

DAVID NAGUIB PELLOW is Professor and the Don A. Martindale Endowed Chair of Sociology, University of Minnesota. He is author of *Garbage Wars: The Struggle for Environmental Justice in Chicago* (MIT Press, 2002) and *Resisting Global Toxics: Transnational Movements for Environmental Justice* (MIT Press, 2007).